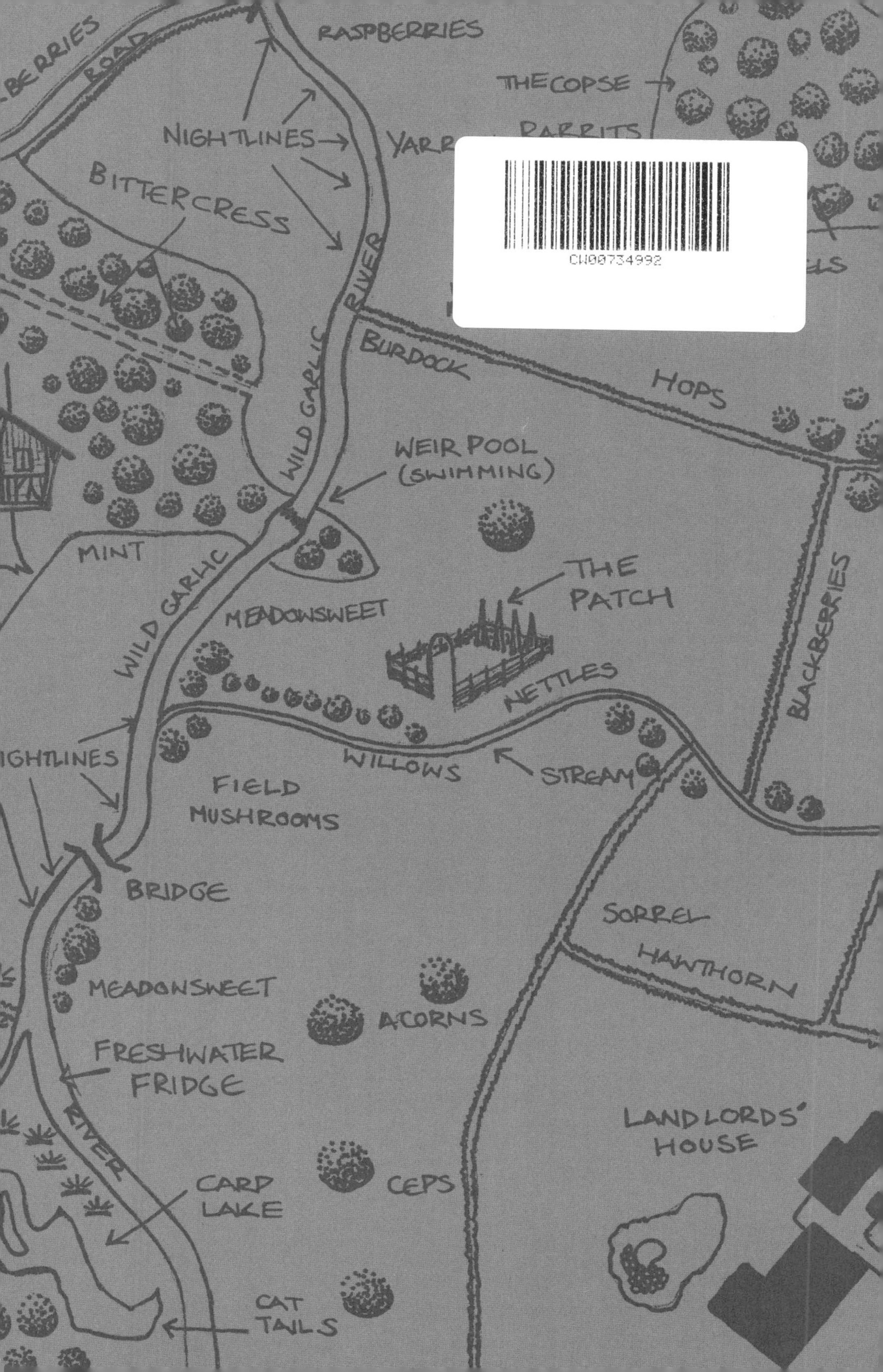

-BERRIES
ROAD
RASPBERRIES
THE COPSE
NIGHTLINES
YARR
RABBITS
BITTERCRESS
CW00734992
RIVER
WILD GARLIC
BURDOCK
HOPS
WEIR POOL
(SWIMMING)
MINT
WILD GARLIC
THE
PATCH
MEADOWSWEET
BLACKBERRIES
NETTLES
IGHTLINES
WILLOWS
STREAM
FIELD
MUSHROOMS
BRIDGE
SORREL
HAWTHORN
MEADOWSWEET
ACORNS
FRESHWATER
FRIDGE
RIVER
LANDLORDS'
HOUSE
CARP
LAKE
CEPS
CAT
TAILS

THE TREE HOUSE DIARIES

The Tree House Diaries

Nick Weston

COLLINS & BROWN

First published in the United Kingdom in 2010 by
Collins & Brown
10 Southcombe Street
London W14 0RA

An imprint of Anova Books Company Ltd

Distributed in the United States and Canada by Sterling Publishing Co.
387 Park Avenue South, New York, NY 10016-8810, USA

ISBN 978-1-84340-564-1

A CIP catalogue for this book is available from the British Library.

10 9 8 7 6 5 4 3 2 1

All photography and illustrations by Nick Weston except: Greg Funnell (64, 65, 187 bottom, 269, 297, 299, 308, 310); Al Humphreys (110, 112, 174, 179 top right); Tom Kevill-Davies (31 middle, 88 right, 89 left and right, 185 top right, 192 top left, top right and bottom right, 193, 210, 212, 215, 219); Nick Murray-Willis (219–320 tree house illustration); Nick Sandham (242, 243).

The following images are reproduced with kind permission of Frank Lane Picture Agency and Nicholas & Sherry Lu Aldridge (162 bottom); Richard Becker (204); Nigel Cattlin (71, 76, 127, 156, 208); Bob Gibbons (10, 234); Toomas Ili/Minden Pictures (93); ImageBroker (223); Mike Lane (109); S & D & K Maslowski (95); Phil McLean (101); Derek Middleton (133, 138, 298); Erica Olsen (82); Malcolm Schuyl (164); Gary K. Smith (162 top); Martin H. Smith (115).

ADVISORY NOTE The methods and activities described herein have been used by the author but by no means represent authoritative or definitive guidance on the subjects. Reasonable care has been taken to ensure the accuracy of the information and processes described herein however it is for general interest and in no way replaces professional advice as to the relative safety of carrying out the activities or eating wild plants, fungi and other wild foods. Neither the author nor the publishers make any warranties as to the safety or legality of carrying out the activities described or the consumption of any wild foods. This book is sold on the understanding that the publishers and the author cannot accept any responsibility for any accident incurred or damage suffered as result of following any of the suggestions contained herein and any liability for inaccuracies or errors relating to the material contained in this book is expressly excluded to the fullest extent permitted by law.

Reproduction by Mission Productions, Hong Kong
Printed by 1010 Printing International Ltd, China

This book can be ordered direct from the publisher at www.anovabooks.com

CONTENTS

INTRODUCTION

IN APRIL 2009 I built a tree house deep in the Sussex woodland, using natural and recycled materials. I lived there for the next six months to see if it was possible to sustain a self-sufficient lifestyle as a 21st-Century hunter-gatherer. With the help of a few basic staples and a small vegetable patch, I spent the rest of my time hunting and foraging for my food, while creating and maintaining a comfortable existence amongst the leaves.

This wasn't my first tree house. That one was little more than a platform: a few pieces of mahogany shelving poached from the garage and crudely nailed into the fork of a small oak tree. Crucially, though, it gave me a place to sit, obscured from grown-ups, in my own little world – king of the castle. I am sure I thought about walls and a roof, but they never came to fruition and a platform was good enough. In fact, the mahogany planks still sit in that oak tree today, perhaps due to my expensive taste in wood (something my father was none too pleased about), or perhaps it is because I am the only person who knows where it is.

I suppose the obvious question people will ask is why leave a perfectly comfortable flat in London to go and live in the woods for six months? The answer is simple: happiness. Countless people suffer the daily grind of a job they can't stand for one simple reason: money. Many people have to, to support a family or pay a mortgage, others because they haven't quite figured out what else to do, and some because they are working towards a goal and you always have to start from the bottom.

And that was literally where I began.

I was at a stage in my life where I didn't have any ties; I had always worked freelance, either as a chef or as a set designer, both in the events industry. But I knew what I wanted to do and where I wanted to be: living in the countryside and writing about my adventures. Neither was going to be found in the big city …

Push came to shove in November 2008, along with the demise of Lehman Brothers and the free fall in the stock market. The recession hit the events industry hard – production and food were the first cutbacks made by every party planner in the country. The six different companies for whom I juggled work didn't have a job between them, and slowly my bank balance spiralled further in to debt – and to add insult to injury I was charged for being overdrawn.

> **'Every man can transform the world from one of monotony and drabness, to one of excitement and adventure.'**
>
> IRVING WALLACE

Many of my 'involuntary' days off were spent pondering my next move. At the time, the only outlet for my writing was a blog that centred on wild food and other self-sufficient bits and bobs. I was never happier than when grubbing around in Battersea Park, taking various parts of the wild larder home and concocting different recipes and homebrews. I also enjoyed it because it didn't cost me anything, save a few basic staples. 'Surely this is the way to live!' I declared one afternoon, while in the kitchen bottling and tasting my first successful batch of nettle beer.

I decided I wanted to try living as self-sufficiently as possible for a period of six months. This would be timed to coincide with the most productive seasons of the wild larder: spring, summer and autumn. I could shoot and fish for all my protein and keep a small vegetable patch. But where would I live? I could build a small shack in the woods, or live under canvas, but those options seemed like muddling my way through. I wanted a proper house, somewhere warm and comfortable, somewhere I really could call home. Something that I had never had but always wanted: a proper tree house!

Now, I am no eco-warrior, nor am I a hippy, a crusty or a tree hugger. The one thing I am, if anything, is a realist. I am well aware of climate change and the various ways in which our existence has managed to threaten this amazing planet of ours. What I wanted to find out was what it would be like to live a low-impact lifestyle that was both self-sufficient and sustainable. If it was perfectly do-able, then why couldn't I strive to live like this in the future?

With next to no money I took stock of the best way to go about building a tree house. I could afford very little on materials and I spent hours trawling the Internet for information on how to build tree houses, log cabins, stoves, furniture, toilets, beds and sink units. Some of it helped, but most of it relied on a trip to the local DIY centre.

During all this planning I laid out a few basic ground rules: this was not supposed to be an exercise in all-out survival, nor was it a trial period as a hermit. Life would go on as normal, except for my diet and living arrangements. I wanted to enjoy this experience; I didn't want to struggle through some ridiculous challenge I had set myself, feel miserable most of the time and have to keep telling myself that with hindsight I would truly appreciate my time in the woods. That would be a waste of time. I had spent the last six months doing that in London and felt none the better for the experience!

I would be allowed a few staples to help convert fresh produce into more appetising meals (olive oil, flour, water, salt, pepper, vinegar, tea, coffee, sugar, rice and yeast); I would try to use recycled and natural materials as much as possible in the building of the tree house; and I would report back the joys and practicalities of self-sufficient living through my blog and any other means possible.

I moved back to Sussex in mid-April as spring was in full flow. What money I did have left in my bank account was spent on brand-new wood for the foundations and some fixings (bolts, screws, etc.). Sometimes you need something to give you a gentle shove into taking action, and for me it was signing the delivery note for a stack of wooden planks on 24 April 2009.

Nick Weston

February 2010

APRIL

SATURDAY 4th APRIL

My first obstacle is to find a place to build my tree house – I need a wood I can use for six months. Today I took the opportunity to speak to some family friends who own a sizeable 250 acre (101 hectare) farm, where I used to go shooting, and explain my predicament. Ideally I am keen for no money to change hands, in the spirit of this whole enterprise, and instead offer my services as an odd-jobber. Barter is still a common currency in the countryside and I think many people, where possible, are more than happy to keep this ancient economy alive. My new landlords were intrigued by my idea, perhaps more out of curiosity than anything else …

ENGLISH OAK (QUERCUS ROBUR)

DESCRIPTION **Found in drier woodlands in the south and east of England, the common or English oak has grey, deeply fissured bark, and can reach up to 148ft (45m). The leaves are irregularly lobed and appear from March/April. Catkins appear May–June, followed by clusters of acorns on very short stalks.**

USES **English oak is a tough, durable, close-grained wood and has been used for furniture, ship building, timber frames for houses, and even barrels. As a fuel it burns slowly and gives off a lot of heat; it is also used for smoking fish and meat. Acorns can be boiled and roasted to make a coffee substitute.**

They took me up to the wood they felt was most suitable and they couldn't have suggested a better spot. There is a diverse range of trees: tall, strong oaks (perfect for holding a tree house), ash, hazel, chestnut, larch and a few evergreens. There is a lot of fallen wood that could be used for fuel, as well as plenty of hazel stands in need of a little trimming (coppicing) that could be used for building. Now the land has been secured it is time to begin this whole crazy adventure.

Friday 10th April

Technically I am still a London resident, but the lack of freelance work has left me with empty days that are best spent down in Sussex preparing for the next six months. The first thing on my 'To Do' list is a wood burning stove – the heart and soul of any woodland dwelling. Thus far, research has proved demoralising, as it seems the cheapest stove I could buy (including the stovepipe, flash plate and rain hood) is around £400–500, and I simply don't have that kind of money.

The thought of building my own stove fits more comfortably with my plan of using recycled materials where possible. Scouring the Internet has turned up a few options, mostly involving recycled gas canisters, and the use of a heavy-duty welding kit. Eventually I came across an interesting set of plans by a chap in the US that was produced for an online countryside and small stock journal.

The plans are very basic and involve using very low-tech materials: he made his stove using a 55 gallon (250 litre) steel drum (the kind usually cut in half and used as a barbecue), a bit of nip and tuck using a jigsaw, a drill, pliers, bolts, a hinge and a few L-brackets.

I thought sourcing the steel drum would be harder than it was. On a trip to my local town to get a few fixings I drove past a garage with a couple of drums sitting outside. I pulled in and asked the owner if they might have any for sale. 'S'alright, mate, you can 'ave it for nufink.' It was that easy. He told me to pop back and pick up the drum that afternoon, once they had drained any remaining oil.

I have decided to call my stove Bertha after the extraordinarily capable factory machine in the 1980s' TV show *Bertha* that I watched as a child. Hopefully my version will be just as effective …

HOW TO BUILD BERTHA

1 Drill a hole at the edge of the top of the drum (the end with the screw-on caps). Using a jigsaw with a metal cutting blade, cut around the edge of the drum and remove the 'lid' (this will eventually be bolted on as the firebox floor). Bear in mind before making any cuts with the jigsaw, that you will have to drill a hole to insert the jigsaw blade (as above).

2 In an open area, make a small fire in the bottom to burn off any excess oil or residue still clinging to the insides (remember to stand well back). Once it has cooled, you can begin work.

3 To make the stove door, cut two rectangular openings in the front of the barrel, on the side opposite the seam. Before you start cutting, remember to mark out the openings using a thick felt-tip pen. There should be two raised rings running around the barrel, dividing it into three sections. The smaller rectangle (8in x 12in/20.3cm x 30.5cm) should be cut in the top section and will be the opening of the firebox. Keep the smaller rectangle to use for the draft plate. You will also need to cut out a larger rectangle (10in x 14in/25.4cm x 35.6cm) from the bottom section; this larger rectangle will be used for the firebox door (see step 6, p.14).

4 The hole for the stovepipe should be positioned on the top surface of the stove near the back edge. You will need a stovepipe with a diameter of 5in (12.7cm). Position a section of the stovepipe about 1in (2.5cm) in from the seam and draw around it with a felt-tip pen. Next, draw a 4in (10.2cm) circle inside the 5in (12.7cm) circle. By cutting out the smaller circle, you can cut the remaining 1in (2.5cm) into tabs that can be bent up when fitting the stovepipe. You can then fit the stovepipe with L-brackets or self-tapping screws.

5 The firebox floor can be made using the round disc that was cut out of the top of the barrel (see step 1). This will be supported by 3in x 3in (7.6cm x 7.6cm) L-brackets. Six brackets spaced evenly, with an extra one at the door, work well, but if you want to use more, it does not hurt. Drill holes in the barrel about 1in (2.5cm) below the upper ring. Make sure they are all the same distance from the top, about 2in (5cm) below the door opening. Bolt the brackets to the sides. Be sure they hang below the floor and cannot be seen from inside the firebox. Place the disc on the brackets, drill holes, and bolt the floor into place. This is a lot harder than it sounds, and is an easier job for two people rather than one. There will be a crack around the edges on the inside that can be stuffed with aluminium foil or sealed with exhaust pipe filler.

6 The air draft at the bottom of the door is quite tricky to make. Cut a piece of curved metal from the smaller rectangle left over from step 3. This should be 2½in (6.4cm) high and 9in (22.9cm) long. Make vertical markings ½in (1.3cm) wide from end to end. This draft slide is held in place by six carriage bolts. These have a round shaft with threads, topped by a square, which is then topped by a rounded head. If in doubt your DIY shop can help you locate them.

Drill five holes (two at the top, two at the bottom, and one on the left end) big enough for the shaft of the bolt to pass through, but not big enough for the square to pass through. The slide will move back and forth in the space between the stove door and the round heads of the carriage bolts. Install the five bolts and move the slide to the left as far as possible. Then drill a hole in the centre through the slide and the door. The size of the hole will be dictated by the knob you use. Through this hole, bolt the slide to the door. This will hold everything in place while you drill the air holes. Next, drill four air holes, ⅜in (1cm) in diameter, ½in (1.3cm) apart. Be sure to drill through both the slide and the door at the same time so the holes will all line up when the draft is open. The ½in (1.3cm) spaces between the holes will cover the holes in the door when the draft is closed. Remove the slide and drill or cut an opening in the door to allow for the movement of the knob screw. Replace the slide and install the sixth carriage bolt on the right end. Allow space so that the slide covers all the holes in the door when the draft is closed. Finally, attach the knob. This step involves a lot of drilling, but it results in a great air draft.

7 When fitting the door to the drum, attach the door hinge to the other side. Ideally, use an old, well-worn hinge to allow for thermal expansion (not entirely necessary).

The door latch is made using two 3in x 3in (7.6cm x 7.6cm) L-brackets. Cut one L-bracket down to 3in x 1in (7.6cm x 2.5cm) and carve a ¼in (0.6cm) notch into it that will accept the other 'latch' L-bracket. It's a bit fiddly to get a snug fit, but make adjustments until the door stays tightly shut.

EXTRA INFORMATION

It is important to test the stove outside a few times to ensure there are no weak points or cracks. Do check that the draft works and draws the smoke out of the stovepipe without any escaping; remember the stove will be used indoors! The stove does give out a fair bit of heat so make sure the floor and walls around it are fireproofed or at least a good 12in (30.5cm) away. For further information see web link on p.317.

MONDAY 20th APRIL

'Gardening requires lots of water – most of it in the form of perspiration.'

LOU ERICKSON

Before starting the tree house build in earnest I have been planning my vegetable patch. Over the last couple of years in London, I have converted our small garden into quite a productive kitchen garden: in salad production alone I was cutting plenty of money off our weekly food bill. The vegetable plot I have in mind for my woodland home is different – the aim is for it to produce 40% of my tree house diet, so there is no margin for error.

I turned up at the spot designated by my landlords with a spade, fork, machete, axe and ball of string. The area I had been allocated was a grassy patch on the edge of a maize field. There was a small stream too: a great source of water. Alongside the stream were plenty of willow trees, their buds just breaking with the coming of spring.

The first job was to mark out a 16ft x 20ft (4.9m x 6.1m) plot with string. I then began turfing and digging the plot. By the end of the day my arms and back were screaming with fatigue. I had reached my target and, though at times I wanted to, I did not decide to reduce the size of the plot. Bangers, my landlords' enormous 500lb (227kg) pig who shares the same field, was initially a great help snuffling up the turf sections for me. However, once I had removed them and stacked them in a rudimentary wall around the patch, she promptly destroyed my efforts – thanks, Bangers!

I know I will sleep well tonight, but tomorrow I'm going to be in a world of stiffness and pain …

BUILDING THE TREE HOUSE

The deep green of the woods in early summer; I wouldn't want to be anywhere else.

THE FOUNDATIONS

1 Brand-new wood for foundations. Cost: £170.
Two lengths at 17ft (8in wide x 2in thick) (5.2m [20.3cm x 5.1cm])
Nine lengths at 14ft (6in x 2in) (4.2m [15.2cm x 5.1cm])
Two lengths at 14ft 4in (6in x 2in) (4.3m [15.2cm x 5.1cm])
Two lengths at 17ft (6in x 2in) (5.2m [15.2cm x 5.1cm])

2 The first plank is always the hardest to fix. We had a person at each end holding it up and checking the wood was always level, and one person in the middle drilling holes for the coach screws and then using a ratchet to screw them in.

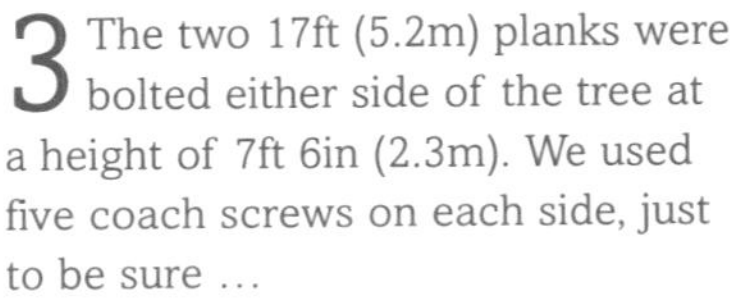

3 The two 17ft (5.2m) planks were bolted either side of the tree at a height of 7ft 6in (2.3m). We used five coach screws on each side, just to be sure ...

4 We then rested two 14ft 4in (4.3m) lengths on top of the first two planks; these would determine the width of the tree house. Up to five coach screws were used in each plank, and attaching these planks brought the platform height up to 8ft (2.4m). The planks were not fixed to each other, thus allowing them to run on each other so that they would flex and move on windy days.

5 The front and back planks were fixed on using 'L'-brackets to hold them in place until we could bolt on the side planks. Once the sides were fixed to the front and back, we were able to get an idea of the overall size of the platform.

6 A good reason to have rough plans: a conveniently placed hazel tree was bolted to the foundations for a little extra support and gave me a chance to test the platform.

7 The roof/support posts for the four corners were 15ft (4.6m) long and cut down from the surrounding woodland. The metal stanchions were an enormous help in keeping the platform level while the support posts were lifted and bolted onto the frame.

8 Each support post was fitted with a 'foot' – a wooden block that was bolted to the bottom to spread out the final weight of the tree house. These were dropped into a pit 1ft (30.5cm) deep and covered with soil, which we then packed down using our feet.

9 We put up eight roof/support posts: three on each side at 16ft (4.9m), and one each on the front and back at 20ft (6.1m) to form the apex of the roof.

10 At the end of day one the main frame of the platform was up and four corner supports fitted, but for now the tarp in the background was home!

11 To fill the frame, which would support the flooring, we used the 14ft (4.2m) planks and spaced them at 2ft (61cm) intervals, starting with the two either side of the tree. Each plank was fixed with two coach screws at each end and then with 'L'-brackets to the central beams.

12 Not bad for two days' graft: the two 20ft (6.1m) roof apex supports were last to be fitted. I could now begin work on my own quite comfortably!

The Balcony

1 The task of cutting 119 pieces of reasonably straight 5ft (1.5m) lengths of hazel was definitely a labour of love! Each piece I cut down had to be able to provide me with at least two or three sections for the balcony floor. I did test to see if they were strong enough first.

2 So that it was possible to use the hazel lengths for the balcony, they were supported by three of the platform beams. Each length needed a hole drilled through it over each beam to prevent the wood from splitting before it was nailed into place.

3 Aesthetics are just as important as functionality. The banisters were made from dead oak branches I found around the wood. Both 'Y'-shaped and straight pieces were laid out within the frame before being cut to size.

4 The frame was fixed to two lengths of wood underneath to keep the correct width before arranging the oak in an order pleasing to the eye. Some fitted perfectly, others not quite so well …

5 Before being fixed into place I removed the weathered surface of each branch to reveal the true character of this beautiful wood. This 'skinning' and sanding was the most labour-intensive part of the job, but well worth it.

6 The finished banister sections were hauled up onto the balcony and fitted between the roof/support posts with 'L'-brackets; small wooden blocks were used to hold them up off the hazel floor. The result was a completely natural balcony, which blended into the surrounding woodland.

THE FLOOR

1 The area to be covered with floorboards was 14ft x 12ft (4.2m x 3.6m). I had tried to get as much 18mm plywood as possible, but beggars can't be choosers, so I did end up using some 12mm as well.

2 The start of the jigsaw puzzle: a pile of recycled offcuts sits ready for distribution. Still, it cost nothing!

3 I began with the biggest pieces (so it felt like I was making progress more quickly!). The edge of each board had to cover just half the surface of a foundation plank and was then screwed down using 50mm screws.

4 In most cases I had to add these extra sections into the foundations. Because of the erratic size of the recycled plywood, the pieces didn't always fit. By screwing in these 'bridges', I was able to add a surface and a support into which I could screw the flooring.

5 I couldn't let rain stop play. Because I used the big pieces first, the jigsaw puzzle became ever more complex when it came to fitting in all the smaller bits. Annoyingly, this meant using more screws, and occasionally having to scour building sites for more wood.

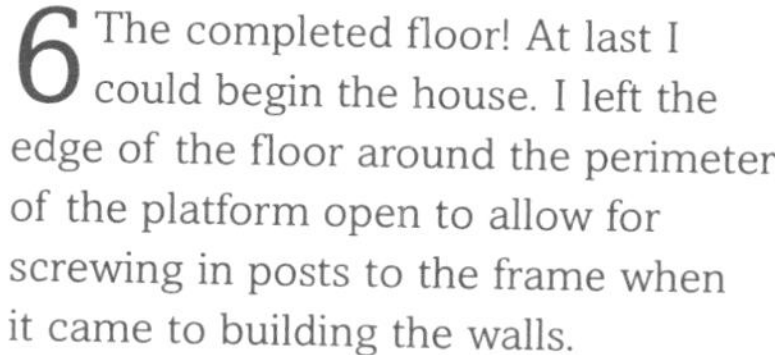

6 The completed floor! At last I could begin the house. I left the edge of the floor around the perimeter of the platform open to allow for screwing in posts to the frame when it came to building the walls.

THE FRAME

1 My first job was to put up the roof lintel. As there was a tree running through the middle of the house, I had to attach a block on each side of the tree to fix the two sections of the lintel to, once again with the use of my big coach screws (and notice the all-important use of the spirit level!).

2 The heavy roof lintel ready to be lifted into place. Once in position, one end of the lintel was attached using 'L'-brackets, while the other end sat in a convenient fork at the top of the roof/support post and was screwed into place with builder's band.

3 The other section of lintel was fixed in place with a coach screw straight through the roof/support post. One of the more precarious Health & Safety moments of the build …

4 The front and back rafters were the first to go up; this was because the side beams would need to rest on them at each end. Then the rafters covering the main body of the tree house would rest on the side beams … are you with me so far?

5 The side beams were single 18ft (5.5m) lengths of wood and rested on the front and back rafters. I bolted these into place using coach screws. The frame uprights were spaced to the exact size of the giant pieces of Perspex I had obtained for my windows and were screwed onto the foundations (in the gap I had left). They were then fixed to the side beams on top using coach screws.

6 The rafters were 10ft (3m) lengths of birch and came from a different area of woodland that was a little overcrowded. They were spaced at intervals of 22in (56cm); I put up 20 rafters in total, but cut down only ten trees. When I put the rafters up I kept them in order as each pair represented two halves of the same tree.

7 The rafters were tricky to put up due to working at height! First I had to cut the end that joined the roof lintel at the correct angle. I then rested one end on top of the side beam, and climbed the ladder with the other end and a drill to pin it in place with a screw, before securing it from the top with a length of builder's band. (Notice I took the precaution of screwing a block of wood into the floor to prevent the ladder slipping!)

8 Framework complete. Because the roof didn't have to support an enormous amount of weight, the fixings used were fairly light. The framework was made exclusively from natural round wood, mainly birch with a few lengths of ash. Finally I had a frame to put up the roof, so I could start to think about moving upstairs!

THE LADDER

1 The ladder, made from hazel, was 9ft (2.7m) long and had seven rungs. First we cut notches for the rungs in the sides of the ladder using a saw and a chisel. The rungs were split in half at each end to ensure a tight fit and a flat surface so they could be fixed together with screws.

2 Nick testing our handiwork. If there was anything that could cause an accident at the tree house, it would be the frequent use of the ladder; thankfully it was built to last!

THE ROOF

1 I got my roofing from a demolition yard; the corrugated iron had come from an old Sussex barn. Unfortunately they had only 8ft (2.4m) sheets, so I bought 22 sheets at a wholesale rate of £3 a sheet, £66 in total – a bargain!

2 There was a lot of debate over the best way to put up the roofing, so Chris and I tried them all. We found putting the sheets together on the floor and then hoisting them up was the easiest, but this didn't work as well when it came to fixing them in place. Running along the length of the rafters were two rows of hazel lengths that were screwed down to the rafters, so we screwed the corrugated iron sheets down onto them.

3 Here are the first two sheets in place over the balcony. The camouflage tarp, which had been my base camp up until now, was stapled over what would become the inside of the tree house to act as extra waterproofing. The tarp was stretched taut over the roof and stapled down using a staple gun I still had from my set-design days.

4 Corrugated iron is a series of peaks and troughs. All the holes for the screws were drilled in the troughs to get the best fixing closest to the wood underneath. When fitting the sheets together for a roof, make sure they overlap by at least two peaks and troughs to form a weatherproof seal.

5 The gap in the middle of the roof was covered with two overlapping sheets that were screwed down lengthways to the roof lintel. The only problem was that once I had screwed them all into place I was stuck without a way down. In the end I slid down a nearby hazel tree!

6 My first night undercover in the tree house. Tom strung up his fancy hammock, while I was confined to the floor. We even brought Bertha up to see how she liked her new home. Notice the window in the background ready to be fitted.

THE WALLS

1 I was very lucky to get my hands on the remains of quite a large shed, which I gradually picked to pieces and used in sections. All the wood used for the walls was recycled; I went through skips, builders' yards and even friends' garages. One of the set-design companies I had worked for donated quite a bit of scrap wood and the Perspex for the windows.

2 Fortunately I didn't have many tree trunks to contend with! I wanted the tree house to fit into its surroundings – I didn't want to remove anything that got in the way. Cutting the wood to fit around the trees was tough, and my efforts were by no means perfect, but nothing a bit of patching wouldn't fix …

3 To prevent the tree house looking like a garden shed in a tree, I tried to break up the walls by putting in lengths of wood running down from the roof. Another jigsaw to complete!

4 I began each wall by putting up a frame for the window, made from lengths of timber 2in (5.1cm) wide and 2in (5.1cm) thick. Having such enormous windows meant I would save myself having to put up more walls!

5 The four massive windows measured 3ft x 5ft (0.9m x 1.5m). I began by screwing 2in x 1in (5.1cm x 2.5cm) timber to the edges of the Perspex to make a solid frame. I then attached the Perspex window to the wall frame with two hinges at the top, so they could swing up and clip onto the ceiling with the help of a couple of metal hooks and some string. I also cut small blocks of wood, which were screwed to the bottom of the window frame and could be turned through 90 degrees to act as window locks.

6 Getting to the bottom of the wall to screw the wood into place on the outside was dodgy to say the least, but it had to be done!

7 Working on the final front wall was a relief, and at last I had something to stand on when screwing wood into the outside! From this point on I was able to be less strict with my recycled wood, as I had more than enough to finish the tree house.

8 Fitting the downward lengths: on the front and back of the tree house I had to mark the angle of the roof slope and cut the lengths to size before screwing them into the rafter. I felt it was important to mix up the colours of the recycled wood to give the front of the tree house a warm look and feel.

9 Four walls almost complete! Note the door resting against the tree ready to go in. Hanging the door would take a few more pairs of hands, so I would have to wait for some visitors.

THE DOOR

1 The tree house door came from a skip and still had the hinges and lock attached. I toyed with the idea of making a stable door by cutting it in half, but decided against it. The door frame was built out of chunky recycled timber from a new block of flats in the local town.

2 I got Nick, the product designer, to chisel three notches carefully in the door frame for the hinges to fit into, and we screwed the door into place with heavy-duty screws.

3 I bought a brand-new rimlock to fit to the door and removed the old one. The handle was made from a conveniently shaped piece of hazel from the offcuts left over from building the balcony. I stripped the bark off the handle using a knife, and then sanded it down until it was smooth and wonderfully rustic.

THE LOO

1 My posh mahogany loo seat came from a trip to the demolition yard where I also got the tree house roof and Bertha's stovepipe. I was a bit shocked by the £10 price tag, but you can't put a price on comfort! All the necessary measurements had to be taken before construction.

2 The toilet design was more complex than I thought. I needed somewhere at the back to screw the seat into, and the top had to have a large enough hole and yet still have an edge for the seat to rest on.

3 To add a nice woodland touch and screen the hole in the ground that the loo would sit over, I delved into the pile of hazel offcuts once again. There were practical problems with a slatted front that soon became obvious after road-testing! The sides were left open for ventilation …

4 I had to build a backrest for the loo seat to rest on when in the upright position. This was made from some more hazel and tied together with jute twine. It also gave me some useful bits to hang the toilet roll on.

5 The toilet unit was designed to sit over a hole dug in the ground. As most of the time I was the sole user, I dug a hole 3ft (91cm) deep and 1ft (30.5cm) square. For numbers one and two I always put a handful of sawdust in afterwards, in direct ratio to the number being executed. Once a week I would clean out the ash from Bertha and tip some of that in too, which helped combat any interest from flies and unpleasant odour.

6 Positioned a short walk from the tree house, the throne was one of the most comfortable loos I have ever used. It was even made to be the same height as a standard lavatory in a normal bathroom, for that added 'homely' touch.

THE BED

1 The wood used to build the bed comprised a couple of chunky ash logs, a few recycled bits of timber, and some thin slats I found in the garage at my mother's house. All I needed to construct was a fixed frame on which I could rest an inflatable mattress. The dimensions for the mattress were 6ft 2in x 4ft 6in x 6in (1.9m x 1.4m x 15.2cm).

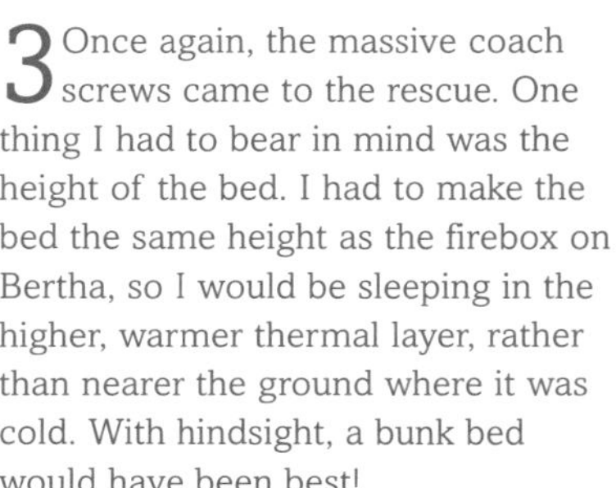

2 For the end of the bed that would be seen (the foot) I made the legs from ash. For the legs at the head end I used the same large timber that I used for the sides of the bed; these were 'L'-bracketed to the wall and floor.

3 Once again, the massive coach screws came to the rescue. One thing I had to bear in mind was the height of the bed. I had to make the bed the same height as the firebox on Bertha, so I would be sleeping in the higher, warmer thermal layer, rather than nearer the ground where it was cold. With hindsight, a bunk bed would have been best!

4 To fix the slats that would hold the mattress, I screwed in a baton the length of the sides and used a thick piece of timber running down the middle for extra support.

5 The slats came from the ceiling of our old house and only needed to be cut to size and put in place, rather than being screwed down. The entire inside of the frame needed a thorough sanding – splinters and air beds don't mix!

6 The bed was incredibly comfortable. I had a single duvet over the mattress, a double duvet over the top and three pillows! I had a sleeping bag on stand-by, but never had to use it. I often slept with my head at the bottom of the bed – that way I could keep an eye on Bertha …

THE KITCHEN UNIT

1 I was lucky enough to find this old sink unit in an ancient tip in the corner of the wood. After a good scrub down it passed the hygiene test and just needed something to rest on. I built the frame using a mixture of hazel and ash. To begin with, I built a rectangular frame to support the sink, and then added the back legs and a crossbar that I could use to hang things on. I added the front legs, and then worked on putting in crossbeams and struts to make the frame stronger.

2 Other than the ladder, my first major undertaking in building something from round, natural wood was difficult. I had to make a lot of notches to fit various bits of wood, drill holes so the wood wouldn't split when a nail was hammered into it, and work out how to use as few supports as possible to make a rigid frame that would support the weight of the sink and the 5½ gallon (25 litre) water barrel that would sit on top.

3 The completed structure. Unfortunately the rectangular frame the sink sat in wasn't quite level, but a few small chocks of wood later and all the water went straight out of the plughole.

4 Originally I had wanted the kitchen unit inside the tree house. Eventually, though, I decided it would be more practical to keep it downstairs. Despite looking everywhere for a plug big enough, I ended up using a shaved-down disk of ash and some sphagnum moss – a method developed by some ingenious guests, Ben and Katie.

5 The sink unit still in working order after five months. I fitted a metal bucket underneath, which hung off some rope with butchers' hooks: when the bucket was full, I simply unclipped it and emptied the water into a nearby drainage ditch. As you can see, the crossbar certainly did come in handy!

The Clay Oven

1 After a disastrous bread-making episode I decided I needed a proper oven. First I dug a shallow pit and lined it with bricks. Between the bricks I pushed hazel saplings into the earth, arranged in a circle. I began by bending down two opposite lengths, tying them together in the middle, and cutting off any excess hazel to create a dome.

2 Once the dome shape was complete, I began weaving smaller, shorter saplings, starting at the top and working down. The plan was to make a woven frame that I could cover with a thick layer of clay. The size of the oven opening was determined by the larger of my two roasting pans. When the clay had dried out, the plan was to make a fire inside that would gradually burn away the wooden framework and set the clay hard, leaving a solid clay dome – cunning!

3 Processing the raw material, clay, from the wood was hard work. First I had to find a source of dry clay. Rabbit burrows were a good source of fine, dry, pre-dug clay, as was the spoil from the hole I dug for the loo. Then it was a matter of pounding the clay into a fine powder.

4 The mix. The three ingredients for the mix were clay, sand and hay. The clay came from the wood, for sand I used silt from the river, and fortunately the farmer was cutting the fields around the wood for hay. For a good clay mix, you need to add 'temper', or sand. The mix that I found worked best for me was two parts sand to one part clay, and then as much hay as I could add so that the mix was still thick and sticky.

5 The reason for adding temper is to give the clay body and to help it keep its shape. The end result after adding both temper and hay is a more durable oven that won't crack as much during the drying-out process. I began by putting a thick base layer over the bricks and then worked from the bottom of the dome upwards, building up layers of clay until it was about 2in (5cm) thick.

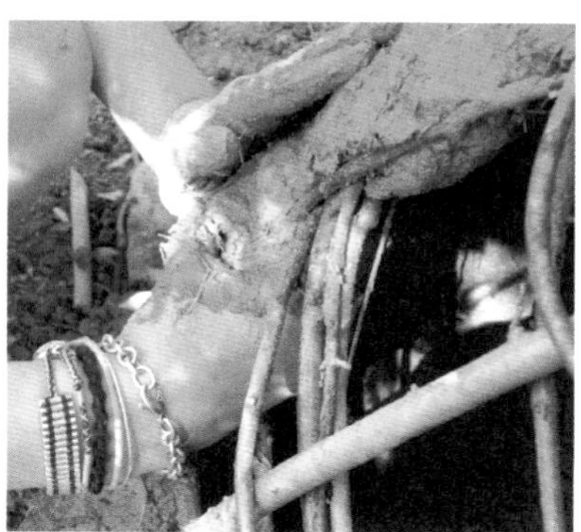

6 When Clare came to help me, she quickly mastered the technique for applying the clay mix. Use one hand on the inside to keep the clay in place and the other hand to press and smooth the clay out over the frame.

7 Rather than seal the dome completely with clay, leave a small, round piece of wood sticking out of the framework and layer the clay around it. This will be the chimney and will help to regulate the temperature inside.

8 As a final flourish, Clare and I used hinges, 'L'-brackets and nails to create our own design around the bottom of the oven. I couldn't light a fire in the oven straightaway as the sudden heat would cause the clay to dry too quickly and produce serious cracks. Instead, I let the oven dry slowly over a week, during which time a few cracks appeared. I filled these in with a pure clay 'slip', consisting of water and powdered clay.

9 When the oven was dry enough, it was time to get it fired up. For the door I used a piece of 18mm ply, which had been soaked in a bowl of water for an hour to prevent it burning. To get the oven working effectively, I gradually built up a small fire in the middle of the oven with kindling and then added some small oak logs. After half an hour with the door half on to retain heat and get the fire burning well, the fire was pushed back in a semi-circle. Whatever needed cooking was then placed in the centre of the oven, and on went the wooden door.

10 The oven performed brilliantly: I could bake a loaf of bread in 25 minutes and roast a pheasant in 40 minutes. Sometimes I even made pizza! Whenever cracks appeared, I sealed them up with clay slip. I did find the dome was a bit too high, so whatever I was cooking had to be raised up on a brick – but these were just teething problems!

THE STOOL

One thing I was keen to learn while in the woods was how to make furniture out of round wood, using traditional methods. Usually wood used to build furniture has been well seasoned (for six months to a year, to allow the wood to dry out and shrink). The wood I used was only about two months old and not fully seasoned.

My first attempt was a small stool for sitting and cooking by the fire. The bottom 'stretchers' were pegged tightly into holes drilled into some timber blocks, and the hazel lengths on top of the stool had holes drilled in each end and were nailed into place. The best thing was that if the wood ever split or broke, there was no shortage of replacements around me!

THE BENCH

1 I found a fallen tree covered with a curved mat of thick ivy and moss. I decided it might make the perfect woodland bench top, as the ivy was so thick it had a natural springiness about it, which was reinforced with the curve it had grown in.

2 To build the pegs that would be the 'stretchers' between the front and back bench legs, I whittled down both ends of four lengths of hazel.

3 I drilled a couple of large holes in each of the bench legs, into which I then hammered the hazel 'stretchers', until they were a very tight fit.

4 The result was two ends of a bench, solid as a rock, and completely free from any fixings. I was amazed at how easy it was and how beautiful it looked.

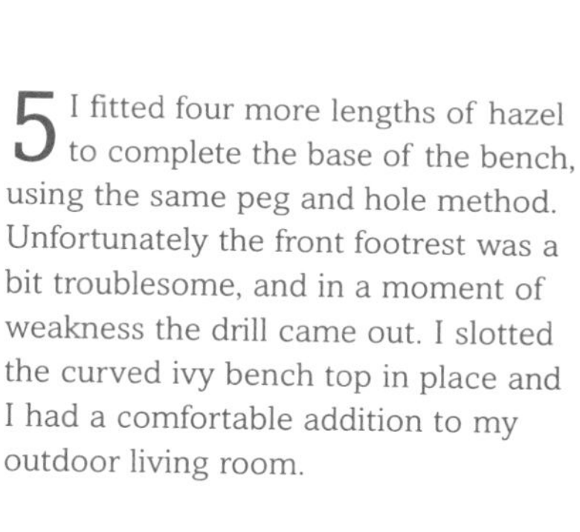

5 I fitted four more lengths of hazel to complete the base of the bench, using the same peg and hole method. Unfortunately the front footrest was a bit troublesome, and in a moment of weakness the drill came out. I slotted the curved ivy bench top in place and I had a comfortable addition to my outdoor living room.

6 My outdoor living room slowly filled up with useful items, and life in the woods became increasingly settled and began to feel like home. Here I am sitting on the bench fixing nightlines.

The finished tree house. By late summer the tree house had taken on a slightly weathered look and was beginning to fit in to its surroundings. The sight of my home lit up at night was very comforting, especially after a fruitless mission to check nightlines at midnight.

Tuesday 21st April

I want to make my patch look as Shire-like as possible, but without as many hairy-footed, pointy-eared hobbits. So I looked to the willows by the river and the hazel in the wood to provide me with enough fencing material to keep out any unwanted rabbits, deer, sheep or large, waddling portions of pork.

To achieve the look I was after I hammered cut lengths of hazel into the ground around the patch at 3¼ft (1m) intervals. I took a pair of garden shears to the stumps of willow, which were laden with thin rods of new growth. After I had sheared four of the willows, I had about six faggots (tied bundles of wood) in a pile ready to be woven between the hazel lengths. It was slow work, but by the end of the day, I had built up two impenetrable walls of willow.

Wednesday 22nd April

I got down to the patch at 8am to continue the fencing. Although it was sunny there was still a chill in the air. My weaving technique, based on the age-old technique of hurdle and wattle making, was becoming more satisfactory. Increasing numbers of willow stumps were given severe haircuts and my hands slowly deteriorated into a bloody mess. By lunchtime (a fitting ploughman's and a flask of tea) all four walls were complete. It was a particularly inspired lunch break, after which I managed to install an arch for a gate from some of the leftover hazel.

The afternoon was never going to be fun: more digging. In order to grow vegetables here successfully, the entire patch needed a good going over to break up the clods of earth, and condition the soil ready to receive seeds. The field on the other side of the stream was peppered with small, dark piles of horse manure. Not being one to waste some free poo, I got my

Hazel (Corylus avellana)

DESCRIPTION
A common shrub or small tree up to 20ft (6m) high. Toothed leaves are heart-shaped and alternate, 3in (8cm) long, May–November. Flowers appear January–March: male flowers are long yellow catkins; female flowers are swollen, red buds. Hazelnuts ripen in early September.

USES **Hazel was traditionally used to make walking sticks, frames for wattle and daub houses, and fencing. It is also good for making skewers and weaving baskets, and very good for fishing rods and for building quick shelters. Small, finger-sized pieces can be chewed well at one end and then used as a rudimentary toothbrush. Coppices well, hence very sustainable. Best cut for use in spring. Hazelnuts have long been a useful source of food for animals as well as people.**

poncho (which will never smell the same again) and ran around the field collecting it up. Back at the patch, I heaved the big bag of dump across the stream and over the fence. Yet more soil conditioning and digging in the manure followed.

As the light faded, it became clear I was never going to be able to work this soil by myself. I wondered if I could get some friends involved? Yes, a digging party! The thing is, no matter how I dressed it up, I couldn't see any of them falling for it. I've realised I can't do everything by hand, and I feel I have grafted enough on this patch so, as I cannot afford for my veggies to fail, I have hired a beast of a rotivator instead.

Thursday 23rd April

As I walked down to the patch today I noticed something was afoot. At first all I could see was a few sheep gathered around the willow walls, but as I got closer, I realised the patch had been invaded! Both sheep and pig were having a grand old time wallowing in the bare earth – my fault for not installing a gate.

Getting the rotivator down to the patch was a job in itself. I had to walk it down in reverse, because going forwards was slower than a relaxed snail sitting in an armchair perusing the Sunday papers. I toiled and tilled for most of the morning, gradually getting used to the shifting of gears and the engaging of rotors. Lunchtime came and with it a patch of fine soil, which at last resembled somewhere vegetables might like to live.

The afternoon was a little more laid back as I set to work making the wigwams for my runner beans. The wigwams were made from eight 6–7ft (1.8–2.1m) lengths of hazel tied together at the top and some hazel withies bound on in an ascending spiral – it's all about the look.

Standing back to survey my handiwork, I was amazed at what a few days of enthusiastic hard work can achieve. I can imagine walking down here on a warm summer's evening to pick and water the vegetables, plucking a few fish straight from the river, raiding the wild larder, and heading back to my woodland home to cook up a fresh and wild feast.

Friday 24th April

The wood for the tree house was delivered today – £150's worth. I kept going back and forth to my landlords' farm only to find it had been left at the top of the wood all along! The enormous pile of planks made me feel daunted – my plan is to get the entire tree house platform up in two days, supports and all. The whole idea has been a bit of a fantasy until now, little more than a collection of excitedly scribbled plans on scraps of paper, formulated at a kitchen table in a London flat.

While I was waiting for the delivery I went for a wander to become more accustomed to my new neighbourhood. In a stream running through the

field nearest to the wood I found lush beds of watercress and some wild mint. I walked up the hill to Birch Grove wood, which was full of birch and pine – and maybe fungi come October. I found a pair of antlers too, which were lying on the ground, arranged as if they had dropped off a deer's head barely moments ago. I am pleased with my surroundings. There is everything a woodland dweller could need: varied building materials, a well-stocked wild larder, and plenty of fur and feather for the pot. In my head I have started to enter the first of many pieces of essential data that will eventually become a mental map of all the resources available to me.

It is strange how this moment has suddenly crept up: spring is here, I have been to get my fixings, and now the wood has arrived. The fact that my bank account is empty clearly states that the tree house is going ahead.

To be honest, I am a touch anxious about living on my own in a wood. I am not scared, just concerned – and I'm wondering exactly what things will go bump in the night. Tomorrow the building will start and I will see just how hard the next few months are going to be.

SATURDAY 25th APRIL

In my excitement I woke up early – 6.30am. I looked outside – rain, bollocks! I went back to sleep and woke one hour later hoping it had just been a dream – no such luck. I hoped this wasn't a sign of things to come, but despite my worries, the weather eventually cleared by 10am.

Two friends of mine, Tim and Chris, had willingly given up their weekend to help me with the foundations. Both had had plenty of experience building camps in their youth, and they were the only people I knew who had ever built a proper tree house with walls and a roof. Tim had guaranteed the use of his Land Rover, which would make getting everything on site much easier.

However, when they turned up there was no Land Rover, just a van. Oh, well! We loaded Bertha, food, tools and ladders onto the van and headed down to the wood. It took 45 minutes to lug the stack of wood and all the rest of the gear down to the tree house site, although we did pause for coffee brewed on a gas stove. I took this opportunity to run the lads through my rudimentary plans, sketched on a piece of A4 paper with the exact measurements of the tree house platform.

I had ordered the wood to these measurements. However, it turned out that my supplier had cut the planks to their own 'nearest' measurements. At only 1ft (30.5cm) or so out, but basically the same, we decided to avoid any extra cutting and go with what we had.

We sized up the tree I had chosen for the tree house and began by laying out, measuring and drilling the first board. A true tree house is generally considered to be one that is at least 20ft (6.1m) off the ground with no support posts in contact with the ground. As I will be building most of the tree house myself, I have bent the rules a touch. I have deemed 8ft (2.4m) a safe working height for me and my builders – just as well, as it turned out, as our two stepladders could only just make this height comfortably.

The first two planks we put up were the two main crossbeams, followed by another pair running across them. I think we may have used too many coach screws – six per board! For the foundations my fixings of choice are M10 x 160mm galvanised coach screws (screws are much stronger than nails and form a tight seal into the tree, and as they are treated they do not rust, so the tree will not suffer infection). First we used a 10mm x 250mm drill bit on an electric drill to make a hole for the coach screw, and then the screw went in with the help of a ratchet. We also constantly checked and rechecked the main crossbeams using a spirit level to make sure all was, well, level.

Next we moved on to attaching the outside edges of the foundations, which would give us an idea of the overall size of the tree house. We used the big coach screws and L-brackets. All four sides went up and even took in two nearby stands of hazel. The bulkiest of the hazel trees were incorporated into the support for the foundations and attached once again with the coach screws.

We broke for lunch – pork pies, a beer, scotch eggs and some ham sandwiches. After a relaxed feed we sat in the glorious spring sunshine. It became clear that the foundations would need some serious support. Originally I had planned to have these supports running down to the tree at 45-degree angles, but this would unfortunately limit the space underneath the tree house. While we discussed the best way to add support, we realised that by cutting down slightly longer support posts we could tackle the problem of roof supports at the same time, thus killing two birds with one stone!

We donned our lumberjack hats and went to look for trees the right size (4–5in/10.2–12.7cm in diameter). To ensure minimal impact on the tree population, these had to be taken from a thick grouping of trees, and this way we would be creating a space that would be beneficial to the neighbouring trees. We ended up with a mix of hazel, ash and sycamore posts, two at 20ft (6.1m) for the central roof supports, and six at 16ft (4.9m). This means that when it is time to put up the roof, the pitch will be fairly shallow, a difference of 4ft (1.2m) spread across 8ft (2.4m).

Chris pointed out that the framework would be sturdier if each support post had an 'anchor' buried into the ground. I had some extra-chunky wood so we cut this into rectangular pieces and bolted them onto the bottom of each post. The posts were then placed into a 1ft (30.5cm) deep hole and raised into position. Tim had brought some adjustable metal stanchions, which were really handy and helped keep everything level as the frame was bolted onto the posts. We developed a good rhythm and, surprisingly, reached a suitable finishing point by 7pm! None of us had ever felled a tree before, and shouting 'Timber!' for real was certainly the highlight of the day.

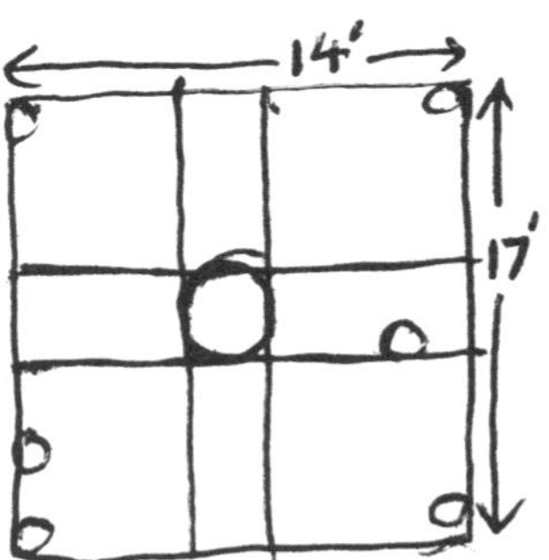

The three of us cautiously climbed up onto the foundations to test their stability and get a feel for the eventual size of the tree house.

It was both enormous and fairly stable. We all perched there, celebratory beer in hand, content with our day's labour.

Tim drove home to get his sleeping bag, while Chris and I set about digging a fire pit and collecting wood for the night. It was still fairly nippy and the fire was going to be the only source of warmth under the 15ft x 20ft (4.6m x 6.1m) tarp sheeting I had erected the week before to act as base camp (see photo, p.52). I felt it was time to road-test Bertha and she worked a treat!

I turned on my new wind-up radio and was pleased to discover all the important stations were available. After the day's hard graft we were all starving and cooked marinated chicken wings, potatoes with mint from the wood, and broad beans with butter. We had a few ales and discussed tomorrow's building before getting into our sleeping bags for some well-earned rest. Tim and Chris had blow-up mattresses (lightweights!), while I had to deal with the cold, hard ground. But to be honest, I think a sore back is going to be the least of my worries.

SUNDAY 26th APRIL

I woke to glorious sunshine on my face. The weather forecast had unreliably predicted rain – and not for the first time. As I rolled over I saw Chris sitting up staring at something. I followed his line of sight and saw what had caught his eye – a muntjac – the smallest of Britain's deer species. It was about 15ft (4.6m) away, having a gentle stroll past our camp. It wandered up to the tree and had a sniff about before Tim rolled over with a groan and a loud fart. The muntjac, startled by Tim's bodily functions, beat a hasty retreat into the undergrowth.

REEVES' MUNTJAC (MUNTIACUS REEVESI)

DESCRIPTION

Britain's smallest deer species, Reeves' muntjac measures just 20in (50cm) at the shoulder. Originally from China, the muntjac was first introduced to Woburn Park in Bedfordshire in the early 20th Century, and escapees have formed wild populations in many parts of central and southern England. It favours wooded areas. The coat is red-brown in summer and grey-brown in winter; antlers are short.

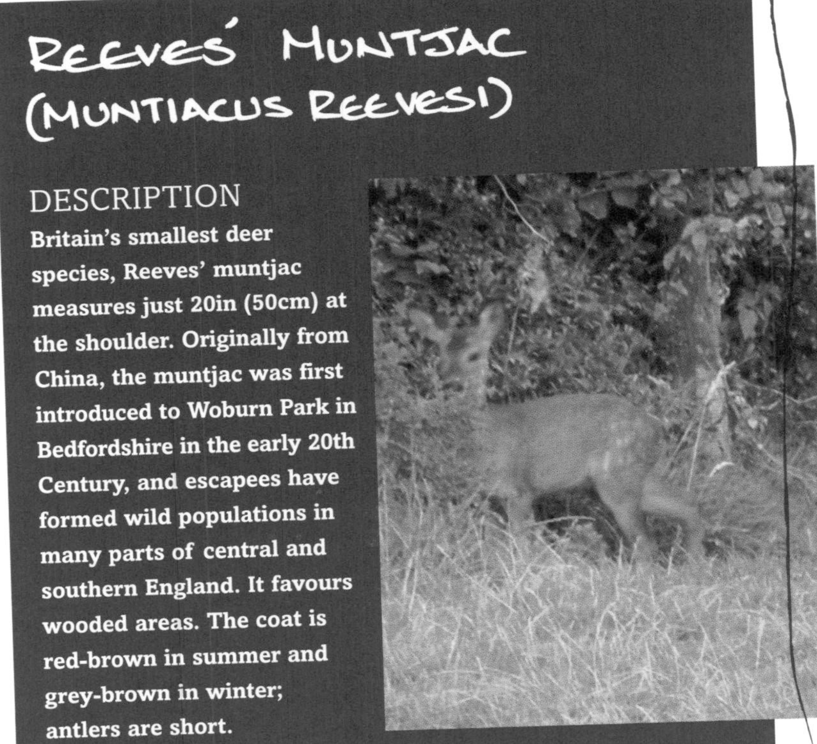

I walked over to the edge of the wood to take a leak and noticed a thick frost had set in overnight – it was a very cold morning. We then cooked a full English breakfast on Bertha; she's amazing – she also boiled the kettle in ten minutes flat! We made a large, essential pot of coffee before getting stuck into day two of the build.

We began work at 9am; we needed four more support posts, and two were the extra-long roof posts. We got back into a good rhythm and by midday moved on to fitting the beams that would support the flooring. We soon realised that, although level, the frame was not a perfect square. We measured 2ft (61cm) between each floor beam and worked along, one of us at each end drilling and ratcheting in coach screws, while Tim screwed in L-brackets in the middle. The foundations were complete by 2pm, bang on schedule.

Chris looked up at the platform and commented, 'This thing is bloody huge, and you have to build a house on there too?' 'Where are you going to get all the wood for the floor and walls? That will cost a fortune!', added Tim.

They had both hit the nail on the head, so to speak. How and where was I going to get the wood? There is one overwhelming factor involved here – I've got no money, so I need to get my scavenging boots on. I need a floor.

MAY

MONDAY 4th MAY

It's been a horrible weekend of goodbyes and cleaning out the London flat – Clare is moving in with some friends. We've been living together for the last four years, and I could never and would never live with anyone else. I love her more than anything and that's what makes doing this so much harder.

So here I am, a new Sussex resident – for now, the family home certainly makes a very luxurious halfway house. I had forgotten what a well-stocked fridge my mother keeps. I was meant to have moved to the woods on 1 May – last Friday – but logistically that didn't work. I have decided to wait before moving all my kit down there. It's not going to be easy to leave the comforts of home!

Clare came down last night so this morning we hit the patch and planted some vegetables. After a croissant and buckets of real coffee we packed up her little car with plants. It was a relief to get my kitchen garden on the move – until now the patch has looked cold and empty with just the green fringes of the first early potatoes. Today Clare and I dug in 15–16 runner beans (x 2), 6 broad beans, 1 chicory plant, 2 courgette plants, 1 chive plant, 3 sweet pea plants for colour and 3 garden peas.

I still have to put in the red onions – I'm a bit late with these. The farmer has ploughed and raked his soil so I'm one step ahead of him, and Bangers the pig has been put under house arrest, which will put an end to any more attempted break-ins. We did the planting in some steady May drizzle – I was not impressed. Clare was more than happy and said I was being pathetic. 'It's just a little bit of rain!', she kept saying.

When we returned, damp and muddy, to the family home for a ploughman's lunch, we found my friend Nick standing in the kitchen. Quite how I had managed to drag him away from his latest lady, I really don't know. Rather than lumber him (a product designer) with the dull task of laying the platform/balcony flooring, I felt he would be better suited to making the ladder – it was certainly going to be one of my most essential items.

Back at the wood we found a couple of crooked hazel trees that I decided would do the job. I fired up Bertha so I could show her off, and we spent about four hours sawing, chiselling and drinking tea in true builders' fashion – perhaps that's why it took so long! As we left the wood, I saw a group of very straight hazel saplings that would have been perfect – typical! Clearly I haven't mastered my surroundings just yet …

TUESDAY 5th MAY

First night living in them woods! It is midnight and I'm still picking the remaining bits of rabbit meat from my teeth. All I can hear is the crackle of the fire and the faint screech of an owl doing something, somewhere …

Today has made me realise just how much work needs to go into the opening stages of a project like this. Spending the day gathering and cutting materials for the build, working on the tree house, and then having to hunt and forage for my food is a real nightmare (the patch is still way off providing me with any veg) – I'm not sure there are enough hours in a day!

My name was added to the insurance on my mother's car today. On went the old roof rack and I whizzed down to a local builders' yard owned by a friend of my mother's who is one of those 'aunties' you acquire in your youth. I explained my tree house project to her and she was only too happy to help. I was allowed to take anything I wanted from the skip, and two of the fellas in the workshop pointed out all the wood they no longer needed – it was quite a haul! I was after any bits of ½in (12–18mm) ply board for the floor of the tree house, regardless of size, shape or quality (in retrospect I should have been more

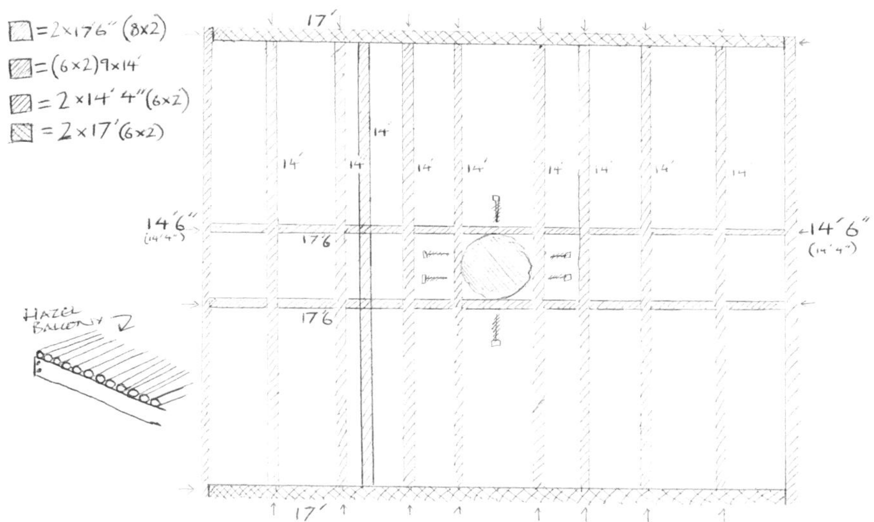

discerning). I also plucked an old, heavy window frame from the skip, possibly the base for a future loo?

Once back in the wood, I had to spend a good hour unloading and manhandling my plunder down to the site, something I knew I was going to become very familiar with over the next month. Lunch was just a couple of slices of bread filled with wild garlic leaves and some bittercress – I'm sure even vegetarians don't stoop to the level of a salad sandwich, do they?

The tree house frame looks enormous. What scares me is the fact that I am going to have to scour all the surrounding woodland (and perhaps the rest of Sussex) for the materials to build a house on top of it – a daunting prospect indeed! The only things fixed to the frame at this stage are six 5ft (1.5m) lengths of hazel that I have attached as test pieces to see if they would work as the balcony flooring. The fresh-cut hazel lengths proved to be the most forgiving, and I found I could actually jump up and down on them without fear of breakage, or loss of any limbs. Unwittingly I have set myself the task of covering 15ft (4.5m) of balcony with 1in (2.5cm) diameter hazel rods.

HAIRY BITTERCRESS (CARDAMINE HIRSUTA)

DESCRIPTION **A common weed, with rounded, pinnate leaves in a basal rosette, and a slightly hairy stem carrying a head of white flowers and long brown seedpods. Up to 12in (30cm).**

USES **The wild version of rocket, with a strong peppery taste that will liven up any mouthful. Generally considered the gardener's nemesis – use it as an edible crop and you will always have clear flowerbeds. It is especially good in salads and when I was in London I used to pick a handful from the garden to put on top of my eggs Benedict.**

I wandered around the wood trying to select the most economical lengths of hazel (the longest and straightest, in order to avoid having to cut down too many). I also took only a couple of rods from each stand of hazel, trying to follow the coppicers' code of ethics as closely as possible. If this meant going further afield to find raw materials for the good of the wood, then so be it. When I got the hazel rods back to the site I stripped them of vegetation, cut them into 5ft (1.5m) lengths on the sawhorse, and then casually launched them through the air onto what would become the balcony. All the remaining offcuts were piled up, either to season for burning in a few months' time or to be used in future building projects.

First I laid down the hazel rods so they roughly matched up and there was a slight gap in between each one (to save wood, and to save me time). I drilled holes in the ends and in the middle of each rod, and then screwed them into place. Near the end, I ran out of screws and moved on to nails, which actually did the job better! In the end it took 119 hazel rods to make the balcony floor (with 19 half-size to allow for the trap door entrance).

I set myself the target of finishing the balcony floor by 7pm, and at 6.30pm I lay back on the first part of the tree house floor with a big fat grin on my face at what I had achieved – it looked so rustic it was ridiculous. I had a small celebration and treated myself to a pint of my recently brewed nettle beer. Both grin and satisfaction disappeared quite quickly when I realised that as far as supper was concerned, I had none!

With the fishing season not kicking off until 15 June, my only option was the gun. What would I shoot: rabbit, squirrel or pigeon? It would depend on what was foolish enough to attract my attention first. I set out across the fields, creeping down hedgerows and sneaking around corners. After an hour the only creatures I had seen with the slightest hint of fur or feather were a few crows and a farmer sitting atop his big red Massey Ferguson. At this point I started to feel panicky and helpless at the possibility there might be no meat to go with my meal.

I have had these feelings before. The last time was when I was thrashing about on the reef in the Cook Islands with a bamboo fishing rod, a dental floss line, and a hairgrip fashioned into a hook with a snail attached. My time as a 'survival expert' on the Channel 4 programme *Shipwrecked* back in 2008 gave me a taste of what it was like to have to hunt and fish for all my protein, so when I embarked on my tree house project I was vaguely familiar with what I was getting myself into. I particularly remembered what a horrible feeling the prospect of nothing really satisfying to gorge on was at the end of a busy day.

Just as I was about to admit defeat and gather a bumper crop of nettles for an uninteresting meal, my luck changed. Near a gate I had climbed over some time earlier a rabbit sat munching away on the grass. I got down low and crept along the hedgerow until I was close enough to lie down, take aim, and … 'bang' (although a silenced air rifle doesn't actually go 'bang') – one fat rabbit rolled over stone dead. My spirits lifted and I had a meal! After skinning and gutting it, I stuck the liver on a whittled hazel skewer, and enjoyed the first of many rabbits that would inevitably come my way – this kind of gluttony and indulgence I could live with!

After a carnivorous meal of rabbit followed by steamed nettles, I updated my diary with the day's events, threw a few more logs on the fire and settled into my sleeping bag for my first night as a woodland dweller. I had expected to drift off straightaway after a day of hard building, but my mind was still buzzing with 101 questions, most notably: 'How am I going to feed myself properly and build a tree house at the same time?'

It is all very real now – and certainly not what I had envisaged back in London. Something is going to have to give if I am going to move into a completed tree house by the end of the month.

Wednesday 6th May

I woke at 4.30am. The fire was out and it was freezing. I had to get out of both my sleeping bags to nip to the loo. It was hard to get back to sleep afterwards as a nearby pheasant decided to start crowing. I toyed with the idea of loading the shotgun and putting an end to his dawn chorus. But then the blackbirds joined in along with the rest of the woodland orchestra – it was so loud! I'm sure I will get used to it eventually. When I finally got up at 9am my first job was to get Bertha fired up and put the kettle on for an energising cup of coffee. I badly need a bed down here – I don't mind sleeping on the ground as long as it is just every now and again.

While the kettle was boiling I wandered down to water the plants – they all seem to have settled in well. I am a bit concerned about the potatoes, which seem to be turning yellow – perhaps the horse manure is giving them nitrogen burn. Losing my crop of early spuds would be a disaster! I had some coffee and a banana, and set about building my kitchen unit, entirely from hazel. I have managed to recycle a lot of the hazel and ash that has already been felled here. I was running very low on screws so I ended up using some nails and 'borrowing' some screws from my balcony build. I must go and buy some more before I end up taking apart everything that I have made so far!

My mother came down at 4pm to see exactly what I have been up to. She kindly mustered the knowledge that all mothers have when it comes to cleaning and helped me bleach the enamel sink – it now looks almost second-hand! As I am thinking about putting the sink unit inside the tree house I had to work out a way to get the water to run out of the sink without causing a flood each time I empty it. I could have used some guttering, but instead I went for a big metal ice bucket, which is attached to two butcher's hooks underneath the plug. Once it is full I can just unclip it and empty out the water – ingenious!

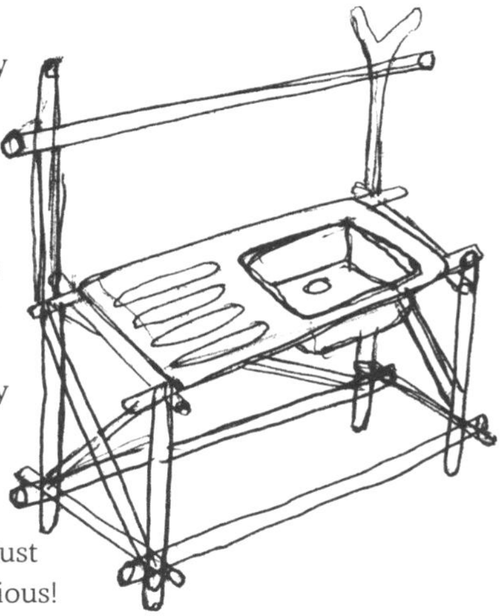

I made an important decision today, although it feels like a bit of a cop-out – I am not going to live in the wood full time until the tree house is finished. At present I have no crops and no home. Spending a whole day on the build as well as having to hunt and forage for my meals is not sustainable – one can only run on enthusiasm for so long.

I got home and crashed out in bed completely exhausted. Tomorrow I have a 6am start – I have promised to help out a friend. It had better be worth the early kickoff.

THURSDAY 7th MAY

The early start *was* worth it! Today, in return for £70, I helped Dan, who owns a campsite on the South Downs, set up his shower and loo, and make some other last-minute adjustments before a 16-strong hen party arrived. The campsite is home to two yurts (large, round Mongolian tents complete with stoves) and a collection of bell tents. In these beautiful surroundings urban types come for a couple of days of fresh air and to learn a bit about foraging – my new job. It should be a good way to earn some money during the summer and will pay for some extra things for the tree house. I spent a while tinkering with the shower and loo – good research for when I come to make my own. The shower design is ingenious, and the loo uses sawdust to minimise the smell.

Something else happened today: a publisher wants me to write a book about my tree house life!

HOW TO SKIN, GUT AND JOINT

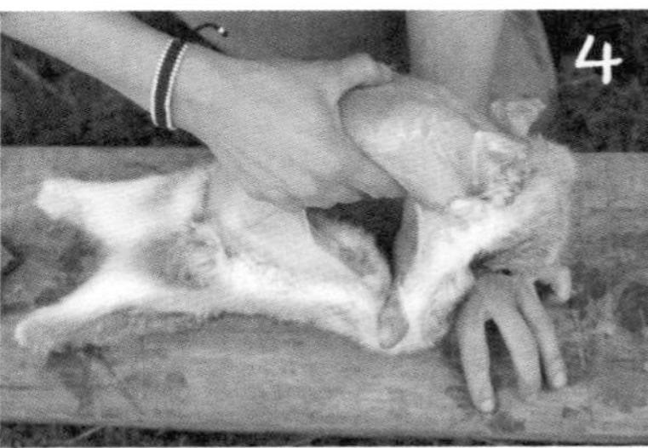

1 Lay the rabbit on a heavy chopping board or block of wood and, with a meat cleaver or old knife and hammer, chop off all the feet just above the 'knees'. Cut off the tail and then, using the same tools and technique, remove the head (the most unpleasant bit).

2 Lift the fur at the belly, make a horizontal incision, and pull the skin away from the rabbit. Insert the knife into the horizontal cut, taking care not to pierce the stomach, then, holding the knife upside down so the sharp edge faces upwards, slowly cut the skin from the belly up to the neck.

3 Gradually pull the skin away from the rabbit's flesh, which, if fresh, should come away easily. Work your way around the body of the rabbit to begin with and then upwards to the front legs. The legs must be popped out through the skin. The best way to do this is to pull out the skin around the leg and push on the stump of the rabbit's leg from the other side – a bit like taking off a jacket.

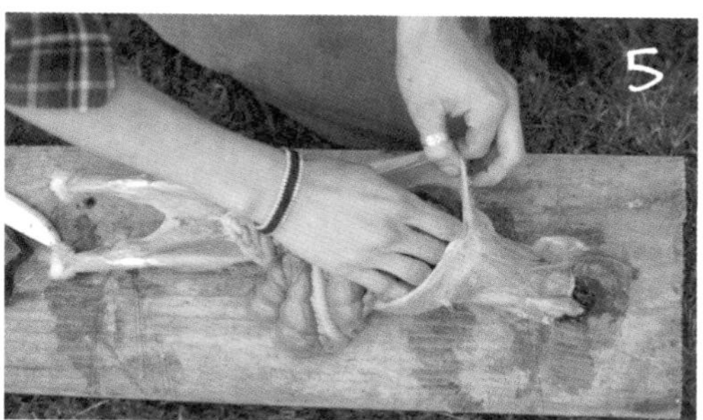

4 The final stage is to grip the shoulders of the rabbit and pull the skin down over the back legs – again, like removing an item of clothing.

5 Next you must paunch or gut the rabbit; this will prevent it from spoiling. Make another horizontal cut across the belly (again, try not to pierce the intestines), and gradually slice open the stomach. Reach in and upwards to the ribs, grasp the intestines, and remove with one firm tug. Put aside the rabbit's liver for eating – this is the best bit! Cut through the diaphragm and pull out the heart and lungs. With a knife, cut out the rabbit's 'bottom'; make two cuts to form a 'V'-shape where the tail was and remove any remaining droppings from the rectum. Give the rabbit a scrub under running water; it is now ready to be jointed or cooked.

6 A rabbit is usually jointed into five sections: the two hind legs, the saddle, and the two front legs and ribcage. The first chop is made just above the hind legs. Once separated, chop down the middle of the hind legs. Then chop the top of the saddle, just below the ribcage, and finally split the front legs and torso down the spine.

SATURDAY 9th MAY

Today I went to Lewes with Clare for a few bits for the shower, and ended up buying a T-shirt, a 1934 copy of *Robinson Crusoe* and a hardcore head torch. For some reason I had put off investing in a good head torch because of the £25 price tag, but in the end I realised it would be essential when living somewhere with no power – what an idiot! I went with Clare

MEADOWSWEET (FILIPENDULA ULMARIA)

DESCRIPTION **Widespread and common in damp habitats such as marshes, alongside streams, and wet woodland and grassland. Usually 2–4ft (60–120cm) high but can be taller. Leaves are dark green on top and hairy white underneath with a red stem and feature up to five pairs of large leaflets with smaller ones between. The creamy-white flowers grow in scented, frothy clusters, June–September, although the leaves can be found in late winter and spring.**

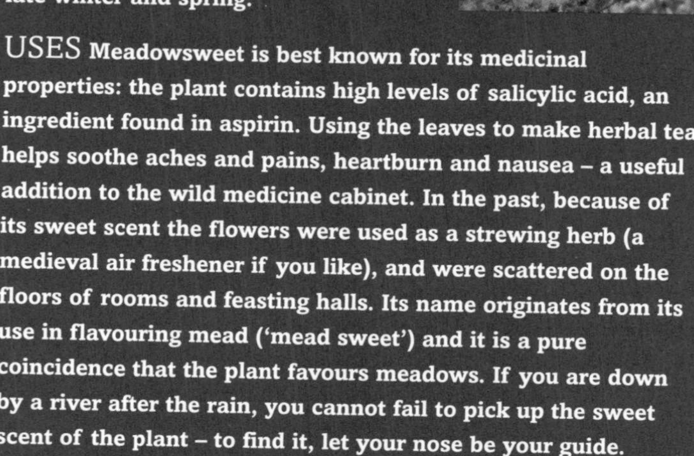

USES **Meadowsweet is best known for its medicinal properties: the plant contains high levels of salicylic acid, an ingredient found in aspirin. Using the leaves to make herbal tea helps soothe aches and pains, heartburn and nausea – a useful addition to the wild medicine cabinet. In the past, because of its sweet scent the flowers were used as a strewing herb (a medieval air freshener if you like), and were scattered on the floors of rooms and feasting halls. Its name originates from its use in flavouring mead ('mead sweet') and it is a pure coincidence that the plant favours meadows. If you are down by a river after the rain, you cannot fail to pick up the sweet scent of the plant – to find it, let your nose be your guide.**

to her house so she could get ready for her first night in the woods. Her wardrobe isn't very well equipped for outdoor living – but why would it be?

When we got to the woods, I lit a fire under the tarp, and we sat with a glass of wine before going for a wander at dusk so I could demonstrate my manly hunter-gathering skills. What I actually produced was a dainty, fully foraged salad of primrose flowers, sorrel, wild garlic, golden saxifrage, chickweed and hairy bittercress, all found within 650ft (200m) of camp. Sadly Clare wasn't all that impressed by my macho display – perhaps next time I need to do it bare-chested with a knife in my teeth. For dinner we had steak and potatoes with the salad, and then washed it down with a calming, wild infusion of mint and meadowsweet tea.

MINT AND MEADOWSWEET TEA

Mint makes a good partner for meadowsweet, as it too has soothing properties, and is particularly good as a digestive aid. Steep a few leaves from both plants in a mug of boiling water for five minutes and enjoy.

Damn caterpillars! The little buggers are everywhere and on everything! They seem to have appeared overnight. Brown, green, big and small, they have been dropping from the trees on lines of silk like mini-paratroopers. They seem particularly partial to anything made of metal. Bertha was covered with them – until she was fired up, that is! It was Clare's first night sleeping in the open and I was very proud of her. I am not sure she will stay again until there is a proper loo and a tree house to sleep in, but she did seem to enjoy it … I think.

SUNDAY 10th MAY

I found out the best way to get Bertha going for morning coffee is to use small kindling – this produces lots of flame. I sat in the field this morning and watched a fox eating a pheasant egg – it must be difficult without a spoon. I think I will call him Frank – he looks like a Frank. It might be a good idea to create my own community of animals around me, or is that a little bit mad? I am also thinking of making a bird table for my leftover bread. I gave Frank the remains of a rabbit the other day and I heard him barking his thanks at 5am the next morning.

This afternoon I put the shower together. It consists of a metal bucket, a watering can rose, a gas valve with lever, and a few plumbing fixtures.

How to Make a Shower

My shower consists of a metal bucket, with a few plumbing bits fixed to a gas valve on/off lever switch, and a watering can rose (head) attached to the end with a J-clip.

For the perfect woodland shower, first I have to heat up the water on the fire in my big pan to the desired temperature. The bucket is then placed on top of the sawhorse (there is a gap for the shower head to fit through) and filled with water. The shower is clipped to a sling or some rope using a carabiner and hoisted up into a fork in the tree.

The shower lasts for about three minutes with the switch on halfway. I find the best method is to soak myself for 30 seconds, turn the shower off, scrub down thoroughly with soap, and then turn it back on to rinse off until the shower runs out. The shower has a great spread and is perhaps one of the most liberating cleansing experiences you can have!

MONDAY 11th MAY

Today was all about flooring. With the hazel balcony done I needed to get cracking on finishing the platform. I started early, around 7am, and so I could keep the car for the day, I had to drop my mother at the school where she teaches – how the tables have turned!

I spent most of the morning driving around looking for wood. My first stop was another family friend who worked at a building firm. He found my tree house idea a bit bizarre, but gave me access to plenty of plywood scraps, which I greedily stashed on the roof rack. Most of the boards were slightly worn, while others had remnants of cement plastered across them, but they were almost full sheets, which was what I was looking for.

I dropped my haul off at the wood and then went to look for building sites that might have some wood going spare. I found one on the outskirts of a nearby town that had loads, and it was good-quality timber too – I can't believe they were going to throw it away! Most of the wood was in the form of beams and rafters – not great for floors, but good for joists to support the flooring and any future framework.

I made sure I had a good cover story for my mission: I would speak to the foreman and explain that I was creating an art installation using recycled materials. The story worked well and it reminded me of a childhood scam that involved writing to sweet companies to request samples for an imaginary sweet-based school project – it worked every time!

At a builders' merchant, where I purchased some screws, I took the opportunity to ask if I could go through their skip. 'Ask the lads in the yard, but they might call you a skinflint …!' Cheers, mate. I am getting used to being called that. I'm the one who's laughing though – haven't had to pay a penny for my wood so far.

I spent the afternoon ferrying ply down to the tree house site – exhausting, especially in the wind. The floor is going to take a lot of work: there are so many small bits that it is going to be a real jigsaw puzzle. All my fixings were delivered today and I think I have collected enough recycled wood to complete the floor.

TUESDAY 12th MAY WIND

I got down to the tree by about 8.30am, put a brew on and began carrying down the mountain of wood I had accumulated yesterday – by the end my arms were tired and my hands full of splinters; I hope they get accustomed to the graft. Although it is work and I suppose the tree house build is my new job, it doesn't really feel like work; it feels more like the ambitious camp-building days of my youth. It's a shame I don't still have the ballsy, gung-ho, no-fear attitude of those days – kids are so lucky!

Today was all about building the tree house floor (see pp. 24–25). I used the biggest sheets of ply first and quickly found I would have to put in lots of joists underneath to have something to screw the misshapen wood into. I think I may need to get a new saw. My grandfather's antiquated piece just doesn't cut the mustard, let alone any wood. The bow saw is quite effective but only for small cuts and firewood.

It was another windy day. The wind constantly wafted over the sickening smell of manure – one of the nearby farmers was muck spreading. It has been so long since I was in the country – I used to love that smell! The wind made the tree house foundations creek a bit, and when I sat with my back to the tree I could feel everything gradually moving back and forth, like it was breathing – very weird. The foundations slide perfectly on one another where they are connected to the tree. It appears my genius arbor-engineering has paid off (or is that just a happy coincidence?).

I have started to think through the next stage of the build – the roof. I already have a tarp, hazel is plentiful, and with the number of barns being turned into fancy new conversions there must be stacks of corrugated iron lying around Sussex just waiting to be recycled. It would be nice to thatch or shingle the roof, but I just don't have the money or access to the materials – or the time!

Wednesday 13th May

I woke to a mist of drizzle, but I can't let poor weather get in the way of building a house. As I walked down to the patch, clad head to toe in waterproofs, I couldn't take my eyes off the hedgerow. What I had originally assumed was bindweed were in fact hundreds of straggly hop shoots steadily intertwining themselves around anything in their path. And what can you make with hops? Beer!

I had to finish the platform today – it involved lots of tinkering but I got there. The next stage is the house frame and the balcony railings. Originally when I nabbed some fine oak planks from a nearby builder's skip, I thought they would make good balcony railings. But now I have

HOP (HUMULUS LUPULUS)

DESCRIPTION **This hairy climber can often be seen amongst hedgerows, fences and shrubs, most commonly in England and Wales. The toothed leaves with 3–5 lobes grow in opposite pairs up to 4in (10cm) long. Male flowers are greenish hanging clusters; the green, cone-like female flowers (hops) ripen brown. Flowers July–August.**

USES **Hop shoots were highly regarded as a vegetable during Roman times. In spring they can be harvested and eaten raw, pickled or steamed for a minute or two until tender for a tasty side dish. From July onwards, the female flowers can be used for brewing. First introduced in the 16th Century to flavour beer, the bitterness initially was unpopular (Henry VIII banned brewers from using it); however, these days bitter is adored by many. Hop flowers are also useful for those suffering from sleep disorders: tie up a bunch of dried hops in a muslin bag and put it under your pillow for a thoroughly good night of slumber.**

decided to use natural wood for my railings so they fit with the surrounding woodland atmosphere. The wood I am now going to use caught my eye at quite an ironic moment – while I was cutting it up for firewood. There are an awful lot of dead, weathered oak limbs lying around the wood and they come in all manner of gnarled shapes and

sizes. I really like the 'Y'-shaped ones. I had a go at cleaning one up and it came out well – I think they will do nicely.

While I was working away during the afternoon, I suddenly heard a noise: 'clomp, clomp, CLOMP!' I nearly jumped out of my skin, but it was only my landlord coming to check on his tenant. He seemed very impressed with the proceedings and commented on the balcony floor and how it must have been 'very time-consuming.' He stood on the platform, and for a minute he seemed slightly overwhelmed by what I was creating – funny really, for something that is not much more than a shed in a tree. He then gave me a list of my rent-paying jobs. He seemed reluctant at first – he probably felt I had enough to do. Good fella!

I finished up around 6pm and met Chris in the pub for a quick ale. He presented me with something I might find useful: a bright, shiny kettle that had been knocking around in his garage for years – a new friend for Bertha and a timely replacement for my crap, dented, flimsy, gas stove kettle.

I got the first two dates for my new foraging job – that should bring in some much needed cash for tree house construction.

THURSDAY 14th MAY 

Today Paul, a friend from back in my school days, came down to stay. It seemed like one minute I was on the phone asking him if he wanted to drive down to give me a hand and sample my nettle beer, and the next minute, there he was! I thought Beaconsfield was the other side of London!

We went to get some sandpaper to use on the oak railings. I was pleased to be using the dead oak in the build. It felt like I was paying homage to my host tree – also an oak. I was turning these fallen victims into something beautiful. I didn't tell Paul that; he would have thought I was weird, or worse – a hippy.

Once the cut oak sections were whittled down with a knife, so that all the moss and rot were removed, they were then sanded down. It took ages, but the result was a rock-solid, smooth, clean and dappled finish. After all the hard work I had a good mix of 'Y's and straights. I was really pleased I was able to recycle these write-offs into something that added enormous aesthetic value to the tree house.

A quote of Kevin McCloud's from an episode of *Grand Designs* came to mind: 'I expected it to look rustic, but I wasn't prepared for it to be beautiful.' After I'd said it enough times it became hilarious to both of us – simple minds ...

So much rain today. Paul and I took the decision to camp out. The rain was relentless, almost tropical. We sat under the big tarp around a roaring fire and the drumming of the rain was so loud we could barely hear each other speak. But, we were warm, dry, and had a fair few bottles of nettle beer for comfort. We took turns winding up the radio, until Paul forgot to push in the aerial before commencing wind-up, and that was that. Around dusk a very wet pheasant came in close – I think I may have a new pet. Paul and I talked about our school days and drank my homebrew well into the night.

I like it when it rains; the scent of the soaked earth wafts into the air and all the forest smells are magnified. It also means I don't have to go and water the vegetables. I found another antler today too – six in total now.

Saturday 16th May

As the saying goes, some men are great and some have greatness thrust upon them. Others are just about the most colourful characters you ever have the good fortune to meet. The owner of my local demolition yard is one of those people, and everything and anything you could ever need can be found in his domain.

Eric was dressed in navy all-in-one overalls and a stout pair of wellies, his teeth were crooked, he sported a mop of black curly hair, and he had a lazy eye to boot; he also had a true Sussex accent, and I liked him immediately. His enthusiasm probably had a lot to do with it. I told him what I was after and he took me straight to it – this was a man with a good head for mental mapping, I took note.

I had come for a stovepipe, and Eric managed to find me a complete set: a stovepipe, flash plate and rain hood, all for £84. He was slightly bewildered by my request for a well-worn loo seat, but I found what I needed, even if I did have to unscrew it from a toilet that certainly was 'well worn'. My mahogany loo seat set me back £10. I tried to haggle in light of the dodgy stains on the back but Eric was having none of it. I also enquired about getting hold of some corrugated iron for my roof, and this time I got the bargain I was looking for. Eric said he could do 22 sheets at £3 a sheet. I will come back another day to pick them up.

£94 was a bit more cash than I wanted to part with, but I handed over the money, bid him farewell and went on my way. I drove over to see Clare's house. Her father gave me a Black & Decker workbench and her mother gave me some leeks to add to the patch – all useful stuff!

MONDAY 18th MAY

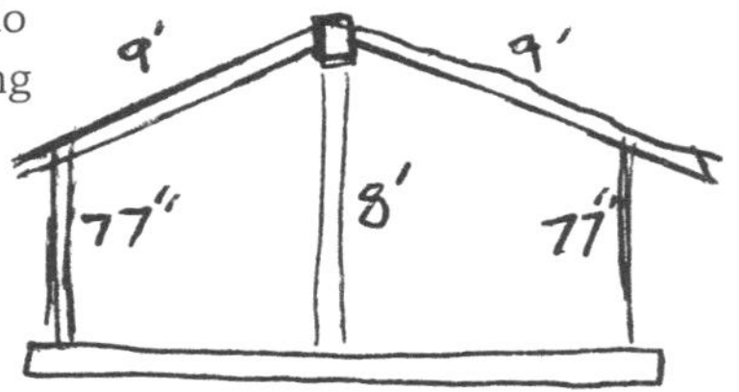

Early this morning, as I walked down to do my watering duties at the patch, something spooky happened: I coughed and immediately afterwards I heard something else cough – no idea what it was. I do know that cows long ago learned to trick hapless loners in the countryside by mastering the exact tone and pitch of the human cough, but there were no cows around. Am I being watched?

The patch looked splendid. I spent a bit of time tying up the beans (both runner and broad), dug in two tomato plants, some rocket, and all the leeks I had been given by Clare's mother. I tried my best to spread some plastic over the salad, hoping for a sort of greenhouse effect, but the wind made life difficult. Eventually I managed to create something that resembled a rubbish poly tunnel and then I walked back to the tree.

Today I started work on the tree house frame and the roof lintels were first to go up. I had wanted to use round wood but felt life would be easier using big square lengths of timber instead – this time practicality and stability overcame aesthetics. It was hard work on my own and a purple sling of mine came in very handy. I got the front lintel up and then put together the workbench. It was a right pain and in the end I didn't use it.

As I worked away on the tree house platform I paused to watch a series of cockfights between two male pheasants. They didn't seem to mind having a spectator, and I even managed to give so much encouragement to the smaller of the two (I think he is my new pet) that he ended up smashing the other one's face in. The bigger of the two scurried off into the woods never to be seen again.

I finished up around 5.30pm and went to pick some wild garlic for pickling, as both that and the bluebells are slowly disappearing with the end of spring. As I went about potting up the wild garlic leaves before pouring

WILD GARLIC (ALLIUM URSINUM)

DESCRIPTION **Quite often you can smell wild garlic, also known as ramsons, before you see it; it tends to grow on riverbanks and occasionally in woodland. It grows up to 14in (36cm) high and has spear-like leaves. The stems carry umbels of white, star-like flowers from April to June.**

USES **Of all the wild plants available to us, this is perhaps the most gastronomic. It can be used in absolutely anything you would normally use cultivated garlic for: flavouring oils, meat, soups, stews, etc. The whole plant is edible – the bulbs (root) can be used in the same way as a standard clove of garlic, but the most popular part of the plant is the leaves, which present the flavour of garlic in a different form. Although the bulbs can be gathered year-round, if you know where it grows (dig them up only if they are in abundance and you have the landowner's permission), the leaves appear only during spring. For long-term use, the bulbs are best preserved in oil or pickled in vinegar, and you can pickle the leaves. Finely chopped, the leaves make a fantastic garnish, as do the pretty white flowers. Combining the leaves with sorrel or nettles can produce a wild twist on pesto or *salsa verde*. As this plant has so many applications the best advice I can give is to be experimental in the kitchen as its versatility is unstoppable!**

over the vinegar, I heard the distant rumbling of the train – probably packed with commuters. I couldn't help but smirk; that had been me not so long ago – poor buggers!

I then went over to my mother's house to post an entry on my blog. By the time I finished it was rather late so I spent the night there.

TUESDAY 19th MAY

This morning I had a little lie-in (until 8.30am) and made the most of my mother's washing machine – this is the last chance I will have for a while to have really clean clothes. On my way back to the tree house I caught sight of an old shed stacked in pieces against a tree next to a couple of

YARROW (ACHILLIA MILLEFOLIUM)

DESCRIPTION **A common, ferny, wayside plant (20in/50cm). Finely divided, long, feathery leaves are dark green; clusters of white flowers with a central yellow disc appear June–November.**

USES **The leaves of this plant are present all year round, which is handy because when made into a herbal tea yarrow is a fantastic remedy for severe colds. The plant is incredibly common and will grow almost anywhere. Its Latin name is derived from the warrior Achilles, who is thought to have treated his soldiers' wounds with yarrow. It has quite an aromatic flavour, which is released when crushed. You can eat it raw in salads with a light dressing, but in my experience it is best in a mug with boiling water and a slice of lemon for a refreshing cuppa.**

farm buildings. I will have to go and see if the farm owners want to get rid of it. I also noticed plenty of yarrow in the hedgerow by the wood, another useful ingredient for herbal tea.

I went straight up onto the platform to continue with the back rafters and roof lintel. Yesterday I had thought that the tree house was starting to look like a proper structure, and by the end of today it began to look distinctly 'house-shaped'. I am getting into a good routine with all my useful tools bagged up ready to go.

I cut down three trees today and coated the stumps with clay to keep infection at bay. Hopefully they will sprout some new shoots in time. I used one for a rafter and the other two for the 17ft (5.2m) side beams.

Builder's band (a heavy duty fixing band made of galvanised steel) got top marks today – the stuff is incredibly useful! I used it to put up the rafters. The uprights for the sides (what will eventually become walls) came out of the recycled timber pile. Incidentally, the pile is starting to look rather depleted – I think I need to down tools for a bit and go on a quest to find more recycled wood. I can check the usual skips and builders' yards, but I might need to find some new spots.

I have decided I am going to have four massive windows (two on the sides and two on the back). It makes sense, as the bits of Perspex I was given by my old employers in the set design trade are huge, and this way I won't have to cut them down to size – and it means having less wall area! I have noticed that being up in the trees makes the animals on the ground really quite bold. My prize-winning pheasant literally walked underneath me while I was up on the platform today. I suppose the tree house is part of the wood and the wood is part of the tree house.

At around 4pm I put down my tools. The frame is nearly complete, and all I need to do now are the rafters to support the roof. I walked down to check the patch and it appears the greenhouse effect has worked! My spinach is reaching for the sky, the other salad vegetables are putting in the effort, and even my runner beans are beginning to take hold of their hazel wigwams.

One pressing issue at the moment is homebrew. As Paul and I made quite a dent in my nettle beer reserves I felt some time off building and a bit of effort on the brewing front was necessary to keep up the morale of my one-man building team. A vast array of nettles has taken up residence next to the veg patch – a sort of wild extension to my cultivated greens. I spent a bit of time collecting the nettle tops and shaking off the insect life. Unfortunately I made a major schoolboy error – I didn't have any gloves.

COMMON NETTLE (URTICA DIOICA)

DESCRIPTION **Upright and unbranched, up to 4ft (1.2m), the familiar stinging nettle is common in every type of environment. Leaves are toothed and pointed, up to 4in (10cm) long and covered in long, stinging hairs. Greenish flowers hang in tassel-like clusters, male and female on different plants, June–September.**

USES **The first lesson every child learns about nature is to avoid the unpleasant bite of the stinging nettle, a cunning plant with a built-in defence mechanism. It is possible to harvest nettles without using gloves, as long as you grasp the plant firmly; too tender a touch and it will smell your fear and sting you for being hesitant. The second nature lesson most children learn is that the dock leaf contains the alkali to soften the blow of the nettle's bite, and that this usually grows in close proximity to stingers; nature provides the remedy close to hand. The nettle has much to offer: those who suffer from arthritis and rheumatism often use nettles to alleviate symptoms. Nettles have other health benefits: they are rich in Vitamin C, iron, calcium and natural histamines. Consuming nettles enriches the body and purifies the system. The best time to harvest nettles is during their primary and secondary growth: spring and autumn. During summer a chemical change in the plant renders them bitter and unpleasant. Harvest the nettle tops – not below the first four sets of leaves. The stringy dark stalks of nettles in late summer make an excellent source of fibre; they need to be stripped of leaves first and then crushed flat. To render the nettle defenceless, heat is by far the most effective method. Nettles can be waved in the flames of a fire a couple of times and then consumed without fear. To use them as a vegetable, boiling in water or steaming for five minutes are the prescribed methods. Nettles can be used in so many different ways in the kitchen; my personal favourites are to turn them into beer or a punchy stinger pesto.**

Nettle Beer

Ingredients

100 nettle tops (first four sets of leaves)

2½ gallons (12 litres) water

3lb (1.4kg) white granulated sugar

2oz (50g) cream of tartar

½oz (15g) brewer's or beer yeast

Makes 2½ gallons (12 litres)

1 Once you have picked your nettles, give them a quick wash and place in a big pot with the water. Bring to the boil and simmer for 15 minutes.

2 Strain the liquid into another pan or bucket and discard the nettles or, if you're feeling thrifty, serve as a green vegetable for your next meal.

3 Bring the liquid to the boil again and add the sugar and cream of tartar. Simmer and stir until dissolved.

4 Remove from the heat, transfer into a brewing vessel or bucket and allow to cool to blood temperature; this may take some time. Then add the yeast and stir well.

5 There is a lot of debate about the next stage. Most recipes say you should cover the bucket in muslin and bottle after 24 hours. Even with my limited knowledge of the mysterious art of brewing I know this is foolish – unless you want exploding bottles or a fizzy firework.

What worked best for me was to get out my hydrometer and take a reading every two days so I could calculate the alcohol percentage. I covered the bucket with a pair of Clare's tights, and left it for about a week, until the hydrometer reading had dropped from 1.050 to below 1.000. This told me that fermentation had finished, bottling could go ahead, and explosions would be kept to a minimum (not in the case of the missing tights).

6 If you can, leave the brew for 2–3 weeks before drinking. It is ready to drink a week after bottling though! My brew came out at 6.45%. (To calculate alcohol by volume, multiply the drop in specific gravity – from the initial reading until it falls below 1.000 – by 129. In this case 0.050 x 129 = 6.45%.)

7 Serve chilled in a jug with a sprig of mint, preferably in a green, leafy place at the end of a busy day. It is deceptive stuff, so do watch how many you have, especially if operating heavy machinery like a hammer or drill, and working off the ground.

Wednesday 20th May

I believe a house is not a home until it has a damn fine lavatory – for relief, thinking time, and to keep Clare happy when she comes down to stay. And if I'm being honest, I have no intention of squatting behind trees for the rest of the summer, leaving a series of landmines dotted about this lovely wood of mine. I definitely need a loo.

To take my mind off the prospect of putting up the roof rafters, I started the toilet build. I had taken the liberty of measuring the exact height of a loo seat the last time I was at home – to be well within the 'comfort zone' a height of exactly 16in (41cm) is recommended. I gave my lovely mahogany loo seat a thorough scrub down and a soak in disinfectant, and I put the loo together over the next few hours.

I was going to construct a small outhouse next to the tree house, making it convenient for any 'pressing issues' that could arise in the middle of the night. But then I thought it was probably better to have it further away – downwind for one – I had no idea if it would smell or not. Also, I can't imagine any future guests would be all that keen to pop to the loo in full view of the campfire.

Having made this decision I then had to lug the toilet frame 160ft (50m) away from the tree house and position it behind a few holly bushes. I set about digging a hole – the spot was full of clay and roots, just my luck! After much perspiration and spirited hacking at roots with the hatchet, I had a hole 2–3ft (61–91cm) deep, which should last a while.

Before trying it out I went to the local sawmill and asked if I could pinch some of their sawdust. I ended up with a bin-bagful of mixed tropical hardwood sawdust, enough to last me my time in the woods. To help break down any solids and prevent any nasty odours I may also have to empty the ash out of Bertha every now and then and dump it down the loo.

Finally I gave it a test run – what a loo with a view! All I need now is a magazine rack full of *Private Eye* and *National Geographic*, and some wood-panelled walls covered in old school team photographs. I felt very regal sitting atop the toilet – I think I shall call it the 'throne'.

THURSDAY 21st MAY

I got up early to go and buy more screws; they just keep disappearing and I have no idea where. As I came back through the local village I saw a poster on the door of the village hall that read: 'Country Market, Every Thursday 10–11am'. I thought it could be the perfect place to flog some wild produce and make some much needed cash.

I went in to pitch my idea and found myself surrounded by old ladies. The smell of bad coffee and Imperial Leather hung thick in the air. I located the people in charge and explained what I proposed to sell. They were very kind and gave me the necessary forms, and told me where to send them once I had filled them in. I headed back to the tree house visualising jar upon jar of nettle pesto, homebrew, blackberry jam, pigeon jerky and *confit* of rabbit. And then I decided it sounded like a lot of work for little return. Perhaps I should concentrate on feeding myself first!

I spent the rest of the day cutting, collecting and installing the rest of the rafters. The next wood along, over the hill, consists of tightly packed birch trees. I felt it would be more sensible to go and remove a few trees from there, where they needed space, as opposed to taking them from my wood, where space wasn't an issue. This meant having to lug 20 large (10ft/3m) birch rafters back to the tree house, but the pain was worth it, I think.

The birch wood will be a great source of kindling and birch bark for the coming months – there is so much fallen wood strewn between the trees. Back at the ranch I continued the dull task of putting up rafters. I finished at 5pm, at which point Chris came to have a gander. I think he was quite impressed – it now actually looks like a house.

Over the past week, I have noticed a lazy, white-necked cock pheasant hanging about, always in the same spot. It is the same cock that won the fight the other day. He's not scared off by my work – perhaps he wants to be my new pet. As a child I had a pet pheasant called Ziggy that I used to feed by hand; I will call this one Jeff. As there is no need to shoot him for the pot just yet, I have been feeding him my meagre leftovers, and the odd handful of rice – I might as well fatten him up before the day of reckoning … should it ever come.

PHEASANT (PHASIANUS COLCHIUS)

DESCRIPTION

Probably introduced by the Romans back in the 11th or 12th Century, the common pheasant feeds on farmland with some cover and roosts in trees. The male (31½in/80cm including tail) is unmistakable with red, wattled head parts on the sides; the rest of the head is dark, glossy blue-green. The rest of the body is orange-brown with black markings and the tail is long with black bars. The female (23½in/60cm) is buff-brown with dark spots and a shorter tail.

FRIDAY 22ND MAY

I went on a wood mission today. I headed up to the farm to see if they would be interested in parting with the bits of shed I spotted a few days ago. Luckily the farmer was more than happy to be rid of them. The bits are huge – more like a house than a shed! The pieces wouldn't fit in the car, so I went to ask my landlord if I could borrow his trailer, but of course the car didn't have a trailer hook – bugger! My landlord offered to help me move them with his Land Rover and trailer in return for some manual labour. I obliged. After dropping the bits of shed up at the wood, I spent the next few hours moving four enormous traveller's caravans out of their barn, in preparation for my landlord's daughter's 21st birthday party. After that I was completely knackered.

I was enjoying the building but I felt it was time for an afternoon off. I reached for the fishing rod and the nettle beer, and spent a relaxing few hours lying on the grass, a beer in one hand and a book in the other, watching the river trickling by, while my line dangled in the water. In my mind's eye I could see a summer of lazy afternoons stretching before me – but this wasn't just fishing for fun, it was fishing for food. This *was* work!

SATURDAY 23RD MAY

I taught my first foraging class today. Dan asked if I would be able to provide some rabbits for the day, but I had to refuse. The rabbits in my neck of the woods are few and far between, and any I do manage to find are destined for *my* table.

I took my class out for a forage and pointed out a few useful plants. I then took them back to the camp and rustled up some stinging nettle pesto and damper bread (twisted around a stick), and showed them the finer points of skinning and gutting a rabbit. We also put together a classic rabbit stew. Dan turned up with a load of snails he had been collecting from his garden and had purged for a few days to get rid of any toxins. We boiled them for ten minutes, plucked them from their shells with a toothpick and gave them a good wash in salted water. The rubbery morsels were then fried in a little butter, garlic, parsley and some salt and pepper – delicious! I'm not sure the punters felt the same way …

As I was in the vicinity of Eric's scrapyard I thought I should go and collect the corrugated iron for the tree house roof; I had even remembered to attach the roof rack to the car. I took my earnings for the day, which included a handsome tip, and went to purchase my second-hand roofing. The sheets come from an old barn not far away and feature just the right amount of brown rusty patches to add to the aesthetics of my woodland dwelling.

Eric helped me sort through the pile to find the best sheets and we loaded them onto the car. I gave him the £66 for all 22 sheets. As I drove out of the yard I looked at the other people rooting about in the sheds and barns, all on the lookout for a second-hand something or other. All I could think was, this guy must make a killing!

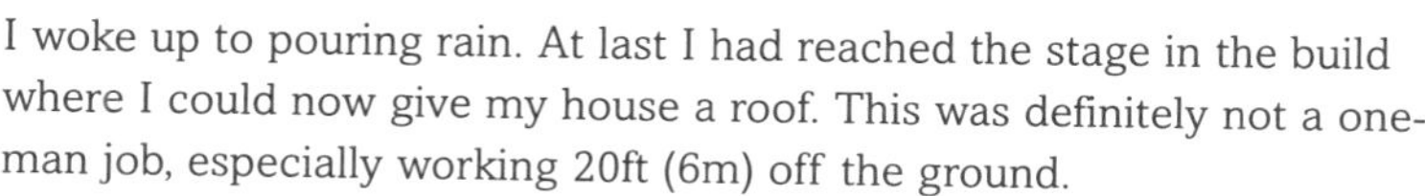

MONDAY 25TH MAY

I woke up to pouring rain. At last I had reached the stage in the build where I could now give my house a roof. This was definitely not a one-man job, especially working 20ft (6m) off the ground.

Chris came over at 10am and kindly gave up yet another of his free days in pursuit of my foolish escapades. With fingers crossed that the weather would improve, we donned some heavy gloves, and began manhandling the roof sheets from the top of the wood down to the tree house.

Eventually the rain went away, leaving lots of mud behind – so crossed fingers do work occasionally.

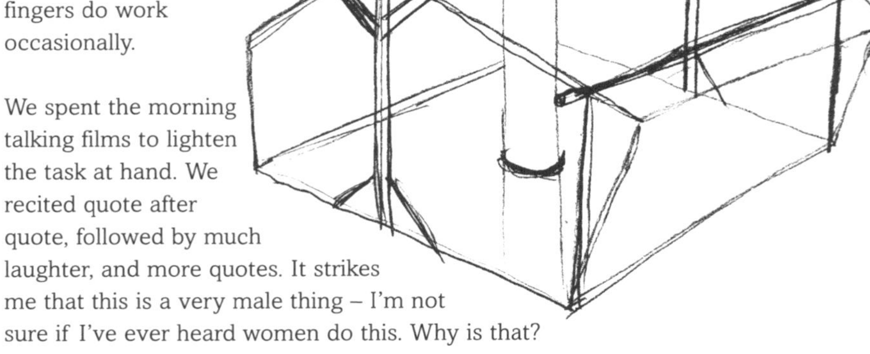

We spent the morning talking films to lighten the task at hand. We recited quote after quote, followed by much laughter, and more quotes. It strikes me that this is a very male thing – I'm not sure if I've ever heard women do this. Why is that?

The roof has to go up as quickly as possible because the enormous tarpaulin that is currently acting as base camp and my regular sleeping quarters is going to be integrated into the roofing. The idea is to cover what will be the inside of the tree house (apart from the balcony) with the tarp to provide an extra waterproof layer should there be any flaws in the corrugated iron sheets (which there almost certainly will be).

After trying a few ways of fixing the tarp, we settled on stretching it taut and pinning it with a staple gun. Once the tarp was pinned, we screwed down the two rows of hazel lengths into the rafters, and then attached the roof sheeting.

Like most of the different stages of the tree house build so far, once we had found a good working rhythm, the roof began going up quickly. The pitch of the roof was shallow and I could happily wander about on top, which was just as well because most of the work had to be done from up there.

I was expecting my first official visitor today – the Hungry Cyclist was riding down from London for a couple of days. Tom, as he is better known, was a few years above me at school and we had got to know each other through a mutual love of food. By the time Tom was due to arrive, Chris and I had almost finished one side of the roof.

Tom managed to miss the turning to the wood a few times. Chris and I walked up and down between the entrance at the top and the entrance at the bottom, but there was still no sign of him. If Tom had managed to find his way from New York to Rio de Janeiro on his epic 2½-year bike journey, I was sure that he would be able to find a wood in Sussex, even with my sketchy directions. Sure enough, on the third walk through the wood, Chris and I came across a set of fresh bike tracks in the mud – it had to be Tom.

The Hungry Cyclist was most impressed by the progress on the tree house. He had seen some pictures on my blog but said they simply didn't do it justice. The three of us spent the rest of the afternoon finishing one side of the roof and then laid out the tarp on the other side in case there was any more rain.

At around 5pm we went up to the local pub to give Tom a taste of the greatest ale in the country. Every Sussex lad remembers their first taste of Harveys – whether they liked it or not! For me, it is the nectar of the gods – an ale you can grow old with. After a couple of jars, Chris dropped the pair of us off at the wood and went on his way muttering something like: 'Some of us have work tomorrow.'

Tom had brought me down a few gifts for my new life as a tree dweller. Somehow he managed to fit all this in his panniers: two Tabasco chilli plants and two courgette plants for the patch, a jar of coconut milk, some bay leaves and dried chilli flakes, a bottle of Spanish mead and a mini chessboard (not sure who my opponent is going to be exactly – Jeff perhaps?). I was most grateful for the presents, but he still had one more surprise up his sleeve – supper!

He produced a large pile of chicken hearts and a block of Halloumi cheese. I hadn't had chicken hearts since my time in the Cook Islands – oh, the memories! We got a fire going outside and roasted the chicken hearts over hot coals, and then mixed them up with a dash of Tabasco, a squeeze of lemon juice and a little salt. They were every bit as good as I remembered – a texture like frankfurters, with the unmistakable taste of chicken. And you can't argue with the price: £1.99 per kilo!

As we munched away on chicken offal, warming our bare feet hobbit-style in front of the fire, the first drops of rain began to hit the canopy of leaves above us – just a passing drizzle, I thought. Wrong! It became a deluge of biblical proportions! Quick, to the tree!

It was the first time this haphazard jigsaw puzzle of recycled and natural wood had felt like a proper tree house. The rain hammering down on the tin roof was music to my ears! We took Bertha with us and continued our feast upstairs. I gave Tom a bottle of nettle beer to open, but despite a warning, he unscrewed the cap without due care and attention, and immediately received a face full of explosive homebrew! After much colourful language and emptying of nostrils, we drank what was left in the bottle, and then settled down to the first night sleeping off the ground. Tom slung his hammock between the rafters, while I was just happy to be off *terra firma* and sleeping on a level surface for once, free from roots, leaves and bare earth. We chatted for a while about our various travel and food experiences while supping on the Spanish mead, but eventually Tom fell asleep mid-sentence – and snored.

I sat up for a while, listening to the rhythmical drumming of the rain, and wrote my diary. The tree house is completely watertight – at least for now. It felt more like being in a rainforest than the Sussex countryside. I gradually drifted off, content with the progress that was being made and really excited at the prospect of embarking upon a life of high-rise self-sufficiency.

Tuesday 26th May

'Is it still bloody raining?' was the first thing Tom said as he lay in his hammock. Yes, it was still bloody raining; it had rained hard for a full 12 hours. The chances of putting up a roof in the rain seemed both foolhardy and unpleasant. The rain still hadn't made its way through the roof. I lit Bertha and got my new kettle on the boil to brew up some coffee. We treated ourselves to an egg and bacon sarnie – I am still allowing myself non-foraged meals because of the on-going, energy-sapping build. I reckon I have about a week left on normal grub before caveman sustenance takes over.

At about 10.30am the rain finally stopped and the sun came out. I took Tom to the patch and we were able to have a taste of my first peas – all this rain is certainly good for the veggies. We dug in the chilli and courgette plants that Tom had brought with him and then went back to continue working on the roof. We struggled to carry down five sheets at a time from the parking area, but with only ten left to bring down, two trips were definitely better than three!

We made good progress and took a couple of hours off in the afternoon. I suggested going to the birch grove to gather more fuel for the evening and Tom decided he wanted to make a classic witch's broom for the tree house. With a handful of fresh birch twigs, some string and a piece of hazel, he made quite an effective one, with a great sweeping action. He promptly went upstairs and gave the tree house a good sweep to prove the broom's effectiveness.

By 5pm the tree house had a complete roof! I collapsed onto my sleeping bag for a snooze, while Tom produced some watercolours and went downstairs to do a small artist's impression of my new home.

In the evening we decided to make an *umu* – a traditional underground oven of the Pacific islands. The *umu* or *hangi* (different cultures have different names for it) is the true mark of caveman culinary perfection: a method of cooking for which no equipment is needed. You need to source only one thing: rocks. They must be igneous rocks, like basalt, which will absorb and hold heat without splintering or cracking. To my knowledge, the best place to find rocks like these is by railway lines, which are always lined with basalt or something of similar quality.

Not far away from the wood is an old, disused railway line, which is now a well-trodden footpath. There were rich pickings to be had so we filled both our rucksacks with rocks and struggled back to the wood. On the way back we paused to pick a load of large burdock leaves and then, once back, set about the preparations for the oven.

Tom de-boned a leg of lamb, which we stuffed with wild mint from the wood, and then rubbed the outside with dried chilli flakes, olive oil, and salt and pepper. We wrapped the meat in burdock leaves, buried it in the oven and left it well alone for 2½ hours. After about an hour a meaty, earthy aroma wafted up to where we were sitting on the tree house balcony. Once again, this transported me back to the South Pacific and the smell of succulent pork gently cooking under layers of palm leaves and Polynesian sand. They say a picture paints a thousand words, but nothing makes a memory more real than a familiar smell.

Not much more to mention, apart from a serious bout of meat sweats from gorging on pure flesh, and a stomach fit to explode!

HOW TO MAKE AN

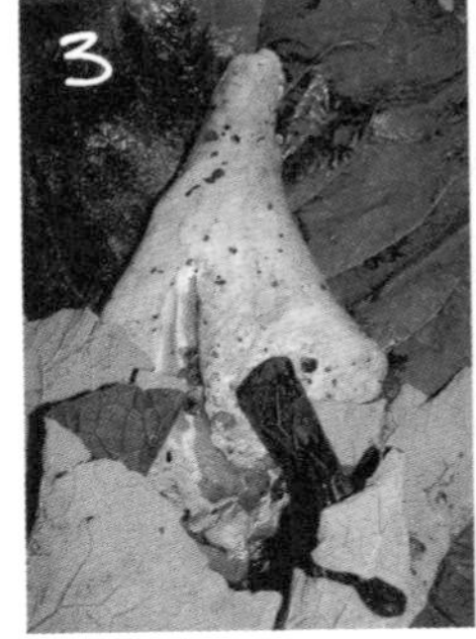

1 **Dig a rectangular pit, 2ft x 4ft (61cm x 122cm) and 1½ft (46cm) deep. You must have everything ready to hand before you start. You need a bag-load of basalt rocks (or similar), a pile of small kindling, a pile of medium-sized wood, and a pile of large, thick limbs of oak. None should be bigger than the size of the pit.**

2 **Collect lots of burdock leaves, about 20–30; you will need them for wrapping the meat and covering the oven. Cut down a few fresh lengths of hazel – they need to be cut to size so they can form a wooden grill inside the pit that you can rest the meat on. Build a small fire in the bottom of the pit and gradually build it up, going from smallest to largest in fuel size until the pit is full. As the fire picks up, start piling the rocks in the middle, on top of the wood. You now need to wait until the fire has burnt down and sunk into the pit under the weight of the rocks, which will slowly heat up to cooking temperature; this can take anything up to 30 minutes.**

3 **During this time you should prepare your meat; legs and shoulders (big joints of meat) are most suited to this type of cooking. If you remove the bone, the cooking time will be reduced. Wrap the meat in burdock leaves; this will help keep the juices in and retain moisture.**

UNDERGROUND OVEN

4 When the oven looks ready and the rocks are kicking out plenty of heat, place the cut hazel 'grill' over the top and then the wrapped bundle of meat.

5 Start laying on the remaining burdock leaves until the entire pit is covered, and carefully begin pouring over the soil left over from digging the pit.

6 Cover the burdock leaves until not even the slightest wisp of smoke emerges from the soil. So no unsuspecting guest treads on the oven, stick an 'X' over the top with two sticks and leave the oven to do its thing for 2½–3 hours, or longer if you have larger joints. Underground ovens are not an exact science; only experience will help you perfect timings.

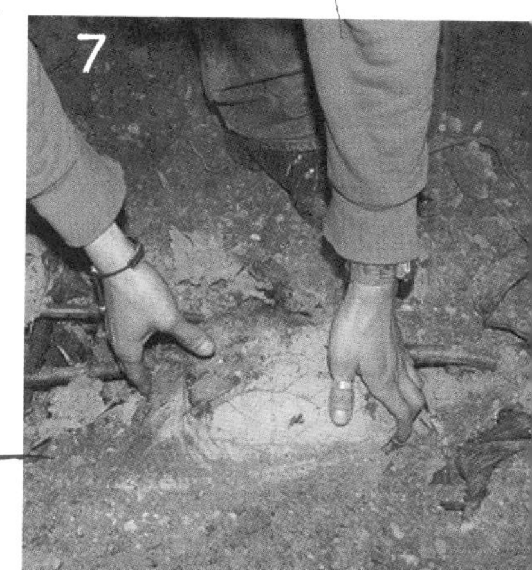

7 When it is ready, simply scrape back the soil and gradually remove the leaves. A word of warning: they will be very hot! Take out your meat, unwrap and tuck in. Quite often, you will be left with some top-quality charcoal in the pit, so be thrifty and make good use of it for your next meal.

WEDNESDAY 27th MAY

This morning the rain was back with a vengeance, and to make matters worse, I had to get up bright and early to head to the South Downs to take some happy campers out foraging. Tom had agreed to come and help me out, and learn a little about foraging himself.

It was wet when we got to the yurts and it got progressively wetter. To be honest, I felt sorry for the campers having their precious few days of countryside idyll ruined by the weather. I wouldn't have wanted to stay at the campsite either, and I live in a half-built tree house!

The campers were certainly upbeat about the weather and got stuck into the foraging. I kept to the original menu of stinger pesto and flatbreads (which Tom made with the kids), and I showed everyone how to take apart a rabbit and make a stew.

As we left, the weather took a turn for the worst as the wind began whipping across the Downs. Tom and I went to sample some cider at a nearby farm, and Tom bought me some Lindisfarne Northumbrian Mead as a thank-you for having him to stay. He bought himself some ginger wine so he could enjoy a whisky mac in the bath when he got back to London. I had no such luxuries waiting for me back at the tree – except the mead …

During the evening I got a phone call from Dan: 'Nick, your rabbit stew is fantastic!' 'Why are you eating it, Dan? I made it for the clients.' 'Oh, they left … adverse weather conditions.'

Back at the tree house, huddled next to Bertha, with the entire structure creaking and twisting in the maelstrom of 'adverse weather', I didn't blame them one bit. The only thing going through my mind is whether or not I will wake up in the morning amongst a mass of broken wood, back on the forest floor!

THURSDAY 28th MAY

I can't believe how quickly the weeks are going! Today I went on another mission to find wood for the walls, and then I patched up all the screw holes and worn rust patches on the corrugated iron roof. I also dropped in to see my folks and to check e-mails – 150 of them! I felt rather popular. I started to write a list of the stuff I need to pack so I can bring it to the tree house – I quickly realised how much crap I have. I am such a hoarder!

FRIDAY 29th MAY

Ladies and gents – we have a wall! With the roof done – apart from the stove corner – I toiled on the first wall for most of the day. The windows (58in/147cm across) are huge and take up a good bit of space. I began by taking apart bits of the shed I had acquired. Some of it was the perfect size already and simply needed a thorough going over with the hammer to remove bent nails and screws.

However, it soon became clear that I had chosen to start with the only side of the tree house that has to accommodate the curved limbs of a hazel tree. I drew a rough outline of the branches on the panels of timber surrounding the hazel and set about sawing out the shape, checking it, and sawing some more. I wasn't happy with the poor job but I will patch it up at a later date. The Black & Decker workbench has finally come into its own and is my new best friend, along with Jeff, who keeps his beady eye on everything I do. I fed him a slice of bread today and he ate it all!

When I went down below to view my progress, the completed side of the tree house did look distinctly shed-like. Not quite the look that I was going for. I started patching the top of the wall near the roof with planks of wood screwed on vertically to try to break up the horizontal lines. It worked quite nicely and I have made a mental note to use the technique more often when constructing the other walls. I managed to put up a window, but with no hinges to hand, I had to fashion some wooden blocks to slide down and hold the window in place. It has been a good day in all and, even better, Clare is coming over later. Unfortunately I have to be up at the crack of dawn tomorrow to teach foraging.

SATURDAY/SUNDAY 30th – 31st MAY

An interesting bunch for foraging today; I will say no more! We managed to get a good haul from the hedgerows and cooked up a storm back at the camp: elderflower cordial, elderflower fritters, pan-fried rabbit with rosemary, a hedgerow salad, nettle pesto, yarrow tea … the list goes on.

I spent the rest of the weekend doing very little down at the tree house. Clare and I made the most of the fine weather and sat out in the fields sunbathing and reading. We found an old double duvet cover from one of our previous flats and Clare ran it through her sewing machine so I could turn it into a hammock – just what a tree dweller needs for down time! This week I will finally move in to my new home – about time too.

JUNE

MONDAY 1st JUNE ☼ 26°C!

I am writing this by paraffin lamp, surrounded by moths, and an extremely creaky tree house. If it is this noisy with one wall, what's it going to be like with four? The wood settled into silence at about 9.30pm. Dusk was announced by the scolding 'tak-tak' of the blackbird as my feathered neighbours went to bed.

The moths are a little worrying to look at when I point my torch at them. Their eyes glow red and they also have a long, sharp nozzle protruding from their head that looks ready for injecting or biting. I hope they don't get violent; perhaps they are waiting for me to go to sleep so they can get me.

I have been working on the back wall today, and it is coming on quite well. I wasn't too comfortable with the way I had to dangle out of the window to put some of the screws in. At one point, to reach a particularly awkward screw, I actually tied a piece of rope around the tree and then to my waist. It is a good thing I don't have to answer to health and safety officers – they'd be having kittens.

For dinner I sat on the floor next to Bertha and enjoyed my first salad from the garden: Lollo Rosso and cos lettuce, with spinach topped with wild garlic and hairy bittercress. I cut up a handful of my garden peas and added them to a bowl of rice cooked in stock. It was incredibly fresh, but did lack a vital ingredient – meat. I still hadn't had the chance to go out hunting, although I did give Jeff a second look!

The moonlight shining through the window is so bright I can almost write by it. Looking out of the window at the moonlit wood is a bit unnerving; the shadows form familiar shapes and I keep waiting for movement, but there is none. The wood is silent. The most dangerous wild creature in Britain is a bee, for goodness sake. But adders are poisonous and badgers can get aggressive if cornered, although neither of them can climb trees … zzzzzz.

Buzzard (Buteo buteo)

DESCRIPTION **The UK's most common bird of prey, the buzzard feeds over farmland and moorland, and nests in nearby woodland. A medium-sized raptor with a wingspan of 43–52in (110–132cm), the buzzard has rounded wings that it holds in a shallow 'V'-shape when it flies. Plumage variable but usually brownish with barring; it is paler beneath with bands on the tail. It has a hooked beak and yellow feet.**

Tuesday 2nd June ☼ 24°c!

One and a half walls are better than none, so says the ancient Belgian proverb. I slept well last night on my blow-up roll mat, snuggled up in the sleeping bag in the walled corner of the tree house. I was rudely awakened at 6am by something running up and down the tin roof, making a hell of a racket; I think it must have been a squirrel. If it does the same tomorrow morning, I'm having it for breakfast.

Yesterday evening, while watering the patch (I am having to water it twice a day to cope with the 'heat wave') and picking a few things for supper, I spiked my right forefinger right in the joint on a hawthorn spike. Nothing was stuck in my finger, but it has swollen up like a balloon! It is so swollen I can hardly move it. As I am right-handed, trying to use the saw was an interesting experience.

The buzzards that haunt the wood were in full cry today, constantly circling above the tree house, and their distinctive call became the soundtrack to my afternoon. I realised there is a nest in the oak next door – a big 3¼ft (1m) tangle of twigs and sticks. I haven't seen them in it so far, but apparently they can use as many as three alternative nests in their extensive territory, which can stretch up to 62 miles (100km). There you go – you learn something new every day!

I continued work on the back wall and window. My landlady and her daughter dropped in to see how I was getting on; they were surprised at the size of the tree house, but impressed with the progress. We also arranged a bit of back scratching. I am hoping to go on a brief research mission to Scotland in July, and in return for them watering the patch, I will look after their animals when they go away at the end of the summer.

I was hoping to take the gun out to arrange a bit of protein for my meal this evening, but found myself too engaged in the build – dinner was another veggie special.

Wednesday 3rd June

My life here has become virtually timeless, and my only parameters are day and night. I'm just glad that there is a lot more day than night at the moment!

Thursday 4th June

I now have three walls! It was very hot and sticky today, and even the shade of the trees didn't offer much protection. I walked down to the bottom of the wood to have a dip in the river. It was more than a little refreshing! The pool I have designated for swimming is deep and has a flat, shingle bottom. Along the bank are a couple of large alder trees with enormous roots that I use for sitting on and diving off, and they also provide a convenient ladder for climbing out of the river. Today a couple of brown, furry creatures bounced along the thickest of the roots, engaged in some sort of playful fight: mink. I watched them for a while. They came very close and didn't seem in the least bit concerned about a semi-naked human frolicking in the middle of their river.

During the afternoon I put up half of the last wall and another window. I have used all the Perspex, so I will need to find some more; this has been added to my 'To Do' list. I also started to make a bench using some leftover bits of hazel. I was down to the last of my good screws and had to raid my emergency stash for some chunky silver screws with flat tip ends. Unfortunately these proved to be the most frustrating screws I have ever tried to use: the screw tip on the drill kept flying out and digging into the wood – and, occasionally, into my hand that was holding said wood in place. By some miracle I managed to finish the bench and then spent a good few hours lying on it reading.

MINK (MUSTELA VISON)

DESCRIPTION

Originally from North America, the mink is not native to the UK, but has escaped into the wild from fur farms. Found near water, where it feeds on birds, fish and mammals. Slimmer than an otter, the mink resembles a ferret, and has a long body, covered in super-soft, slightly shaggy dark-brown fur. It has small ears and a short tail.

FRIDAY 5th JUNE

Why is it that the one type of wood I need I don't have? Today I drove over to a timber company to raid their offcuts bin. I managed to get plenty of small scrap timber, but it is really only good for patching and shelving.

I went to try my luck at the scrapyard on the other side of the town; this was a *proper* scrapyard ... Amongst the usual ancient golf clubs, broken toys and 1980s-style 'How To' manuals, I spied something that could be of use to me: two beautiful wooden farmhouse chairs in perfect condition. I asked how much they were and the bloke scratched his head and asked for a tenner – a bargain! I neglected to inform him that they may well be worth a hell of a lot more; he didn't look as if he had an eye for antiques, only for big, sparkly things that looked expensive. Wooden objects simply slipped beneath the radar.

After I dropped off the chairs at the tree house, I carried Bertha up to the car and took her to have a bit of a manicure. Tomorrow I am planning to install Bertha – stovepipe and all – inside the tree house, but she still has one minuscule flaw that could, potentially, become a major fire hazard. The inside of the firebox needs sealing around the edge to prevent hot embers or sparks dropping out. Even though this is unlikely, knowing she is properly sealed will help me sleep better at night.

My godfather runs a classic car garage in a nearby village. In my youth, his son Rupert and I used to spend hours tinkering about with various car parts, and pretend we knew what we were doing. Fifteen years on, Rupert does know what he's doing as both he and his older brother work alongside their father: a great example of a traditional family business.

Rupert was surprised at what I had done with an old oil drum, and, of course, had the necessary tools to fix Bertha. So out came the welding kit, but unfortunately the heat of the welder nearly burned through the thin steel of the drum. Rupert then had a brainwave, and came back with a tin of exhaust pipe sealant, which he immediately began applying to the underside of the firebox. It was the perfect solution.

On the way back to the wood, I went to the DIY shop to buy some more fixings and a rim lock to fit to the tree house – tomorrow the tree house will have a door!

SATURDAY 6th JUNE

Two hands are better than one, and six are better than three. Chris and another friend Nick came down for the weekend to help me with a few final bits: fit the last wall; hang the front door; and install the stove and chimney. By the end of the weekend I was hoping to have a complete tree house, with a roof, four walls, and central heating to boot!

Chris turned up at 10am as arranged. Nick had managed to lose his phone, as well as receiving a fat lip while trying to stop his car from running him over, having forgotten to apply the handbrake. When he eventually made his way down from London he began to complain about how cold it might be at night. 'Mate, it's not exactly Alaska, is it', I said. 'No, but it's not Tahiti either!', he replied. Point taken.

I was very grateful to have the boys to help me carry down the remaining bits of wood destined for walling, patching and door hanging. First, we worked on getting Bertha settled in. She had cost next to nothing to make; her stovepipe, complete with rain hood and flash plate, was the most expensive part. Yesterday, at the garage, I had taken it upon myself to construct a rough circle in some old corrugated iron to fit the stovepipe through the roof – rough being the operative word.

I had grown rather accustomed to traversing the roof, 20ft (6m) off the ground. It was glorious up there – the canopy sat below and the sun shone on the roof constantly (perhaps I should have built the tree house higher up). We fitted a few pieces of corrugated iron to the walls surrounding Bertha to act as heat absorbers. I then noticed a sudden flaw – Bertha sat right in the way of one of the windows and stopped it from opening. So much for best-laid plans!

Once fitted, I fired Bertha up to look at the draw from the stovepipe. As soon as she started to smoke I ran downstairs so I could see the chimney. Sure enough, Bertha was belching out more smoke than a smoker with a 60-a-day habit. What a glorious sight (the stove, not the smoker)!

Our next task was hanging the door that I had been lucky enough to find in a skip. Nick, a phenomenally good designer with a keen eye for precision, was left to chisel out the notches for the door to fit the hinges that had belonged to it in its previous life. After half an hour of chiselling, checking and re-checking, the door was screwed onto the rigid frame. Unbelievably it fitted first time with no alterations.

Once the door had been hung I fitted a fat rim lock to provide tree house security. (To be honest, I had chosen the lock for the big 'Hogwarts'-style key that came with it – after all, why not?) I then whittled and sanded a conveniently curved hazel door handle from my 'hazel to recycle' pile.

By the time we had finished tinkering it was 7pm. So with a lockable door, but no walls on either side of it, we called it a day. This was just as well, as with the close of play came the rain – not just a pitter-patter, but a tropical-style hammering of precipitation. The boys cooked up their offerings of chicken wings and lamb chops on the stovetop. It was great to see Bertha working as a true indoor stove at last: not only for cooking, but as a central heating unit – the heat Bertha kicked out was extraordinary and, in the midst of inclement weather, very welcome.

The rain persisted until the early hours, but curled up in sleeping bags, lying on some 25-year-old goat skin rugs from Haiti, and with Bertha going full blast, we didn't care. We slept as soundly and happily as if we had been in the presidential suite at the Dorchester. Although a day of hard, fiddly graft, and a few bottles of red wine probably helped too.

SUNDAY 7th JUNE

It rained hard all last night. The drumming of the raindrops on the tin roof had been delightfully soothing, like being in a tent in a downpour, with the smug feeling of knowing you are warm and dry.

The only water inside the tree house was on top of Bertha. The water had run down the corrugated iron roof, underneath the conical flash plate and down the outside of the stovepipe, making a nice pool of water around the edge of the stovetop. This isn't a problem when the stove is burning as the water evaporates instantly, but if this happens every time it rains, the stovepipe seal will need addressing before Bertha starts to rust.

After a full English breakfast of epic proportions, the three of us finished the last bit of wall. Nick carried out some interesting carpentry and fitted a triangular piece of shed next to the door. It was the only piece of the tree house that wasn't a horizontal or vertical line and it didn't feel right to me. Nick's inner designer had obviously got the better of him and he accused me of 'being too conventional' – conventional, my arse; I live in a tree, for goodness sake!

The final touch, the crowning moment if you like, was when we hung my antlers. They had come from an estate in the Scottish Highlands I had visited when I was 12. My first salmon fishing trip was hugely exciting – I was obsessed with fishing as a child. I also had the opportunity to go stalking on the estate, another first. I returned home with three huge salmon and the antlers, which I had mounted and fitted with a plaque. They have adorned the walls of my rooms at university and, much to Clare's disgust, our flats in London too. But they have never hung in a place more appropriate than they do now: on the front of a tree house, in the middle of a Sussex wood.

As I was in the mood for hanging things, I also put up my two hanging baskets, which I had filled with herbs, at either end of the balcony. Rather than have the herbs down at the patch (where they would probably do better), I thought it would be more convenient to have them to hand while I am cooking, so I have planted thyme, parsley, oregano, rosemary and sage.

Clare came down after the boys had left. She has just returned from a brief trip to the south of France and has brought me back a hammock chair to hang on the balcony – nice touch, m'lady!

MONDAY 8th JUNE ☁

The only thing left to do to make the tree house complete is to find some Perspex for the fifth and final window above the bed. I have been trying, but I haven't been able to find Perspex at any of my usual recycling outlets. I bit the bullet and went to my local DIY shop, but having to pay £15 for a flimsy piece of transparent plastic was a real pain in the backside – funds are low.

Once I had installed the window, I started work on updating my sleeping arrangements. For over a month now I have been sleeping on the floor of the tree house, with the luxury of a night in a bed on my weekly blogging mission to the family home.

My plan was to build a frame to hold an inflatable double air mattress, which I already have from my surfing trips to the West Country. I did toy with the idea of a proper mattress, and I have even thought about stuffing a double duvet cover with the leftover hay they have cut from the surrounding fields. That would obviously be the ultimate in self-sufficient comfort, but there is one snag – I tend to suffer from hay fever at the beginning of the summer, so making a bed out of the stuff would be like inviting the plague into my bedroom.

There was one issue regarding the bed build that I had not even considered until now: thermal layers. I have now realised why proper wood burning stoves sit very low to the ground – because hot air rises and will therefore heat the room from the floor upwards. Bertha's firebox is at least 2ft (61cm) off the ground, meaning that below that height the air will remain cold.

To put me well within the warm layer, I needed to make sure my sleeping height was at least 2½ft (76cm) off the ground. I suppose a bunk bed would have been the most practical choice, as the higher you go the warmer it gets – but it is summer and I don't foresee having to get through any really cold nights until October. Even though I say it myself, the finished product does look good – sturdy, rustic and, above all, comfortable.

With the bed complete I organised the bedding – you can't put a price on comfort when you are living in the middle of the woods. I've got plenty of stuff stashed in the loft at home left over from school and university. I put a single duvet over the mattress to sleep on, then added a double duvet to sleep under, three feather pillows, and I've also got a three-season sleeping bag for emergencies. When I lay down to test it out, I sank into all the soft layers and very nearly reached for a book to have a read and a snooze – but then I would have had nothing for supper.

As I lay on the bed thinking about food, I heard a flurry of wings in a nearby tree followed shortly by a familiar 'Coo-coo-coo'. I sat up on the bed and peered through my new window. About 20ft (6m) away a pigeon had landed in an oak tree and was sitting with its back to me. Supper, I thought. As slowly and as quietly as possible I reached under the bed for the air rifle. I cocked and loaded the gun, and then, ever so carefully, undid the latch and lifted up the window.

Pigeons have a reputation for being reasonably bullet-proof. Even a savvy shot with a shotgun can sometimes fail to bring one down. As I looked through the telescopic sight, I had only one option: the head. Was the gun sight zeroed? I had scrawled this on my 'To Do' list earlier this morning. There was only one way to find out.

I waited until the bird gave me a profile of his head and then pulled the trigger. Success! The pigeon folded and dropped like a stone to the forest floor. It was an incredibly jammy shot and I had a feeling Mother Nature was smiling on me. Either that or the pigeon was depressed and looking for an easy way out.

I took my kill down to the patch, sat on the big fallen oak, and plucked the pigeon in the early evening sunshine. While I worked I had a think about

WOODPIGEON (COLUMBA LIVIA)

DESCRIPTION **A common resident in rural areas in woods, on farmland and in gardens; now also seen in urban areas. The woodpigeon is a plump blue-grey bird with a pink-tinged breast (16in/41cm). There is a distinctive white patch on the side of the neck, a blue-green patch on the back of the neck, and there is a horizontal white stripe across the wing when in flight. Its wings make a loud clattering sound on take-off.**

how best to serve the pigeon. Thankfully I didn't suffer from the options paralysis that faces most cooks – I have what I have and nothing more. Surely basic, limited ingredients are the key to inventive, inspired cooking? I dug up some of my first early potatoes, picked a few courgettes, and gathered a handful of spinach. The prospect of the first of many self-sufficient meals was an exciting one; this is the moment I have been looking forward to since I started digging this place over a month ago.

I roasted the pigeon over hot embers, sautéed the vegetables, and made an improvised mash with the potatoes and some olive oil. What a feed! As it grew dark I cut a load of wood for the night and carried some of the dying embers from the fire upstairs in a pan to light Bertha. I put the kettle on, then got on the bed to tuck into another instalment of *Robinson Crusoe*, and was asleep within minutes.

Tuesday 9th June

What a difference a bed makes! I didn't wake up until 9.30am. As I opened my eyes I was treated to the sight of a sea of lush, green leaves gently moving in the soft breeze. My new nest of a bed was so comfortable that I decided to lie in, have coffee and read for a while. I know I am committing the most heinous of clichés by reading *Robinson Crusoe* while living in a tree house, but I haven't read it since I was a boy, and I am keen to try and rekindle the same level of outdoor enthusiasm the book gave me when I was younger.

By the time I had finished my third cup of coffee it was midday and time to pop to the throne. I then realised I had a column to write and some video footage to put together – it was time to re-enter the world I had just escaped, for a while at least.

Wednesday 10th June

Stepping off the platform onto a train bound for London felt very strange – it has been a month since my last visit. When I got out at Victoria station, a sense of unease descended; it was as if all my security had vanished. The place was heaving – it was 5.30pm, rush hour. Nothing had changed: the smell, the impatience and the unhappy demeanours. Woe betide you if you happen to be carrying luggage!

I can't understand the pent-up anger and indifference of the average commuter. They all seem as though they would be perfectly happy people if they were doing anything else, but it is as if the word 'commute' conjures up a red veil and flicks a switch – talking on a mobile phone, rustling a paper too loudly, or taking up too much breathing space is like signing your own death warrant.

There are the same old cheerful chappies dishing out free papers though – I took every one I was offered, as I am into my recycling and I thought they would be perfect for getting the fire going in the mornings. My habit of religiously using birch bark and a flint and steel for every fire is no longer a novelty. I have to become more efficient in my everyday tasks.

The Piccadilly Line held the same magic it has always done. A tramp was squeezing his way down the carriage asking people for money, but most of them were plugged into iPods and couldn't hear him. But, my God, they must have smelt him! As he drew nearer the odour made my eyes water. Two young City boys voiced their opinion on his cleanliness a little too loudly and spent the next minute receiving a full-on lecture packed with all kinds of expletives from the smelly passenger. Off went the iPods, and everyone listened in with great interest at the heated rant – all but the City boys enjoyed the entertainment.

My brother was over from New York for a couple of days on business and had taken a few hours out from his hectic schedule to have a beer with his tree-dwelling younger sibling. We met in Covent Garden at 9.30pm, in a pub opposite my favourite London restaurant, Rules. Game has always taken pride of place on their menu, and I found it strange when I realised that my woodland dining experiences have started to emulate theirs, even down to the wood panelling – but without the fancy tableware and, more importantly, the hefty price tag ...

THURSDAY 11th JUNE

Nothing much to report. I spent the day running through footage and editing it into a passable show-reel with my friend Justin, who is a real whiz at that sort of thing. I raced across London to drop it off with my agent and then went back down to Sussex. Felt good to get on the train home. I decided to walk from the station back to the tree house. As I climbed the ladder, unlocked the door and stepped over the threshold, I thought of the bizarre transition that had just taken place. Central London one minute, a tree house in the woods the next ...

Before firing up Bertha, I put on the head torch and filled up my four-year-old hurricane lamps. I am immensely pleased with these antique contraptions; they run on paraffin (kerosene) and can last up to 15 hours, depending on how high the flame is. Just four bathe the tree house in plenty of warm light, and paraffin is cheap too – £6.99 for almost a gallon (4 litres) of the stuff!

FRIDAY 12th JUNE

Today I taught another foraging group. This time it was a group of enthusiastic teachers from the local school. As country dwellers themselves, they already had most of the common wild food knowledge, so I had to dig deep and rely on dazzling them with my culinary creations. Thankfully it worked!

ELDERFLOWER CHAMPAGNE

INGREDIENTS

10½ pints (6 litres) water (in total)
2lb 3oz (1kg) white granulated sugar
30 elderflower heads (in full bloom)
2 tbsp white wine vinegar
Juice and zest of 4 lemons
½ tsp dried champagne yeast

Makes 10½ pints (6 litres)

1 Mix 7 pints (4 litres) of hot water and the sugar in a sterilised container (a normal bucket is fine), stir until the sugar is dissolved, then add cold water to top up to 10½ pints (6 litres).

2 Add the elderflower heads, white wine vinegar, and lemon juice and zest. Give the mixture a good stir. At this stage, cover the bucket with a tea towel and leave in a cool, well-ventilated corner for 2–3 days.

Back at the wood I spent the afternoon organising my living arrangements and even made some coat hooks out of hazel to screw onto the back of the door. One of my concerns about this experience is that the tree house will not be truly finished until I leave … there will always be one more thing to add somewhere.

SATURDAY 13th JUNE

Another morning teaching foraging. I had a fine group today, all very eager to learn. The old coach road, where I usually take my merry band, was lined with elderflower – small, fragrant bursts of white peppered the overgrown hedgerows. I managed to get my foragers to pick lots of flower heads to turn into cordial and fritters, with plenty left over for me to make champagne back at the tree house – nothing like free labour.

---

3 The elderflowers contain their own natural yeasts, so the aim is to try to let these do their magic. If in a few days the brew doesn't look slightly foamy or mouldy-looking, then add the ½ tsp of yeast, give the brew a gentle stir, re-cover with a tea towel, and leave for a further five days.

4 It is worth getting a hydrometer to check the specific gravity so you know when the fermentation is slowing down – this will prevent explosions occurring when the champagne is bottled. Keep checking the brew until it has reached 1.010 (a further five days) – you want it to have a bit of fizz!

5 Strain the liquid through a sieve lined with muslin and decant into plastic sterilised screw-top bottles. Leave the champagne for a week before sampling.

6 Serve chilled and open with caution!

After I had got my brew on the go, Clare, Chris and I spent the afternoon at the South of England Show. As a child, the main attraction of the show was the Army assault course, the birds of prey, the candyfloss, and how many stickers I could collect for my T-shirt from the various stalls. This time I was approaching the show from a hungry, tree dweller's perspective, and so I headed straight for the food hall.

Brimming with a huge variety of gastronomic goodies from across the country, the food hall (if you go around enough times) can deliver a feast of countryside tapas: samples of cheese, pork pies, dips, vinegars, relishes served up with crackers or bite-sized chunks of bread, smoked salmon, smoked duck, pork scratchings and home-cured charcuterie, all washed down with a sample shot of cider, local wine or even a whisky liqueur. This cheeky way of gaining a free lunch was also a good way to share banter with some of the producers and maybe gain a tip or two on products I could make for myself. Once we had our fill, it was off to see the coppicers to watch and learn, and ask the occasional question.

One of the coppicers showed me the correct way to split hazel by levering it up and down when splitting (he used a side axe). It is all about encouraging the wood to go in the direction you want it to – he made it look easy. I walked past a countryside clothing tent and saw a dark green moleskin flat cap for £8; I had to have it. I'm not exactly sure why – too many free shots, I suppose …

We met up with Jamie and Nicole, two friends who had also been raiding the food tent. I invited them down to the tree house for supper and they promised to provide the meat. They arrived with a load of sausages and some steaks they had bought at the show, as well as some rather fruity bottles of rosé from a local vineyard. I provided the potato salad and vegetables fresh from the patch.

Jamie took a long look around the camp. 'So while I'm at work dressed in a suit, you're out here?' 'Yes, Jamie,' I said. 'You're quite a resourceful chap to have done all this …' he added. Maybe it looks that way, but I am still feeling woefully inadequate in the grand scheme of woodland living. It is a start, but then there is still so much more to learn!

SUNDAY 14th JUNE

After a good sleep it was lovely to wake up with Clare in my bed. It would be nice if she could move in full time, but I can't imagine commuting to north London from the tree house every day would be all that practical.

I made some coffee on the stove, and baked some fresh bread for breakfast, using some hastily made dough from last night. Afterwards, the two of us set about doing some work. I began putting up a housing unit for all my tools, fixings and kitchen stuff. It started as a series of shelves and soon became a grand unit built from natural and recycled wood. I even managed to fix my magnetic kitchen knife holder to the wall, as well as plenty of screws and nails to hang up my hammers, saws and axes.

Meanwhile Clare was making the front window on the balcony her own. She was busy with the saw, cutting different-sized disks from hazel and hammering them onto the window frame. During some enthusiastic hammering required by one of the more stubborn discs, she knocked the small mirror off the wall on the other side and it smashed on the floor. Great! A broken mirror in the tree house – this doesn't bode well! It was worth it though; the window sill certainly has a female touch to it, and what I thought would look rather twee, ended up looking quite nice.

Clare headed back to London after lunch and I spent the afternoon searching the wild larder for brewable commodities. I gathered 100 nettle tops and another 35 elderflower heads. If all goes to plan, in a couple of weeks I will have 21 pints (12 litres) of nettle beer and more than 10½ pints (6 litres) of elderflower champagne to add to my expanding cellar.

To me 14 June has always been an important date: the night before the start of the fishing season! Although you can fish most still waters year-round, rivers have a strict no-fishing policy between 15 March and 15 June, so fish can continue their natural breeding cycle. Until now, the stretch of water at the bottom of the wood hasn't really pulled its weight, other than for washing or swimming, but now it is time for the river to deliver …

I got two more brews under way, and then had plenty of time to prepare for that magical first cast, which wouldn't be legal until after midnight – I was in for a late one. I made four new nightlines as my ones from last summer have seen better days.

HOW TO MAKE A NIGHTLINE

The nightline is an ingenious concept for the idle fisherman. Born out of desperation in bygone days by the poaching fraternity, it is simply a 1ft (30cm) long peg of hazel, sharpened at one end, with a 10ft (3m) length of fishing line tied to the other end. A hook and two weights are tied to the end of the line and baited with a fat juicy worm – irresistible to even the fussiest of fish.

At 11.55pm I got down to the river, having already chosen during daylight hours where I was going to set the lines. Armed with all my nightlines, and a bottle of nettle beer to see in the fishing season, I set up shop on the roots of the big alder. I needn't have bothered giving the beer a shake; as I twisted off the cap, the froth exploded out over the river at midnight – a fitting toast to the river's health and mine.

I set all the lines in their designated spots and 15 minutes later I was back up in the tree house. I sat there counting the minutes … well, in actual fact, I read for a while and drank what was left of the nettle beer. Then I opened another – might as well have a party.

At 1am I stumbled through the trees back to the river (because it was dark – not because of the beer). Few things fill me with more excitement than creeping up on a line to see it stretched taut into the water – and that is exactly what I found with line no.1. The next bit is equally exhilarating: you never know what is on the other end of the line. Will it be a tiddler you can tug up to the bank? Or will it be the start of an epic battle between man

WOODEN STAKE
STRONG FISHING LINE
2 X AA WEIGHT

and denizen of the deep? Quite often, it is an eel. And it was with no surprise that I hauled one very angry, slimy *Anguilla anguilla* up the bank.

Unlike my furry and feathery protein providers, you don't have to kill fish as soon as you get your hands on them. This is where the freshwater fridge comes into play. Quite simply, it is a keep net: a series of rings with netting wrapped around them. They are often used by the most pointless of fishermen – match anglers – who sit on top of boxes and throw endless bait into the river, in the hope of catching as many small fry as they can, to win the match with the greatest weight. For people who think fishing is dull, this is the perfect example. When the fish you seek are for food, fishing becomes an entirely different ball game.

The freshwater fridge is my way of stocking up on fish so there is something ready to dine on rather than having to go on the hunt. From the fish's perspective it can't be too pleasant being locked up in a keep net, so I will make sure they are never in there for more than 24 hours.

The second line had also been taken, but was snagged around something under the bank – when will I learn to set my lines away from snags! The

DESCRIPTION **A thin, brown, snake-like fish, up to 3¼ft (1m) long, found in freshwater lakes and rivers. The head is pointed, and the lower jaw extends beyond the upper jaw, which contains many small sharp teeth. All eels spawn in the Sargasso Sea, but their exact breeding habits are unknown as none have ever been bred successfully in captivity. The larvae, known as elvers (a delicacy in their own right), migrate towards northern Europe over a three-year period, after which they enter estuaries and swim upstream into fresh water, where they spend most of their lives. In fresh water their belly becomes yellow.**

other two lines held nothing of interest so I rebaited and left them for the morning. I slipped my first eel of the year into the fridge – smoked eel for breakfast, I think.

MONDAY 15th JUNE

This morning I had caught another eel and another line had snagged – not a bad result! I dusted off my portable smoker and prepared the eels. Eels are notoriously difficult customers. Even after you have stunned them by beating them over the head with something heavy, lopped their head off and removed their guts, they simply refuse to give up the ghost. I hung them in a plastic bag while I washed some salad from the patch. I glanced up to see the bag move as the decapitated eels squirmed inside – eerie!

It was one of the best breakfasts I had had for a while: smoked eel, with fresh salad and pickled hop shoots. After that I was ready to face the rigours of the day.

Fed up with eating off my knees, I have been thinking about building a table for the tree house, so today I had a look through the pile of recycled timber and dug out all the offcuts from my bed slats. I wanted a table that I could fold up against the wall as there isn't that much room. By using hinges where the legs attach to the table, and also where the table fixes to the wall, I will be able to put it away whenever it isn't being used.

I managed to construct a fine, fold-up table using four hinges, some pieces of hazel, and a load of short screws. I was so pleased with it I spent at least five minutes trying to work out if it was better up or down, but more than anything it was the action of the hazel legs swinging out as it was lowered that particularly entertained me – has it really come to this?

At 6pm I had a visitor. My mother had come down to see my new high-rise living arrangements. She climbed the ladder and complained about the lack of rungs near the top. She sat on the bench on the balcony and complained about its height and the fact that the edge dug into her legs. I muttered platitudes about fixing things up for her, while tucking into the basket of luxuries she had brought down: gin, tonic, lemon, ice, and a big bag of pistachios – mmmm!

We sat on the balcony enjoying her portable mini-bar complete with snacks and then I gave her the grand tour of my 'studio flat', before bidding her farewell. She tried to give me the rest of the pistachios but I was determined to stick to my dietary arrangements, though now it has got me thinking about luxury items …

Tuesday 16th June

Moving day! I was up at sparrow's fart this morning. After an overnight downpour the top of the stove had grown another puddle. Immediate action was required. As the stovepipe gets extremely hot, I reached for the exhaust pipe filler left over from sealing Bertha's firebox and climbed up onto the roof by shinning up one of the hazels that grows next to the tree house. I then removed the flash plate from the stovepipe and pulled out the rubber gloves to apply the filler. I managed to form quite a good seal, but only time will tell if it works or not.

So far I have been living in the woods with limited kit, but it was now time to bring down the rest of the gear I had earmarked at home, to make life amongst the leaves more sophisticated. I packed all kitchenware, books, staples and other useful items I had boxed up in the loft at home, and dragged it down to the woods. My book collection is very precious to me and I spent an hour or two building some sturdy shelves in one corner to give them pride of place. I have brought every book I thought would be useful reference for a 21st-Century hunter-gatherer: identification guides for plants and fungi, wild food guides, books on hunting and trapping, and of course a few light-hearted titles for entertainment purposes.

By the time I had unpacked and put everything where it should be, the place actually looked and felt like home. Up in London a studio this size would be laughable, but down here in the woods this self-contained unit looks thoroughly well equipped, and at the cutting edge of tree-dwelling luxury – well, sort of …

I couldn't resist hanging up a small Masai shield, a souvenir from my travels in Kenya – perhaps this token from the great hunters of the African plains will do my hunting prowess some good. I also had a tipple of the second batch of bottled nettle beer, although 'beer' is a slight misnomer – it tastes more like white wine with lemonade, or a cider and perry mix.

The vegetable patch is looking good but the potatoes are not. I am also finding that I am over-picking salad. I am feeling very content at the moment, now my living arrangements are sorted – I am on the property ladder at last!

I have decided that every week I will allow myself a luxury item, most likely food-based, in order to create something more lavish for the table.

The practical realities of my new lifestyle are slowly coming to light. Although electricity isn't an issue, water is. My water comes from two places: the river, for washing and showers; and the farm, for drinking and cooking. In this day and age water is a fairly standard amenity, but filling my four containers (16½ gallons/75 litres total capacity) and lugging them down to the tree house once or twice a week is hard work. I don't want to have to waste time purifying my water when I have so much else to be getting on with. If there were more people than just myself, then this might be something worth considering, but with only so many hours in a day I have decided not to make my water source an issue. In the grand scheme of things 16½ gallons (75 litres) is not a lot of water, and I should try to make it last a week. For example, an average five-minute shower (depending on water pressure) can use 6½–10 gallons (30–45 litres) – that's over half my weekly allowance! If I am going to learn anything down here it will definitely be about controlling my water consumption.

After water, fuel is the second most important issue. On an average night, with Bertha on the go, she can easily burn her way through a stacked basket of wood. I know I live in a wood where there is plenty of, well, wood; but it *must* be dry, dead, standing wood (apart from in exceptionally dry weather when any fallen wood on the forest floor is acceptable). Wet wood just doesn't burn! And this means wet in two senses of the word: wet from rain, in which case it would need to be split down; and wet because the wood has recently been cut down and is still classified as 'green', which needs to be 'seasoned'. Seasoning wood involves allowing time for the sap in the timber to dry out to allow it to burn properly.

Different woods burn in different ways, and depending on your need, be it for light, warmth, speedy or slow cooking, this poem gives some useful pointers for efficient wood use:

Oak logs will warm you well if they're old and dry.
Larch logs of pine wood smell, but the sparks will fly.
Beech logs for Christmas time.
Yew logs heat well.
Scotch logs, it is a crime for anyone to sell.
Birch logs will burn too fast.
Chestnut scarce at all.
Hawthorn logs are good to last, if you cut them in the fall.
Holly logs will burn like wax, you should burn them green.
Elm logs like smouldering flax, no flame to be seen.
Pear logs and apple logs, they will scent your room.
Cherry logs across the dogs smell like flowers in bloom.
But ash logs, all smooth and grey, burn them green or old.
Buy up all that come your way, they're worth their weight in gold.

Anon

The farmer was out today in his big red tractor, cutting down all the hay in the fields surrounding the wood, and there was an amazing smell of freshly cut grass drifting through the wood on the prevailing wind. This is a good sign too – farmers won't make hay unless there is at least a week of good weather forecast to dry it out. Also, if the fields have been cut this should make hunting easier.

I tried a 'speedy kettle' experiment this morning. I dug a small hole and put three bricks on their sides around it to hold the kettle. The aim was to use birch wood, the fast burner, to create a concentrated, small fire that would boil a full kettle in the least possible time. But it was rubbish! It took longer than Bertha to get going. A normal fire with a grill on top is the way forward.

I went over to the birch grove today to bring back a couple of faggots of wood. The fallen lengths of birch are a wonderful source of fuel, especially for getting a kettle boiled (if used in the correct way)! If I can get one bundle a day, I will be rolling in it – literally! I designated a stacking area under the tree house and filled it up with the birch.

Had the chance for a little downtime today and spent it the only way I know: fishing. For sport I always use the fly rod and, after a bit of time moving downstream flicking the fly across the water (with marginal success – there was far too much to get snagged up on), I had bagged a few small perch. Not the 'sport' I was looking for, but a tasty snack all the same.

Eventually I came across a pond next to the river. I had seen it before and had always suspected it might hold something of the piscine variety. Today my suspicions were confirmed – several 5–10lb (2.3–4.5kg) mirror carp! Glad I have got my recreational angling sorted out for the rest of the summer. They didn't seem interested in my flies though – perhaps I should bake some bread for them.

On the walk back to the wood I saw Frank the fox in the newly cut field. I assumed he was after mice; he kept pouncing like a cat, and then burying his head in the hay. He didn't have as much success with them as I did creeping up on him; the wind was blowing in my face and he couldn't smell me. I watched his fantastic red hue flickering amongst the vivid green of the flourishing British summer – I am so lucky to be doing this. He was so preoccupied, he didn't notice me until I was 10ft (3m) away, and even then he didn't seem to mind.

Robinson Crusoe was discussing clay ovens today. Now I have finished the tree house I feel the urge to build something new …

Thursday 18th June

Today was a scorcher and by 9am it was already too hot. I made coffee outside – the usual way this time – and read for an hour while I waited for a basic dough to rise so I could make some flatbreads. I decided R&R was the order of the day so I went to the carp pond. For the last 12 hours I had struggled to think about anything other than those fish. I was determined to hook something of a decent size.

The carp didn't appear to have been fished for before, and even the sight of a half-naked tree dweller didn't spook them. I had two casts in all and dragged out two fish within the space of an hour. They were good-sized mirror carp, rich and golden, probably around 8–10lb (3.6–4.5kg) apiece – they put up a hell of a scrap! There was no chance they were coming home for tea; they were just too impressive, and in another ten years they'll be twice the size.

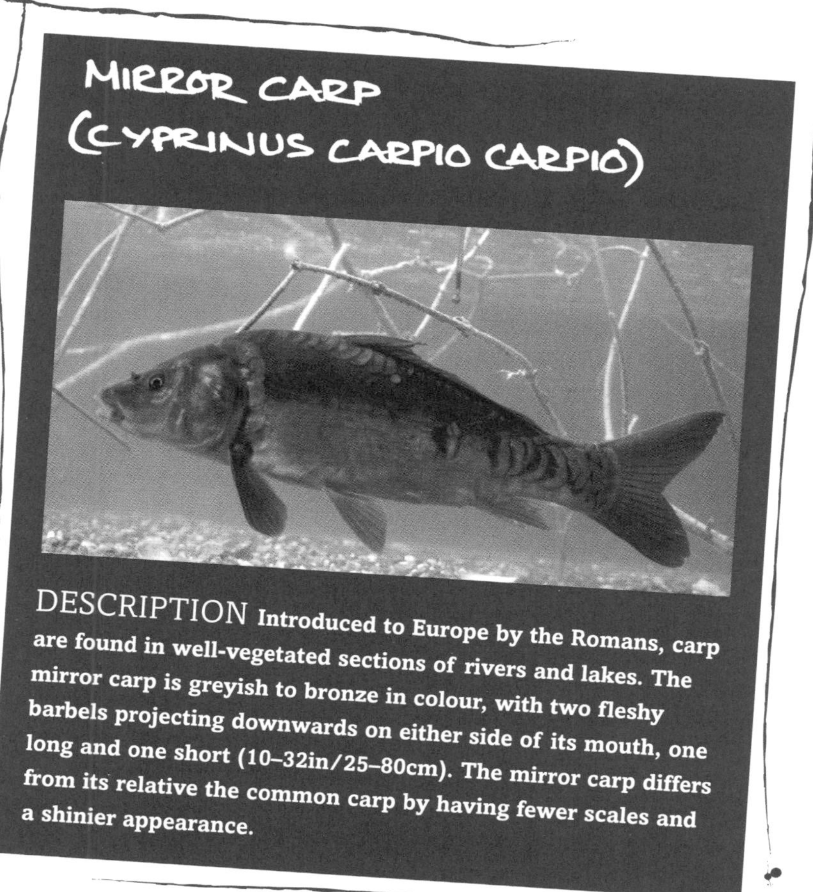

Mirror carp (Cyprinus carpio carpio)

DESCRIPTION **Introduced to Europe by the Romans, carp are found in well-vegetated sections of rivers and lakes. The mirror carp is greyish to bronze in colour, with two fleshy barbels projecting downwards on either side of its mouth, one long and one short (10–32in/25–80cm). The mirror carp differs from its relative the common carp by having fewer scales and a shinier appearance.**

Jew's ear fungus (Herneola auricula-judae)

DESCRIPTION **Associated with elder, this ear-shaped bracket fungus usually grows in clusters. It is red-brown in colour and measures up to 2in (5cm) across. It can be found throughout the year but is more common in October and November.**

USES **The rather politically incorrect name 'Jew's ear' is a reference to the belief that Judas Iscariot hanged himself in an elder tree; these days it is more commonly known as jelly ear fungus. They are incredibly popular in the Far East, and are regularly used in soups or stews, as they do need at least 30–40 minutes' simmering to render them palatable. They are at their best when they are in their jelly-like state, but you can still use them when they have dried out, by reconstituting them in a little warm water. Dried jelly ears can be ground into a powder to use as a flavouring.**

I realised today that the farmers haven't actually been making hay; they have been collecting it for silage to feed the dairy cows – so much for my knowledge of country ways! I swung by the patch to give it a good drink and walked back to the wood with a few veggies for lunch. A great commotion arose as I quietly trod through the wood: 20ft (6m) in front of me a herd of deer flitted between the trees. A train of females was being followed by the most magnificent beast I have ever laid eyes on: a pure white stag. He paused for a moment as I rushed forward to get a better look, and seemed to stare straight at me, then he turned and ushered his ladies onward. I had heard of a white stag in the area, but to have him grace my wood with his presence was a truly humbling experience … what a day.

For lunch I made a Chinese-style soup using some broad beans (I used the skins too as it was a shame to waste them), chives and spinach. I picked some Jew's ear mushrooms off an elder tree at the top of the wood and added them to the broth, along with a stock cube and a teaspoon of red Thai curry paste – my luxury item for the week. I ate lunch swinging in the hammock and washed it down with a refreshing mug of meadowsweet tea. I then stretched out and had a siesta after the terribly gruelling day I had had so far!

I woke with a start, swiftly lost balance, and landed flat on my face with a mouthful of leaves. I have now realised why I don't trust hammocks, especially for sleeping in. It was 4pm and I really hadn't done anything all day, but I fancied some rabbit for supper so it was time to get pro-active. I went upstairs and retrieved the air rifle from under the bed, donned my new flat cap for that authentic country feel (I am not sure I have mastered the look just yet), and stepped out into the fields to look for supper.

Just finished eating the biggest rabbit I have ever shot; eyes were definitely bigger than stomach – mine not the rabbit's!

FRIDAY 19th JUNE

I was back in London today but this time it was for pleasure, not business. At the age of 27 I have managed to achieve something that I never thought possible – I am to become a published author, and this diary is going to be part of it. Better make it good.

Clare took me to Rules for supper to celebrate. It was an excellent meal, and I feel I have become really familiar with all the ingredients. I had a pint of London Pride in a silver tankard (old boy bling, of course) with potted rabbit on toast, followed by venison osso bucco with a fine red wine, and finally a gooseberry and elderflower fool. I was almost as stuffed as I was after yesterday's rabbit, but this time I had some whisky to help ease my digestion. It has been one of the best days ever – didn't like the bill though …

SATURDAY 20th JUNE

I can't believe tomorrow is the longest day of the year – summer has barely even started! The sad thing is, from here on out, the days gradually get shorter and eventually colder. Tonight I hosted a solstice shindig to please the pagan gods and ensure happy tree house living for the rest of my time here.

I opened up the underground oven again and this time I cooked two legs of lamb. I know lamb is not strictly legal game as far as my hunter-gathering goes – it wouldn't be very sporting to go to the nearest field of sheep, grapple one to the ground and lop off its back legs with a machete. I would certainly have a lot of explaining to do to the local farmer. So for this evening I used up next week's luxury item to feed my guests.

Ben, whom I had met on Ray Mears's Assistant Instructor selection weekend (he got the job, not me!), turned up with his girlfriend Katie, after completing his first week at bushcraft school. I thought my own personal hygiene was somewhat in question owing to my occasional bathing habits, but after a week without a shower, Ben stank! Chris arrived with two other friends, Max and Jess, and the six of us got stuck into a spread of underground oven-cooked lamb stuffed with wild garlic and rosemary, and a mix of vegetables from the patch, all washed down with a few bottles of my nettle beer.

My guests had brought down some extra alcohol rations and as the night wore on so did the drunken revelry! We had hoped to see the sun rise at 4.58am, but crashed out at about 2am. Just as well, as it turned out – Sunday morning was cloudy!

MONDAY 22ND JUNE

This week I am going to make a clay oven. You only have to dig down 6in (15.2cm) to hit the clay in the soil here. I don't have access to sand but I can use silt from the river, and as for wood for the dome, well ...

Today the aim was to get some meat on my plate. If this experiment is going to work I must be disciplined: if I want protein I have to hunt it. As far as the tree house armoury goes I am fairly well equipped. I have two fishing rods and two guns: an air rifle and a trusty old 12-bore shotgun. (For legal reasons I must point out that the shotgun was only kept down at the tree house when I was there; when I had a day out teaching or otherwise, it was kept in the gun cabinet at the family home.)

Choosing the correct weapon for the correct quarry is always a matter of debate. An air gun is good for rabbits, squirrels and roosting birds. Ammunition, in the form of pellets, is cheap to buy and the gun doesn't need cleaning as meticulously or as often as the shotgun. It is a great weapon for stalking and allows you to move through the countryside, slowly and thoughtfully, observing everything around you.

The shotgun, although as subtle as a large truck driving through a nitroglycerin plant, has its benefits. It can reach prey that the air rifle cannot, and there is little hope of taking down a bird on the wing without a shotgun. Ammunition is not as cheap as for the air rifle (about £6.99 for a box of 25 cartridges), but then with the spread of pellets from a shotgun you are less likely to miss whatever it is you are aiming at.

Other than taking up the gun or the rod, there is also another avenue open to me: trapping. The problem with trapping is that it can mean you come up against a brick wall. Many of the most effective traps are not as humane as the animal rights groups would like. Hence in this day and age, when you don't have to rely on hunting and trapping for food, it is considered more humane to visit the local supermarket for a packet of intensively reared chicken or a slab of intensively farmed Danish pork. Most traps are illegal in the UK. How our ancestors would have laughed! The notion that it is better for an animal not to suffer in any way and for us to go hungry would seem ludicrous to them.

I resolved to make some traps to catch some pigeons – my favourite meat. I made three Ojibwa bird poles: an ingeniously simple Native American trap. I set them in the field next to the wood where I had seen the odd posse of pigeons feasting on clover, and baited the poles with rice and stale bread. I don't expect much until the pigeons get used to them – they can't be that clever, can they? A few were feeding nearby an hour later, but only a pheasant was bold enough to chow down on the free offerings – a watched trap catches nothing.

While I was waiting to see if I could bring a touch of Native American cunning to the Sussex countryside, I went out shooting – I was after feather *not* fur. Unfortunately, the only bird I saw for the first hour that would have made easy pickings was Jeff, who has continued to hang around the tree house for weeks now, probably because no predators are likely to come too close.

I have added a few new things to my list of staples: mustard and citrus fruits. Mustard, because I am eating a lot of rabbit and the two are made for each other. And citrus fruits, because there is a distinct lack of them growing in this part of the country. They are good for fish and salad dressings, and an orange for breakfast is a worthwhile hit of vitamin C. Best keep the white blood cells in fighting form.

After a poor shooting mission – plenty of squirrels abroad, but I wasn't really in a squirrel mood – I decided to set my sights on the river. I have always been better with the rod than with the gun. I set up the keep net and ledgered for a while (a technique that involves using a couple of weights and a baited hook that sits on the riverbed), feeling the line with my fingers for any sign of a bite. I caught two large gudgeon, which I put in the freshwater fridge. After a couple of hours with barely enough gudgeon to cover half a slice of bread, I decided that later I would set some nightlines to replenish my eel stocks, and went back to the tree house to take the gun out at dusk.

I find I get extremely anxious at around 7pm when I have no protein for the table; it is a horrible feeling, verging on panic. My carnivorous ways are insatiable: no meat, no meal! But sometimes you just have to wait for the right time of day. I took the air rifle to the field on the far side of the wood where there are usually plenty of rabbits and within 15 minutes I had bagged a medium-sized coney with a fine neck shot. I skinned and gutted the beast and cut all the meat off the bone. I made a simple marinade, rubbed it all over the meat and left it for a couple of hours.

I pan-fried the rabbit and basted the meat as it was cooking with the leftover marinade. I had rice with steamed hop shoots and wilted spinach from the patch. A good feed.

MARINADE FOR RABBIT (AND SQUIRREL)

Olive oil

Lemon juice

Wild garlic bulbs, crushed

A dash of cider vinegar

A drizzle of red wine (left over from the solstice dinner)

Sage

Rosemary

A twist of salt and pepper

I have been careful to wash up after every meal otherwise things can get unpleasant very quickly. For tomorrow's lunch, I put the rabbit carcass in a billycan with some stock, a few herbs, and the last of the leftover red wine, and put it on top of the stove for a few hours. They don't call me Thrifty von Thriftenstein for nothing; in fact, they don't at all – but they could.

As agreeable as this lifestyle is, it is a lot of work for one person, although manageable. I think it will be very hard to leave, although I do miss living with Clare. I'm gradually getting set in my ways and establishing a good routine. I'm going to try to fill a thermos with boiling water tonight to make that early-morning caffeine kick come a little quicker.

TUESDAY 23RD JUNE

One of my hurricane lamps packed up last night so today I went to get a new one. Unfortunately the exhaust pipe fell off the car on the way back to the wood …

I began work on my clay oven – or 'adobe' oven, as they are also known. I picked up some bricks and three breeze blocks from a fly-tipping spot that I had noticed on my way back to the wood (*sans* exhaust pipe). I laid out the bricks and started work on the wooden frame using thin, freshly cut hazel rods and jute twine. I made the first one a bit too tall, so I had to cut it down 6in (15.2cm) and then tie it back together again. I also had a go at making a good clay mix. It looks as if it is going to be quite hard work – here we go again!

While clearing out the underground oven, I noticed that the wood from previous fires has become top-grade charcoal – now that's recycling! The bird poles have still not done anything, and there were no eels on the nightlines, so I had to settle for a vegetarian special tonight. Oh, yes, the thermos trick yielded a semi-warm cuppa this morning – I won't be doing that again.

The only company I can depend on regularly are the moths. They really are silly buggers, flying into candles, loving the light, and flitting/crawling wherever they feel best suits them. It strikes me as odd that over millions of years of evolution they are still drawn to the very thing that may prove to be their demise … but who am I to mock them for their shortcomings? To tell the truth, I rather enjoy their antics.

WEDNESDAY 24TH JUNE WIND

The weather has been amazing for some time now, although I'm sure it will change now I've mentioned it. The wind today really made the place feel like a ship – so much creaking! I could hardly hear myself speak (ahem, not that I am talking to myself or anything).

I began the day with coffee and an orange, and after breakfast I went to water the patch. I decided to take the gun – just in case. Almost always, whenever I go out with the gun, word seems to spread around all the animals in the local area quicker than beer turns to piss. Go out without it and the beasts and birds prance about gaily, knowing there isn't a thing I can do about it. Some high-class trickery is called for, methinks, perhaps using the 'concealed weapon' approach.

How to cure a rabbit pelt

To cure a rabbit pelt, all you need to do is pin out the skin, fur side down, with nails on a wooden board. Use a knife to remove any bits of fat or sinew that are still on the skin. The pelt then needs to dry out. If you want the pelt to be soft and flexible (eg. for clothing), you will need to rub salt into it, which will help draw out the moisture; but you must change the salt every couple of days until all the moisture has been drawn out, and the salt no longer cakes. Remove all the salt from the pelt and then finish the skin off by smoking it for 30 minutes. If you don't mind if the pelt is slightly brittle (eg. for a rug), you can let it dry out for 24 hours under a fly net without applying any salt, and then smoke it over a smouldering fire for 30 minutes.

My plan seemed to work. I kept the shotgun as well hidden as possible on my walk across the fields. A pigeon clapped over a tree in a most relaxed manner, up came the gun faster than I could ever have imagined, and 'bang!' The pigeon folded in mid-air and hit the ground with a thud. Perhaps I should resort to this woodland chicanery more often.

With supper taken care of, I set to work on a few of the items on my 'To Do' list. I patched up the floor immediately around the tree to prevent a slight draught that was starting to get tiresome, then I pressed on with the clay oven.

Having perfected the clay mix, I made up a batch in a bucket and laid the base of the oven. I continued to weave fine lengths of hazel into the top of the dome-shaped hazel frame and gradually worked my way down. I noticed the rabbits in the wood had dug up a lot of clay spoil, and I made a note not to shoot rabbits in the immediate vicinity, as a way of repaying their helpfulness.

The patch is really booming at the moment. I gathered a load of broad beans for tomorrow, and took a few courgettes and a handful of potatoes for supper. The potato plants are looking very sad but the potatoes themselves, once dug up, are in mint condition. I also picked some nettles from the wild larder.

For supper I had the pigeon spatchcocked (backbone cut out and laid flat) over the fire outside, fried up some of the courgettes in a pan, boiled the potatoes, and steamed the nettles. I then made a pigeon broth with leftovers for lunch tomorrow.

I do enjoy my evening cup of tea when I write this. I don't usually eat until 10pm – poor, I know – but the day seems to last forever. My first rabbit pelt is almost done, the aim being to get enough to make a rabbit skin rug to lay in front of Bertha.

THURSDAY 25th JUNE WIND

Elgar's *Nimrod* – a good, inspiring tune to fire up the soul first thing in the morning – as is Morricone's *The Mission*. I have allowed myself the luxury of an iPod, but first I had to overcome the issue of how to charge it without power. I found the answer in solar power and have been using a small, compact solar charger. The problem is I don't get much sun in the wood, so I usually put it out in the field or on the roof of the tree house, which sits just above the main forest canopy – it works a treat!

I decided to take the morning off and visit the secret carp lake over the river. As soon as I had set up and hooked a 5lb (2.3kg) mirror carp I got fed up with getting stung by nettles and called it a day. I thought that by now I might have built up some immunity, but no such luck. Time to make some dock leaf serum, I think.

Back at the tree house I had a refreshingly cool shower in the midday heat. After that and lunch it was time for more oven building – a messy job after my shower, but no matter. I went to collect some more hay from the fields to use in the clay mixture. The mixing is not much fun, but the bit I do enjoy is slapping it onto the frame: a sort of grown-up version of making mud pies. I started on the first bit of wall at the base by laying quite a thick foundation, and then gradually worked around and upwards; the hay worked incredibly well at binding the mixture. It was slow, steady work.

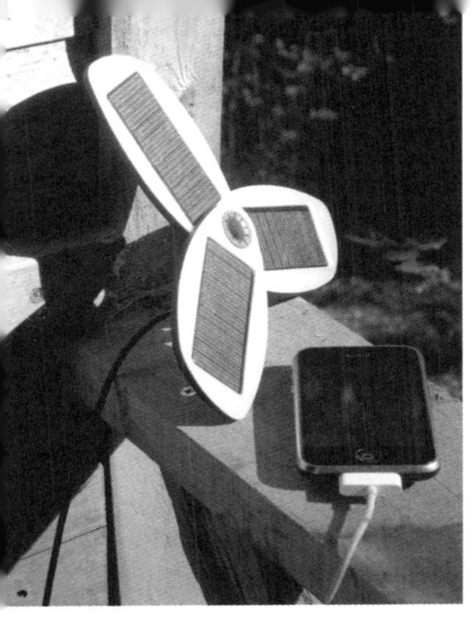

Now, I live in the middle of a private wood, on private land, well off the beaten track, so I was slightly surprised when I spotted a small, sweaty chap, sporting a rucksack and wellies, making his way down the path and staring up at the tree house in bewilderment. He hadn't spotted me, so when I asked him if he was lost, he jumped out of his skin.

It turned out he was from The Environment Agency, and was passing through the wood to check some temperature markers on the river and see if water temperature has any effect on fish behaviour. He was most impressed with the dwelling, so I showed him round my house, and explained what I was up to. I then went with him down to the river, keen to learn a bit more about my hunting grounds. As he left he turned and said, 'I was meaning to ask, actually – I couldn't live in a place like this without beer.' Ah! Well …

Later I visited my parents' house to check e-mails, etc. My publisher is coming to see me next week – I had best impress.

FRIDAY 26th JUNE

At 5.25am I woke to hear distant rumblings and the first 'dings' of rain on the tin roof. Shit, I had a tree house with a metal roof in one of the tallest trees in the wood – surely that was just asking for trouble! I rolled over and tried not to think about lightning. I woke again at about 8am. It was damp outside from the passing rainstorm and there was a fresh, rich, earthy smell when I opened the door. It was incredibly humid.

I spent the day working on the clay oven and managed to get half of it done by mid-afternoon. For lunch I fried up some chopped broad beans (skins on) and wrapped them in a freshly baked flatbread with a couple of crushed wild garlic bulbs. It wasn't much but it was pretty tasty. I am starting to miss the variety of my usual larder; my diet may be fresh and filling, but it isn't always that exciting. Strangely, I miss celery …

The throne smelt a bit more than usual today. While I was collecting some more clay, I could see a 'pile' was developing in the middle of the long-drop hole, so I decided to flatten it out. I grabbed a stick and began my work, but much to my horror maggots were wriggling in the waste! It was time to dig a new hole. We had the same problem in the Cook Islands. As I recall, we made a big fire in the long drop and incinerated everything.

After a few more hours working on the oven, I had a shower to prepare for a visit from Clare. She was on her way down from London with a 'surprise'. While I waited for her I kept myself busy sprucing the place up a bit. I was using the Haitian goat skin rugs I had been given to cover the floor on the 'bedroom' side of the tree house. I beat the rugs out of the window, swept the floor, and cut a large pile of wood for the evening.

Clare arrived with smoked salmon, Prosecco, and Pimms and ice – amazing. We sat on the balcony enjoying a glass of Pimms with all the trimmings. Then we wandered down through the wood to the patch to get some salad for supper. We walked across the maize field in the evening light – it was one of those rare summer evenings when you actually think you could be abroad. Clare seemed incredibly relaxed and happy; I do think she likes being one of the few Londoners (well I suppose there could be others!) to have access to a rustic bolthole like this one.

We had a lovely, chilled-out evening and ate supper on the balcony – it was perfect. Eventually at about 11pm we retired and I lit the stove, for ambiance more than heat, as it was still very warm. Clare was asleep as soon as her head touched the pillow. I, on the other hand, was still wide awake and began reading a new book, Conrad's *Heart of Darkness*.

I have just found out that Michael Jackson died two days ago – I can't believe how out of touch I am with current affairs. I must listen to *Billie Jean* at once.

SATURDAY 27th JUNE ☼ 27°C!

I slept very soundly and had a lazy morning, with coffee in bed at 10am. It is so nice to have company for a change. Clare said she would help me finish the clay oven so I went down to the river to get more water and silt for the clay mix.

I was doing the mixing and clay digging (I began a new long-drop hole to kill two birds with one stone) and in spite of relentless mosquito attacks, we finally managed to finish the oven. Clare said it was like moulding poo, which I did find a little disturbing – how would she know that?

The finished oven looked gloriously Iron Age; Clare said it looked like an old-fashioned beehive. Both spattered with clay, we took advantage of the fine weather, and went to sunbathe in the field for an hour or two.

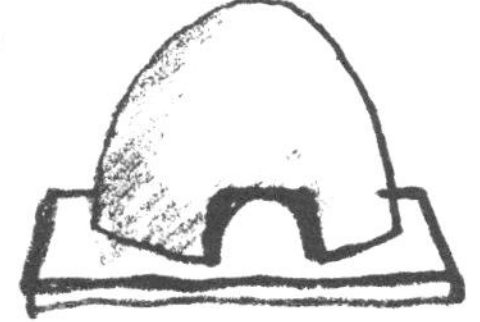

After a while Clare said she might go home for a shower, although she knew full well that there was a shower at the tree house. We went back into the woods and I explained to her the finer points of tree house sanitation. Persuading her to strip naked in the middle of the woods wasn't easy even after I explained that it was the best way to experience it. 'If anyone comes along, I will kill you!', she said. I kept my mouth shut about the sweaty chap who had passed by the other day – she didn't need to know that.

SUNDAY 28th JUNE 28°C!

It was bloody hot today! After a fair amount of Pimms last night, and a good lie-in until 11.30am, I felt rather spaced out this morning. Poor Clare had been attacked overnight by some kind of insect and there was an enormous swollen bite above her ankle. They must have sensed new blood – they don't bother with me anymore.

I made a fire, had coffee, and then I went over to water the patch while Clare washed up a few bits left over from last night. As I approached the bridge over the river I was overjoyed to see the first few ripe wild raspberries! The riverbank by the bridge is a sheer drop and at the top is a sprawling, tangled mass of brambles and raspberry bushes – not the easiest place to reach. A tantalising few were hanging at arm's length from the railings so I gave them a try: they tasted incredibly sweet, with a slight tang. A wild version of a fizzy Haribo sweet: one of my vices from the real world. I will have to wait for a glut, but soon I will be able to turn my hand to jam making or … game sauce? I might have to keep my eyes peeled for duck to go with the raspberries.

After ten or more trips back and forth between the patch and the stream to fill and empty the watering can on my thirsty vegetables, I picked some pretty sweet pea flowers for Clare, and some for the tree house window sill to provide a splash of colour amongst all that wood.

Back at the tree house Clare and I began designing a motif to go around the base of the clay oven. We used a couple of nails, a hinge and an L-bracket, and pressed them into the drying clay. We achieved a good Mexican/Native American look with the design. I now have to wait a few days for the clay oven to dry out before lighting a fire inside it; if it dries out too fast then some severe cracks could develop.

Wild Raspberry (Rubus idaeus)

DESCRIPTION **A slender perennial, usually unbranched, 3–6ft (90–180cm) tall. Stems are arched and woody with weak prickles, and carry groups of 3–7 toothed leaflets. White flowers grow in small, drooping clusters. Fruit is soft and red, and easy to pick when ripe; appears July–September.**

USES **If you can get to them before the birds do, they are best eaten as God intended, perhaps with a generous dollop of cream. If you come across enough, turn them into jam for breakfast or a simple raspberry coulis for drizzling over puddings.**

Clare left mid-afternoon and I was on my own once again. I dragged out my homebrews and measured the specific gravity with my hydrometer to see if fermentation was tailing off – I was pretty certain both the elderflower and nettle were ready for bottling.

First I took the lid off the nettle brew. It smelt a little off and looked a slightly odd colour. There was only one way to find out whether the beer had gone off and that was to taste it. I spat the rancid brew out as soon as it touched my lips; it tasted like urine mixed with pen ink – there was something really unnatural about the flavour.

Then I remembered something I had noticed the day after I had brewed the nettle beer, but until now I had not made the connection. When I had walked through the maize field before gathering all the raw materials, something had looked different: between the 2ft (61cm) maize plants, the standard collection of undesirable weeds, such as fat hen and pineapple weed, had shrivelled up and died. I think at the time I had assumed it must be something to do with the weather.

I went back down to the field to confirm my suspicions. Sure enough, all the weeds were dead and all the nettles lining the edge of the field were on their last legs: the farmer had been using weed killer! The horror … This meant the whole batch of nettle beer was a write-off. This was an appearance by man that I had not been expecting and I was a bit shaken by the unseen encounter. To make matters worse, the elderflower champagne was ruined too. The learning curve has just become a hell of a lot steeper …

Monday 29th June ☼ 28°c!

Today has been difficult. Surely it's not meant to be stressful down here? The weather was stifling; it was not so bad in the woods, but out in the open it felt like the Sahara. I had planned to sort out the patch and do some weeding but it was far too hot for that.

Instead of gardening, I took myself to the river for a much needed paddle. While I was wading through the refreshing cool water, negotiating waist-deep pools, I began to feel like one of the first explorers making their way through an unknown land, an Indiana Jones without the hat – I think it must have been the rope clipped to my rucksack and the machete in my hand …

But it was more than just a passing feeling: it was the landscape I was in. I was surrounded by it. I was struck at just how jungle-like our happy little island can be when the weather is right, with bindweed and hops working their way up trees and bushes – the deep green of summer – and the buzzing patches of insects and constant chatter of birds. It *is* a jungle – a very British one at that.

After my swim I decided to attempt a proper loaf of bread. All the bread I have made since I have been living in the woods has either been twisted around a stick (damper bread) or cooked in a heavy pan (flatbread); it was time for something a bit more substantial.

As the clay oven was still in the process of drying out, I used a large, aluminium pickling pan instead. I made a big fire, placed the dough in a billycan lid, put the billycan lid in the pickling pan, sealed the pan with its lid, and placed it securely among the roaring flames. I packed a few bits of wood around it to get the fire really raging. Happy with my efforts, I sat back in the hammock with a book, looking forward to the sweet smell of baked bread.

BASIC BREAD RECIPE

INGREDIENTS

1lb (500g) plain flour
1 sachet (2 tsp) dried yeast
1 tsp salt
½ pint (300ml) water
2 tsp white granulated sugar
2 tbsp olive oil

I use this basic recipe for all my bread-making exploits. For flatbread, simply pull off a piece of dough, shape it into a ball, squash it on a floured surface and roll it out with a rolling pin if you have one – if not, I find a water bottle or a wine bottle does the job perfectly. The flatbread should be no thicker than a £1 coin. Make sure the flatbread is well floured, and gradually brown it on each side in a heated pan over the fire. The dough should bubble up quite a bit and you will get a few burnt-looking patches; it is basically a pitta and it's meant to look like that ...

1 In a mixing bowl, combine the flour, yeast and salt, and give them a good mix.

2 Fill a measuring jug with ½ pint (300ml) of warm water, add the sugar and olive oil, and stir.

3 Make a well in the middle of the flour and gradually pour the water in a little at a time, followed by a stir with a wooden spoon. Continue until all the liquid has been used up.

4 Put aside the spoon and get your hands involved, ideally just the one, to keep the other clean! You want to create a nice, elastic dough that is not too sticky.

5 Once you have reached a good consistency, flour the surface of a wooden chopping board and start kneading the dough on the board. This should be about ten minutes of pure punishment for the dough. When your arms feel like they can take no more, shape the dough into a rough ball and put it back into the mixing bowl, cover with a tea towel and leave it to 'prove' for 1½ hours.

6 After 1½ hours the dough will have risen substantially. Push a fist into the middle of the dough to expel all the air, then take it out and knead it for two more minutes. Your dough is now ready for use.

After ten minutes I glanced up to check on the baking. The pan was red-hot and melting – shit! I managed to get the pan off the fire but one side of it looked like torn cardboard, and inside was a very burned loaf of … charcoal. It proved to be a good lesson in outdoor baking: stick to damper or flatbreads and don't use aluminium pans! But I suppose I can't expect everything to work perfectly first time.

My shooting fared no better – admittedly, I'm not all that handy with an air rifle. I will never forget a school shooting competition when I was ten. We were allowed to take in our own air rifles, and I was beaten by a girl who had never shot before in her life, with my own gun! Oh, the shame … To make it worse, Chris reminds me about it whenever we go shooting.

I chased a couple of cock pheasants, tried to sneak up on some roosting pigeons, and missed some grazing rabbits. I would have taken out the shotgun but I've run out of cartridges. My freshwater fridge was also empty. I am hoping to have eels for lunch tomorrow so I went back to the river to set some nightlines. Worms were scarce so I tried slugs, but I had no luck there either – not even a ravenous eel would go for a slug!

When I got back to the tree house, feeling very fed up, I was in for a treat. As I opened the door and walked in there was something resembling a mini helicopter circling around inside. At first I thought it was a may bug but then, as it winged its way towards my face, I got a better view – it was a hornet! I have hated hornets ever since I was stung on the ear by one when I was four. But here was my chance of retribution for that cold-hearted attack on a defenceless child. I reached under the bed, keeping low, and felt blindly for one of the recycled newspapers I had stashed away. I grabbed one, rolled it up, and waited for the hornet to settle.

It rested up on one of the birch rafters, so I crept up on it, raised the newspaper baton and commenced my attack with a bloodcurdling cry. The hornet dropped to the floor. I looked more closely and I could see its long sting shooting back and forth as it desperately tried to go on the offensive. I put it out of its misery, picked it up on the newspaper, and flicked it inside Bertha to be cremated later. Revenge was mine.

I had no option but the vegetarian special for supper: broad beans with wild garlic and rice cooked in chicken stock, with a side salad of wild and cultivated greens. I made some delicious vinaigrette to try to cheer myself up. It had been such a miserable day I decided to go to bed so tomorrow would come more quickly.

I haven't seen Jeff the pheasant for ages. I hope Frank hasn't tucked in – that bird belongs to me.

Tuesday 30th June ☼ 29°c!

I can now tell what time it is when I wake up by the position of the sun in the windows. It creeps into the window by the stove at 7.30am, and once it has reached the second window, it is 8.30–9am and time to get up.

Today I stocked up on all my essentials. I had the car, just serviced and fitted with a swanky new exhaust pipe, so I drove to town having just received some money for the first instalment of my magazine column. At the gun shop I bought 50 shotgun cartridges (£12) and 500 .22 air gun pellets (£7.50). I also went to the fishing shop and bought some hooks and weights for the nightlines, and a spinner/lure for the rod (£10). Then it was time to top up my staples: sunflower oil, plain and wholemeal flour, long-grain rice and stock cubes (vegetable, chicken and beef).

While walking down the high street I went into a shop that has been there as long as I can remember: a grotto full of sweet jars and tobacco. I have never forgotten the glorious whiff of my father's pipe smoke while learning to fish when I was small – another smell that is firmly ingrained in my memory. I looked at the bearded shopkeeper and announced that I wanted some pipe tobacco. Judging from all the old tins I have inherited over the years, that I used for storing my fishing tackle, my father was partial to Three Nuns and Condor. I wasn't sure which would be better but I went for the latter because I liked the look of the packet.

I swung by my parents' house, where there is a magnificent collection of pipes that belonged to both my father and my grandfather. I found a long, old-fashioned churchwarden pipe that I really liked. As I am living a Huck Finn kind of lifestyle I felt the time was right to try a pipe and see what all the fuss is about.

Back at the tree house I had my first go on the pipe. It didn't taste that great and as the smoker the smell just wasn't quite the same – the idea of smoking a pipe is perhaps nicer than actually doing it. I sat in the hammock chair puffing away as the sun shone through the wood and, after yesterday's frustrations, this was the perfect antidote. I finished the pipe and had to gargle a pint of water to get rid of the acrid taste in my mouth – probably best saved for rare occasions.

At dusk I went down to the river to set four nightlines. I put one below the bridge and the rest above it, in a long stretch of slow-moving water where there were patches of duckweed. I checked the lines at midnight, and found a fat eel on one, but nothing on the others. I put the eel in the freshwater fridge, happy in the knowledge I *definitely* had something for lunch tomorrow.

JULY

WEDNESDAY 1st JULY ☼ 29°C!

This must have been the hottest day of the year! I woke at 8.30am to the sound of birdsong that seemed louder than usual. I opened my eyes to see a wren perched on the rim of my bedside pint of water. The little bird cheeped, dipped its tail, and then crapped into my water, something I'm glad I witnessed, otherwise I could have had a nasty surprise. When I got out of bed the wren went mental and began flying into my massive windows in a bid for freedom. I promptly opened them all up before the bird caused itself an injury. However, rather than fly out of the windows, the wren eventually escaped through the eaves, which I still haven't patched up.

I began the day with the usual set of chores – down to the patch to give the vegetables a good drink (they needed 13 watering cans' worth), and then I went to check the nightlines. The first one delivered up an eel. I gave it a quick blow to the head so I could take it back for lunch, while the eel from last night lived to die another day. I had hoped the other nightlines above the bridge would fare just as well. Two had obviously been taken, but had snagged on something. With only one line left to check and my publisher coming for lunch tomorrow, I started to worry: I had only one eel in the fridge – and one between two people isn't a great feed.

I had set the last line in a rather inviting pool. As I approached, the line looked taut and, when I gingerly lifted it up, I felt an enormous tug and the water suddenly exploded in a spray of silver, streaked with a flash of gold: a spotty Herbert – also known as a brown trout – had at some point during the early hours, given in to the lure of the worm. It was a beautiful fish of about 3lb (1.4kg) and too big simply to haul up the bank without fear of the line breaking. This was a fish I couldn't afford to lose – the perfect centrepiece for tomorrow's lunch. I had to get it down to the freshwater fridge alive.

There was only one thing for it. I had planned to have a swim anyway, so I grabbed my towel out of the rucksack, jumped over a tangled mass of brambles and into the drink, hoping for a soft landing.

I managed to coax the fish into the wet towel, bit the line off with my teeth, and set off downstream to the freshwater fridge. As I waded through

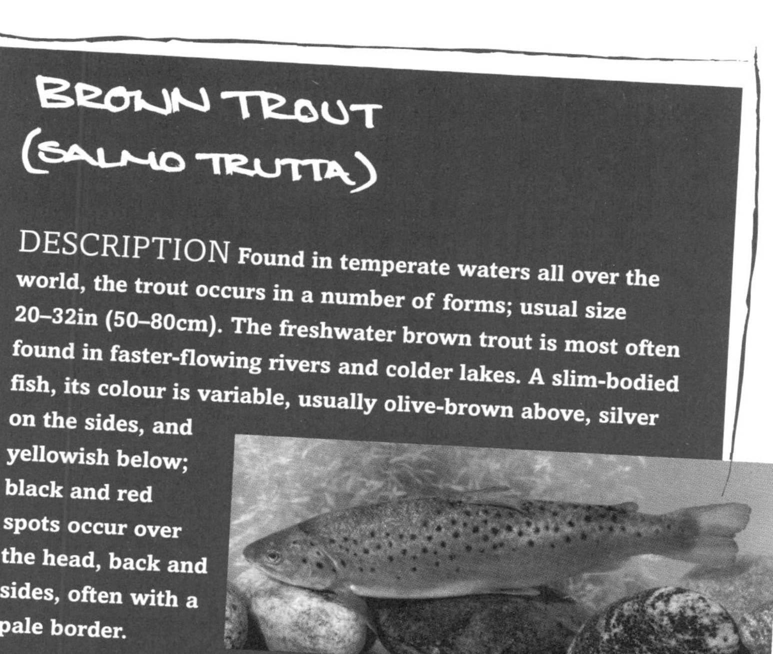

BROWN TROUT (SALMO TRUTTA)

DESCRIPTION **Found in temperate waters all over the world, the trout occurs in a number of forms; usual size 20–32in (50–80cm). The freshwater brown trout is most often found in faster-flowing rivers and colder lakes. A slim-bodied fish, its colour is variable, usually olive-brown above, silver on the sides, and yellowish below; black and red spots occur over the head, back and sides, often with a pale border.**

the waist-deep river, I caught my shin on something sharp underwater, but for the moment the pain was offset by adrenaline as I raced onwards trying to find somewhere to clamber up the bank; but there was nowhere.

In the end I had to go through the tunnel under the bridge and climb up on the other side. I raced across the field to the bend in the river where the keep net was, climbed down the bank and unwrapped the fish over the front of the net, before slipping him back into the cool water of the river. He showed no sign of distress and with one flick of his tail he shot to the far end of the net. Phew! That was that, job done. I left Mr *Salmo trutta* and Mr *Anguilla anguilla* to get acquainted, hoping the former wouldn't scoff the latter. It was only then that the throbbing of my shin came to my attention: a deep gash was spewing blood down my leg. When was the last time I had my tetanus jab?

Back at the tree house I patched up my leg with my compact first-aid kit, and I had pan-fried eel with sorrel dressing, a salad of wild greens and new potatoes for lunch. I spent the afternoon making a bench and trying to master the traditional peg technique. I even found a lovely curved length of matted ivy that would make an excellent bench top. It was still attached to a fallen tree, so I used the saw to cut it off, and walked it back to the tree house to fit it to my new bench.

Eager for more excitement, I took out the shotgun to find supper. There wasn't much about so I waited until it got cooler. As I walked towards the birch wood a cock pheasant shot out and burst into flight. I knew it was the closed season for pheasants, but I needed to eat, and if a pheasant is foolish enough to come within range when I am out with the gun then so be it. I took aim and fired; the pheasant crumpled and fell to earth, landing in the thick vegetation growing around a small stream. After spending 30 minutes looking for the damn thing, I eventually found it had nose-dived into the stream, with just the tail feathers barely visible amongst the rushes. Clearly this is the reason people have gun dogs!

Although I am not generally excited by the idea of fast food, I took my inspiration for tonight's dinner from the most unlikely of sources: KFC. My luxury item for the week (although I hadn't found a use for it until today) is a jar of mayonnaise. I plucked the pheasant, removed the breasts, and chopped them into thin strips. Carefully I heated up some cooking oil in a pan over the fire, and rolled out some dough for a flatbread, which I cooked in another pan. I rolled the chunks of pheasant in seasoned flour and shallow-fried them in the oil until they were crisp and golden. With a handful of salad, and a generous dollop of mayonnaise, I sat back on my new bench and tucked into my hunter-gatherer's equivalent of a chicken wrap. It was a terrific feed!

I have started re-reading *The Happy Isles of Oceania* by Paul Theroux. I do like its pidgin English, particularly the phrase for 'it is nothing/not much': 'samting nating'. I have also bought a copy of a book by Henry David Thoreau, *Walden: or Life in the Woods*. Apparently it is an American classic, and a few people have suggested I read it as I too am living in the woods; I wonder if anything will strike a chord?

THURSDAY 2ND JULY ☼ 28°C!

Important day! My publisher came down from London to discuss how to turn my experience into a book. When it was time to prepare lunch we went down to the river to get the trout from the freshwater fridge. I did my 'Here's one I caught earlier' routine and knocked the fish over the head to pass up to my publisher, and it immediately slipped out of her outstretched hand and dropped back into the river. It was a good thing it was already dead. The eel that was sharing the net with the trout was nowhere to be seen. Either it had wormed its way out of the net, or the trout had already had breakfast.

We had smoked trout and salad from the patch for lunch, and it was a classy dish, even if I do say so myself! The meeting adjourned at about 3.30pm, and I went to write up my notes.

It seems there is a slight eccentricity that is growing in me down here as the days go on: I find myself talking my way through what I am doing out loud. It feels like there is no one around for miles and miles. I suppose it is liberating in a way: I can do as I please and no one tells me what to do, as I am the one who knows everything that needs to be done.

People are always asking if I ever get scared down here, but I think trepidation is a better word. Over the last two months I have fine-tuned my identification of various woodland creatures and have become familiar

with all their sounds and activities. The fox is the most unpleasant with its filthy bark, and then there is the screech of the little owl, and the 'twit-too-woo' of the tawny owl. These are the sounds of my living room and I will certainly miss them when I have to leave the woods. My only real fear is of man, because he is an unpredictable creature. But with a shotgun under the bed, an air rifle, a hatchet and a machete all hanging on the wall, I try not to worry about things too much!

Now I am fully set up there is little I want for, although Clare would be nice (not sure what she would say about living here full time though). Creature comforts I can do without: a comfortable bed and a full stomach are my necessities. I have no need for electricity as nothing down here runs on power. I do feel out of touch with current affairs (especially as my wind-up radio is broken), but as they say, 'no news is good news'. Books are my entertainment down here and all my activities serve to improve my quality of life.

So far, I have been blessed by the weather gods – touch wood (and there is plenty of that around here to fondle). Had I done this during last year's washout summer, perhaps I wouldn't be feeling quite as smug. It has helped me to understand, with this way of life, why our ancestors kept deities for different things – sun, rain, harvest, water, etc. – for these were the very elements that governed their existence and meant they were able to live. At some point in history people became lazy and rolled them all into one – God.

I am beginning to get a little pissed off with the moths and other insects while reading in bed. Once I have turned off the lanterns and put on the head torch, I turn into a bloody homing beacon and spend more time fending off incoming airborne insects than actually turning a page!

None of what I am doing is new, or that different from the way people have lived for thousands of years. It isn't anything we're not capable of – the knowledge must be tucked away in the brain somewhere. With a little imagination, a great deal of reading and a bit of hard graft, you can achieve an awful lot. It is having the willingness, and perhaps stupidity, to go along with it in the first place. Granted, things may bugger up along the way, but I just put that down to the learning curve!

'To succeed in life, you need two things: ignorance and confidence.'

MARK TWAIN

I suppose in the context of 21st-Century living, this is a 'new' way of life: we have become so far detached from our past and have forgotten how to fend for ourselves. This is why I believe tramps are probably the most recent pioneers of self-sufficiency in Britain. They are *the* masters of survival because that is what they do every day (perhaps not all of them, but certainly some!). I have always wondered why they haven't moved out to the country. Maybe life for them *is* easier in the cities, but who am I to judge? I know nothing about their past hardships.

As the old saying goes, 'The best things in life are free', and I would be inclined to agree. All my meat and vegetables cost nothing – I pay for them with my time and effort. For me, a true carnivore, I have found meeting my own dietary requirements difficult. Not every hunt is successful, nor does every nightline yield fish, and the prospect of a vegetarian supper is usually a dismal one. But I do what I can and make the most of what I have. I keep telling myself that no one has to eat meat every day – regardless of incessant blood lust.

FRIDAY 3RD JULY ☼ 26°C!

I went over to the local reservoir this morning on a reconnaissance mission. When I was 12, I did a couple of sailing courses there. They were long, hot, balmy summer days, full of cans of pop, lemon sherbets and *Swallows and Amazons* throwbacks. They also included one of my favourite childhood pursuits: handlining!

On our lunch breaks, a friend and I used to grab our sandwiches, handlines and worms from our bags and sit on the launch jetty, where the biggest perch were always found. We had got permission from the Bailiff to fish there; to the men who paid to fish the reservoir, the jetty was out of bounds. We dangled the worms into the water and the greedy perch would rush out and snatch the bait up in a single mouthful. We used to catch them upwards of a pound, a good size for the species, but we always put 'em back.

With these happy days in mind I returned to my old stomping ground. Much had changed, especially the level of the reservoir, which was looking very low indeed. The perch were still there though and in greater numbers. Lake Geneva in Switzerland is full of perch, and most lakeside restaurants have *filet du perche* on the menu. I am determined to make this dish a staple.

Unfortunately it costs £10 a day to fish the reservoir, but the perch hang out at the rowing jetty, well out of sight from the boathouse, but still off-

limits to paying guests. I figured it would probably take me only ten minutes to catch my fill and £1 a minute was more than I could afford. As it was early in the day I decided to go back later to get my supper.

At 8pm I returned to the jetty. All was still, the boathouse was locked up, and there was no one to be seen, except the odd dog walker on the far side of the water. My rod was already set up and raring to go with a Mepp's 'Black Fury' spinner tied to the end of the line. I convinced myself that this was *not* poaching, it was survival. I could even dress it up as a cull on the perch population as there were so many of the brutes.

The fish were more active than ever and I connected first cast: a good-sized fish of about 1lb (500g). A few more casts followed, with fish all roughly the same size as the first. Then I was out of there; it had been less than ten minutes. A successful hunt, well executed, in record time. I went back to the wood to see to my supper, which was so fresh it was still flinching in my bag.

After scaling and filleting the fish, I made the classic dish *filet du perche*, and served it with some salad from the patch. It was so good I will definitely have to go back for more …

SATURDAY 4th JULY

This morning I had coffee and then a shower to scrub up for work – I had foraging to teach. It had been a while since I had been down there and I welcomed the prospect of a contribution to my funds. It was a fantastic group: six fathers and about twelve of their offspring.

They were in the midst of an energetic water fight when I arrived. I went and introduced myself to the fathers and asked which of them were

FILET DU PERCHE

INGREDIENTS

For the fish:

16–20 small perch fillets (or 12 big ones)

1 cup flour, well seasoned with salt and pepper (1 tsp of each)

2 tbsp unsalted butter

3 tbsp cooking oil

For the sauce:

4 tbsp salted butter

¼ cup strained lemon juice

¼ cup finely chopped parsley

Serves 2

1 **Immediately before cooking the perch, flour the fillets on both sides, shaking off the excess flour.**

2 **Using a large, non-stick frying pan, heat the butter and oil in the pan on medium heat. When the butter foam begins to subside, add the perch fillets, skin side down. Cook for two minutes, gently shaking the pan to prevent them from sticking.**

3 **Turn the fillets over and cook for a further minute on the other side. Turn one of the fillets over and check to see that it is cooked. Cook for a minute longer if needed, then transfer the fillets, skin side down, to two heated plates.**

4 **Discard the cooking oil and add the butter for the sauce to the pan. Allow the butter to heat and foam up, then add the lemon juice, swirling the pan and letting the lemon juice evaporate slightly for a few seconds. Add the parsley, give the sauce a stir, and immediately pour over the fillets on the plates.**

interested in coming on the forage. One or two seemed keen, while the others looked happy to have a couple of 'child-free' hours. 'Anyway, we've got some hookers coming, haven't we, guys?', joked one of the dads. 'Daddy, what's a hooker?', asked one of the kids who had happened to be within earshot. I had fun listening to his father explaining exactly what a hooker was – in the context of rugby!

The boys were hard to rally at first, like most youngsters, and seemed to have fairly limited concentration spans. I took them on a forage and then I showed them how to take apart a squirrel and a rabbit. They relished the gory bits and lost interest once the blood and guts were gone. They snapped up souvenirs: heads, feet, tails, ears – you name it, they took it. I set up the squirrels on a spit roast and left them with instructions on how to cook them slowly during the afternoon.

I was tipped handsomely and so I headed straight for the cider barn; I bought a three-handled ceramic cider mug and some mead, as a pat on the back for such a successful day. Chris came over for a night at the tree house, arriving with 4 pints (2.3 litres) of scrumpy and some chicken wings: 'Thought you probably hadn't had these for a while …'

How right he was. But the strange thing was, the chicken tasted different. My taste buds have become tuned to the flavours of wild meat, not the pre-packaged supermarket pap they sell as an excuse for protein. I ate them because I was hungry, but I am only too aware that things are changing …

SUNDAY 5th JULY

Chris left at about 10am after a mammoth coffee-drinking session. I felt like a bit of recreational angling but, as always, kept supper in mind. I headed to another river about 8 miles (13km) away. This river was different from the one near me: a lot more weed and a fair bit narrower. I fished a big weir pool and caught a few small perch on the spinner, but I deemed them a touch undersized and put them back.

An hour later, I decided I *did* want perch again for supper after all – of course at that point, the fish stopped biting! Two friends, George and Charlie, had asked if they could drop in for supper and, eager for company, I had agreed. I was under pressure to deliver a fine tree house meal.

While I was fishing, some cows came down to the gravel bar at the back of the weir to drink – fine, until I realised one of the cows had an enormous pair of bollocks swinging between its back legs. As if sensing my fear, the bull turned and moved towards me – shit! I was standing next to a fence with the weir pool on the other side, so I hastily hopped over the fence and dangled over the pool, hoping even the bull wouldn't be fool enough to put in a charge – he wasn't. But he did start sniffing and licking my rucksack that I had, in my haste, abandoned. After 15 minutes he buggered off. Phew!

After my confrontation with the bull, I had nothing to show for my efforts. So this time I decided to take the bull by the horns (ha-ha!) and returned to the reservoir. I followed the same drill as my last visit and caught some fine perch. Although the fish weren't quite so obliging this time, I executed my lightning strike with (almost) military precision, and melted back into the woods as if I had never been there.

Back at the tree house I set to work scaling, filleting and boning all the fish. I just can't understand why we don't eat more perch in Britain – it is a readily available source of fish that is completely ignored! The day I see a perch on the slab of a fishmonger's will be the day I willingly put on a dress, stockings and pair of high heels, and start calling myself Susan …

George and Charlie turned up eventually. Somehow they got lost on the way and ended up at the patch – muppets! Neither of them had seen my humble abode and they were both quite taken aback. We sat around the fold-out table for supper and shared a bottle of nettle beer. It was really good to have some company; usually my days hold little in the way of banter.

Monday 6th July

WIND

Some people might think that a dram of whisky with my coffee at 10am on a Monday morning is a worrying sign, but whisky is my luxury for this week and I am making the most of it. I don't think I will make a habit of it – a treat is one thing, but getting on the sauce before the sun is past the yardarm is never a good cycle to get into, particularly with my daily list of chores!

Having finished my Irish coffee, I charged over to the birch wood to get some faggots, and took the gun in case I was presented with any edible opportunities. The pigeons were flying so fast with the wind today that the chance of feather was pretty unlikely.

The woodland fauna, lovely as it is, can be bloody irritating at times.

1. The cows: they follow me everywhere, making it difficult for me to shoot. They have also eaten all my beds of wild watercress – not that I eat it that much (it has to be cooked so it is only really good for soups), but it was a nice treat now and then.

2. The pigeons: by far my favourite meat, and typically always around when I am unarmed. I need to go decoying or must develop the patience to stand behind a hedge for most of the day, hoping one or two will fly my way.

3. The mosquitoes: I didn't think they would be this bad, but they are! As soon as you step into the wood they are everywhere. And woe betide you if you venture to the throne, where they lie in wait for an ambush – you can lose half a pint of blood just by taking a minute's 'thinking time'.

4. The birds: it is good to see the swallows flitting about the fields – I love their fleeting visits – but the others have been devouring my raspberries with reckless abandon. Short of putting a net over the entire bush (impossible), there isn't anything I can do. I will have to kiss goodbye to my dreams of raspberry jam.

Clare is not too well at the moment; she came to Sussex today to see the doctor. I am going to go and see her tomorrow with a bouquet of wild flowers. Today I had to address the cracks in the clay oven. It has dried out really well, so I applied a pure clay slip (clay and water) to fill in the cracks. I think I might be able to get away with lighting a fire in there tomorrow, and maybe even bake some bread.

I made a stool this afternoon (see p. 45) and, though I say so myself, it is very good! I needed something to ease the pain of squatting by the fire every time I cook. I also did a load of washing up, aired the duvet, beat out the rugs and swept the tree house.

For supper I fancied having an eel or two from the freshwater fridge. I took the gun on the way down (you never know). Went to the patch and picked

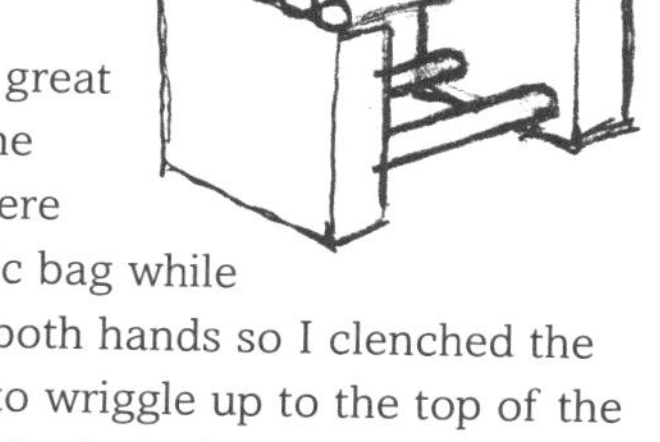

some spinach and a few courgettes. When I got to the river I noticed the biggest eel in the freshwater fridge had died. He hadn't looked great when I put him in, so perhaps he had been the victim of a pike attack. The two other eels were very feisty. I got one out and put it in a plastic bag while I fiddled about with the net. I needed to use both hands so I clenched the bag in my teeth. Somehow the eel managed to wriggle up to the top of the bag and into my mouth, at which point I spat both the bag and the eel into the river, and lost half my supper – good thing I still had one in the net.

I had to cook inside on Bertha tonight as it started to rain. I pan-fried the eel with wild garlic and lemon juice, added the courgettes and spinach, and ate straight from the pan – saves on washing up! I think I prefer perch to eel ...

Tuesday 7th July

The early morning brought heavy rain, which rattled loudly on the tin roof. Although I find this sound soothing when going to sleep, the drumming had me wide awake. All I wanted to do was go back to sleep and hope the weather would clear up. It didn't.

During the morning I was tree house bound. There was very little I could do other than keep the stove burning, make tea and read. After an hour, though, the rain did stop and I went down to the patch to address a straggler that had been on my 'To Do' list for some time: I finally planted my 'maincrop' potatoes. I am not sure if I will need them as I have barely made a dent in the 'earlies'.

Clare is still quite poorly, so after lunch I decided to go over to her folks where she is staying, to try my best to cheer her up – took her some sweet pea flowers.

When I got back to the wood the rain was chucking it down! By the time I reached the tree house I was soaked to the skin; I had to change all my clothes, stoke up Bertha, and hang my drenched garments over her to dry them out. To make matters worse, I heard a distant rumbling, which was echoed by the explosive crowing of every cock pheasant in the area.

I spent the rest of the day studying an old trapping book, simply called *Trapping: a Practical Guide,* by James A. Bateman. First published in 1979, it is a fascinating book and covers traps of every kind, legal and illegal.

Under the Pests Act of 1954, after 31 July 1959 it became illegal to use any trap in the British Isles that was not considered humane by the Ministry of Agriculture, Fisheries and Food. So the use of wire snares for catching rabbits, although probably acceptable in a genuine survival situation, is strictly off-limits. I need to develop some sort of trap that has a bit more compassion for my chosen quarry.

I found a lot of chicken wire and plastic netting fixed to the fences at my parents' house – a measure taken to prevent my mother's last cat, Gizmo, escaping. I took it all back to the wood with a view to putting it to a more practical use.

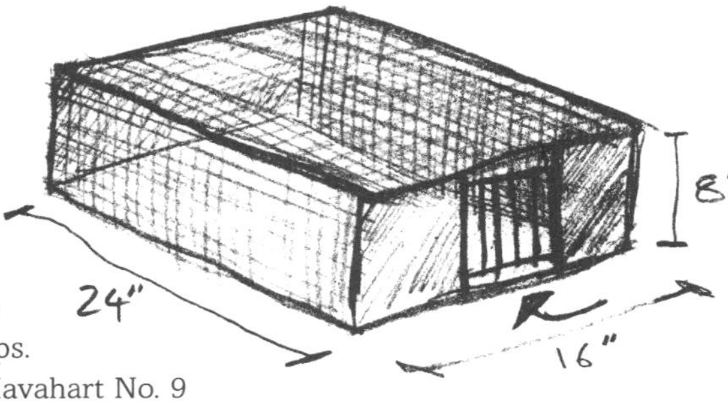

As the pigeons vanish as soon as I step out of the tree house with a gun in my hand, it is time to take them by cunning and stealth. So, tomorrow is to be devoted to building a few traps. The book suggests that the Havahart No. 9 pigeon trap is mandatory for anyone wishing to catch a woodpigeon. And it can hold up to ten birds – wishful thinking! I will also employ the use of the Hawk Island No. 2, a Cook Island chicken trap design, developed by my fellow islanders and myself during our time there. It worked so well it would be foolish not to see if it can't achieve the same results on this side of the planet. I am also keen to try the river for crayfish – there must be some in there – but my bird traps must come first.

The stormy weather continued into the evening: thunder and lightning, and raindrops so fat they would fill a shot glass. The monsoon has broken the stifling humidity at last. The tree house seems to be holding up well to the precipitation. The stove is burning, so there is no run-off onto the top (my repair is holding up), but there is a slight trickle of water running down the grooves of the bark on the oak tree, which has made my duvet a bit damp in one place. My wood store under the tree house also needs to be moved in a bit – sideways rain can be a pain. Other than that – self-contained, self-sufficient! I certainly picked the right week to get the whisky in – nothing better than a hot toddy to keep colds at bay!

WEDNESDAY 8th JULY

Rain woke me again at 6am but I went back to sleep and by 8am the sun was out. There were two things on my list today: traps and the clay oven.

The oven has been drying out for the best part of a week, and I had filled in all the cracks with slip, so it was ready for action. Ceremoniously I placed the first burning log inside – a proud moment! After adding a few more logs, I noticed smoke seeping out of cracks I had missed, mostly around the pressed motif at the base. I added more clay but, as the oven baked away, more cracks appeared. The oven itself seems to be doing its job well so I will keep adding more clay and see what happens. Perhaps a brick dome covered in clay might have been better – too late now …

I had a simple lunch of boiled potatoes, spinach and fried eel with a generous handful of wood sorrel and bittercress. Butter would have been nice. Maybe I could arrange some bartering to get my hands on some.

After an hour of studying and mulling over traps in my head I felt rather peckish again. Snack food is something I don't really have down here so I decided to address the issue: nettle pesto and flatbreads are the answer, and next week's luxury is going to be Parmesan cheese. So to prepare for pesto making I went down to the river and dug up some more wild garlic bulbs for about an hour. I got back to the tree, washed and trimmed the bulbs, and potted them up in jam jars filled with olive oil.

I then got on with trap making. In the end I opted to construct the trap that had proved so effective at trapping chickens in the Cook Islands: the Hawk Island No. 2. In the South Pacific I had spent hours stripping down bits of rope and tying together all the straight, finger-sized pieces of wood I could get my hands on, the result was a truly Crusoe-esque piece of kit. This time, I used a staple gun and it took just two hours!

I went to see Clare, who is feeling a bit better. On the way back I popped into my parents' house to post an update on my blog. Then, at about 11pm, I made my way back to the tree. I didn't even bother lighting Bertha, I was far too tired.

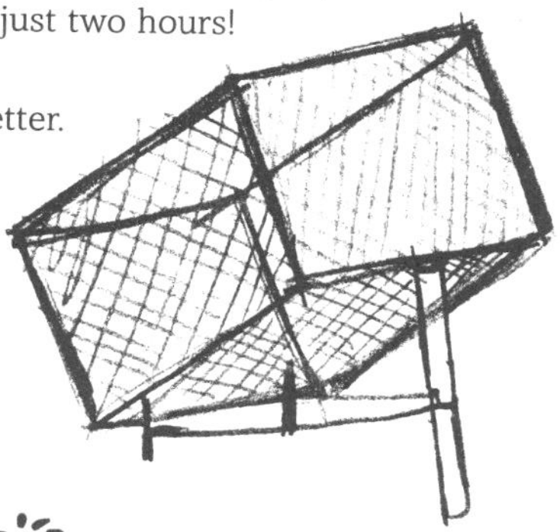

THURSDAY 9th JULY

It has become clear to me why we pay through the nose for food these days. Few people have the time to process, hunt or gather their own sustenance. Food can be cheap, and eating can be cheap, if we have the time to do it. With the modern-day work ethic, and the convenience of walking down a supermarket aisle, Britain can only get worse – who even

HOW TO MAKE A BIRD TRAP

First, put together a rectangular frame using hazel offcuts and jute twine. Then, staple the chicken wire in sections to five sides of the frame (leaving the bottom open), using a staple gun. Once the cage has been made, the mechanism of the trap needs to be assembled. This consists of two parts: two short lengths of hazel with a step cut into the end of each one so they notch together to make a 'stand'; and the trigger, which is a piece of fishing line tied to two small stakes of hazel.

To set the trap, lift one end of the cage and dig the two stakes into the ground at the other end of the cage. The fishing line is then looped around the notched 'stand' and the front end of the cage is balanced on the stand. Bait the inside of the trap with pieces of bread or rice, and scatter a few free offerings about. When the birds come in to feed, they will eat their way towards the trap and eventually, as they go for the pile of bait inside, they will hit the fishing line, which will pull apart the notched stand and the cage will fall, humanely trapping your supper.

has a lunch break these days? Is it not better to eat a civilised lunch off a plate at the table rather than gobble up a crap sandwich in five minutes at your desk?

SATURDAY 11th JULY

Perhaps a six-day trip to Scotland is not technically allowed under the rules of my hunter-gatherer existence, but I have convinced myself this is actually an information-gathering exercise on the delicate art of smoking (fish not pipes). Anyway, Scotland, with its midge-infested summers and propensity for endless downpours, barely qualifies as a holiday destination for many people.

At last I have some company for more than a couple of days: six of us (myself, Clare, Jim, Clare D, Justin and Emma) are going for a break to Emma's family home, near Oban, on the west coast of Scotland. The family business is the nearby smokery, and over the next week I have high hopes of gaining some serious education, along with a little R&R, some good food and plenty of fishing.

The 07.20 from Euston to Glasgow chuffed its way out of the city smoke towards the north, and Justin, fresh from a nightshift in the editing suite, wasted no time getting into the holiday spirit and took three bottles of beer out of his bag: the girls didn't seem interested, so us boys got stuck in. There were four and a half hours to kill, so we slept, chatted, read and slept some more.

> **'There are two seasons in Scotland: June and winter.'**
>
> BILLY CONNOLLY

Emma's dad collected us from the station and we drove the two hours up to Oban. Emma had not told us much about her home, other than that there was some fishing and a smokery. As it turned out, there was a long stretch of river (home to salmon and sea trout), four trout lakes (rainbow trout), an enormous white house, the smokery and a shop! She's a modest young lady …

As soon as we reached the house, the sun came out – despite a forecast of heavy rain for the next seven days. So the shorts went on and we mucked about with the Frisbee and cricket bat. I was very eager to wield a fishing rod, so we all headed to the river, and I had a dabble. I landed a few breakfast-sized brown trout – but nothing to write home about. It had been a long time since I had flicked a fly across the dark, peat-rich rivers of Scotland. The sky was a brilliant blue as I waded through the cool water and watched everyone stretched out on the banks basking in the sunshine.

Living in the tree house – a solitary existence – has made me realise just how much I have missed being with people. Obviously I have the occasional visitor, but most of the time there is just me. I have spent the last two months living in my own little bubble: a house in a tree, a vegetable patch, a river, fields, woods and meadows – that is my whole world. Now I have suddenly been transported to an entirely different landscape and I can't help but compare the two.

While I was wandering around in search of better places to drop my line, I began to get increasingly jealous of just how much is on offer to the wandering hunter-gatherer in the wilds of Scotland. Sorrel carpets the fields – it is impossible *not* to tread on it. At home I have to walk across a couple of fields to find a patch of sorrel. The mushrooms are already here: fairy ring champignons and huge field mushrooms. And that doesn't include the Jew's ear fungi that cover the bare trunks of elder. There are even crowberries and bilberries. Scotland is a wild food paradise!

After our walk we went back to the house and sat in the kitchen having tea and cakes. This week my 'woodland diet' is on hold. I have noticed my weight has dropped: I am now hovering at about 10st (63.5kg), as opposed to the 11st (69.8kg) I was when I started living in the woods. Although I am sorely tempted to spend all my time fishing, it is socialising that I miss more than anything back at home, so I must make the most of it.

That evening we went to sit by one of the lochs, drank 'Highlander' ale, and I showed Jim and Justin how to cast a fly. We sat between the pines and big hills bathed in evening sunlight. This was the first time in a while I had really been able to relax: there was no wood to chop, no fire to maintain and no supper to catch. Having said that, we did catch two rainbow trout (about 2lb/900g each) and took them home for supper.

We needn't have bothered – yesterday there was a photo shoot for the smokery's Christmas catalogue, and there was a veritable feast of smoked products that needed to be eaten up: salmon, duck, paté, mussels, trout and eel. It was time to fatten up – big time!

Sunday 12th July

I woke at 6am to get stuck into the available fishing. It is such a treat to be able to roll out of bed, walk out of the front door, and be fishing on a loch in five minutes flat. I caught two rainbow trout and then went to try out the river. I landed a few more brown trout, but no sea trout, and certainly no salmon. I have decided that to make the most of the company and the fishing, I need to get up and out early with my rod so it doesn't interfere with the day's activities – oh, yes, Jim has devised an itinerary.

When I got back at 10am, showers and breakfast were well under way. There was a magnificent spread of real coffee, black pudding, eggs, bacon, sausages – amazing! I wasted no time tucking in before going for a shower (I had forgotten that the water in Scotland has a rusty brown 'peaty' tinge to it). After breakfast, the boys and I went to fish a small pond near the smokery shop, while the ladies went for some retail therapy – in Oban!

Common Sorrel (Rumex acetosa)

DESCRIPTION **Common in many types of grassy habitats, sorrel varies in size from 4in (10cm) to 2ft (61cm). The smooth stem is upright with arrow-shaped leaves around the base and lower stem. The stalks carry spikes of reddish-green flowers.**

USES **Sorrel is rich in vitamin C, which comes as no surprise considering the tangy citrus flavour of the leaves. This is due to the oxalic acid in the plant (also found in wood sorrel); oxalic acid is not good for you in large quantities, so use sorrel sparingly. It is best served raw, as cooking sorrel reduces it to a green-brown sludge – perfectly palatable but rather unpleasant to look at. It makes a brilliant addition to meat or fish and can be used in salads and dressings or simply as a wayside nibble on a hot day.**

Emma's father gave Justin and Jim a run through fly-fishing 101. He gave them an intro and demonstration, and they began to thrash the water enthusiastically. I moved away to the far end of the pond – the boys' activities scared the fish my way and I landed a couple. After Justin had narrowly avoided a hook in the eye he demanded to know how I made it look so easy. The answer was probably my big, orange, glittery fly – a lure pattern on the end of my line that I was stripping back in a series of speedy jerks; not the most sporting of methods, but fiendishly effective all the same! The foolish stocked rainbow trout could hardly resist …

Emma's dad disappeared and returned 20 minutes later clutching a few bottles of ale for us thirsty fishermen. We fished on: Jim picked it up rather well; Justin may need a bit more work. I hooked one and handed the rod to Justin to bring in, to give him a bit of encouragement.

After an enormous lunch of smoked ham, and buckets of salad and potatoes, we had a brief snooze. I borrowed some waders in the afternoon and took to the river in search of some real sport. I went to a spot under a footbridge where I had been told there would be sea trout. Sure enough, there were and I hooked one but, during the ensuing battle, the line snapped and the fish was gone. Rubbish.

Before supper I took Emma's mum for a quick forage; she loved the sorrel and grabbed a few handfuls to stuff the trout we had caught yesterday. We sat around the massive dining room table in the equally massive dining room and ate lots of food, quaffed buckets of wine and talked about all sorts of things. The trout was followed by sticky toffee pudding, coffee and whisky sours. I do like Scotland.

MONDAY 13th JULY

I had another early start on the river – but with no more luck than before. After toast and coffee we went on a walk to a loch where the water becomes salty. Everyone wanted a lazy day, but I got restless and went off fishing for the afternoon.

We had another big supper: Emma's mum treated us Sassenachs to a traditional meal of haggis and clapshot (a mashed heap of turnips, potatoes, chopped onion and chives with a pinch of nutmeg). I did a starter of grilled mackerel on a bed of roasted tomatoes with a garlic/lemon/thyme dressing, while Clare made an amazing cheesecake with raspberry coulis. Needless to say, I was stuffed once again!

TUESDAY 14th JULY

We woke up to a typical grey Scottish morning so we went on a trip to Inverary prison, which was about as much fun as chewing a wasp sandwich. Loch Fyne was more like it: oysters, Tabasco and lemon juice – need I say more? The real reason for this visit was to find out more about the smokery. As soon as I got near it, the heady aroma of smouldering logs transported me straight back to the tree house. Emma's dad is the Hugh Hefner of the smoking trade – the man is clearly a master of his art – while Emma's mum is the culinary genius behind what to do with the product, as I later saw in her brilliant smokery cookbook.

Emma's dad explained how much time and experimentation goes into each new product. The majority of his cold-smoked items spend around 72 hours in the chamber. Hot-smoked products also benefit from a night of cold smoking before they are finished. There is a whole lot more to it than that: brining, temperature and spice mixes also play a part – don't get me started! It was immediately clear that this was a slick operation that paid serious attention to detail, tradition and, above all, taste.

Emma's dad took Justin and myself down to the smokery to show us how everything worked. At around 10pm we entered the smokery, donned a lab coat, hair net and a shiny pair of white wellies, and then had a good scrub down. After walking through the processing kitchen we entered the heart of the smoking operation. The smoke gave the corridor of chambers an unnatural haze, and despite the amount of fish I knew to be behind each numbered door, there was barely a whiff of fish in the air.

Justin and I tried not to get in the way as Emma's dad checked the temperature of each chamber and went through the health and safety steps associated with the traceability of each batch. Finally he opened up a chamber to remove some salmon steaks due to be 'roast smoked' the following morning. Not even my local fishmonger could have prepared me for the sight of all those glorious fat, pink fillets of salmon fresh out of the smoker – it made my mouth water. Right on cue, Emma's dad broke off a chunk of salmon flesh and we sampled some of the freshest smoked salmon I have ever had the pleasure of tasting.

As we left to go and check on the smouldering urns out at the front, Emma's dad showed us the walk-in fridge. Most of the products were destined for upmarket department stores, but there were batches ready to be sent to some of the best restaurants in London too. Also in the fridge was a crate holding a batch of enormous eels – they made the ones I have been catching look pathetic!

Outside we had a look at the urns that held the wood for smoking. I always thought that only sawdust was used for smoking, but here they use logs, which are placed on top of an urn of gently smouldering sawdust. Emma's dad explained that they use beech and oak as their primary fuel source, and that he had become quite a hero amongst local sawmills, as his wood comes from the tree branches they do not usually have a market for.

As we left Emma's dad to finish his final checks he said, 'Better have a good scrub down, boys, or you won't be getting any tonight!' Luckily Clare has become fairly accustomed to the smell of wood smoke …

WEDNESDAY 15th JULY

At last, some real Scottish weather. This morning Emma, who had a meeting to attend, sent us down to the sea loch to collect some fresh mussels off the rocks. She had told us that they always get buckets of

them. There was absolutely nothing to be found but endless drizzle. The 'mussel bandits' must have already paid a visit – evidently the Loch Ness monster isn't the only myth in Scotland.

In the evening we decided to hit the local pub in search of good times and a few university-style drinking games. The place was so quiet there was tumbleweed rolling down the streets, but that didn't stop play …

Monday 20th July

To the trees! After a refreshing break, the thrill of regular company and easy living, I was really eager to get back down to the tree house. Scotland was more than just a break. I feel so refreshed, as if I am entering into the experience from the beginning, only this time I know what to expect.

> **'He is happiest, be he king or peasant, who finds peace in his home.'**
>
> JOHANN WOLFGANG VON GOETHE

I was also slightly nervous about my return. My landlady has been looking after my vegetables and I had phoned in the middle of last week to check everything was okay. She said there had been plenty of rain, so she hadn't had to do much watering. She also added that the patch was in dire need of a little TLC, otherwise known as weeding. Great – I can hardly wait!

When I got back the first thing I did was to fill up my containers with water, and then I headed straight to the tree house. During my walk down, waddling along, loaded up like a Himalayan yak, I had a good look around and I was surprised at how different everything seemed – long, stringy and overgrown. I've only been away a week!

There were no recent footprints on the paths, apart from a few deer prints. All mine had been washed away so at least I knew there had been no intruders. Everything was just as I had left it – with a few new cobwebs. It is amazing how quickly nature takes over when left to its own devices. Despite all the rain everything inside looked perfectly dry.

After unloading and getting a fire going to boil the kettle, I went to check out my 'overgrown' patch. It was in an absolute state! In the space of a week, weeds had engulfed my lettuces and red onions, and were poking through the rows of spinach. It needs some real attention, but I decided to

leave it until tomorrow. I know procrastination is never a good thing, but on this occasion I embraced it. There were a couple of massive courgettes – what the hell am I going to do with those? The rocket looked like it was well past its sell-by date and was running to seed. I will have to incorporate it into my pesto making. But there was some good news: I am now the proud owner of a small glut of runner beans!

As I was gleaning a few morsels from the patch, I saw some movement in the maize field, which was just hitting the 4ft (1.2m) mark. It was two of my landlords' children. In actual fact, there were three – the youngest one was following his older brothers through the field, but his head wasn't visible above the maize plants. I assumed they were on their way to check out the tree house, and sure enough, when I returned the boys were sitting on the bench in front of a steaming kettle and a smouldering fire.

We chatted for a bit and I gave them a tour. One of the boys pointed at the neatly stacked bottles of nettle beer. 'What's that stuff?' I poured each of them a small glass to taste and gave them a warning about the alcohol content – their glasses were empty in less than a minute. I refused them a top-up and told them not to tell their mother! The boys left in good spirits, no doubt happy in the knowledge that the tree house would be theirs in three months' time.

I don't really need a fridge – my protein is usually consumed in a matter of hours, and my wild food and vegetables are picked as and when they are required. This 'hand to mouth' way of life ensures the highest quality and freshness of everything I eat, and I have no desire to change that.

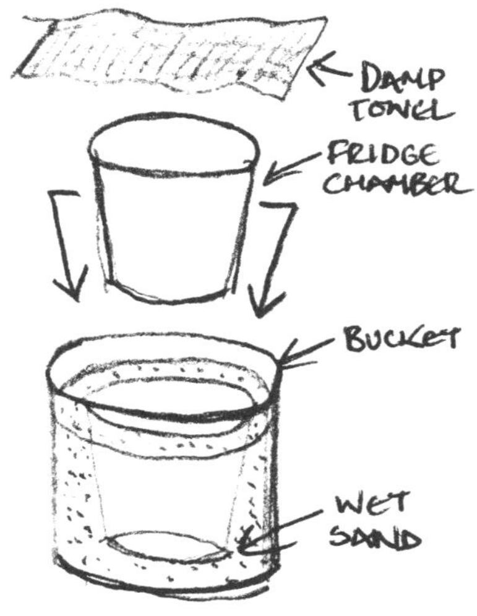

But I am curious about refrigeration without the use of power. I had made a few notes from an online article about a pot-inside-a-pot fridge, pioneered by a Nigerian man called Mohammed Bah Abba. As its name suggests, the fridge simply comprises a smaller pot placed inside a larger one, with a layer of compacted wet sand in between the two. Perishables are put into the smaller pot and a damp towel is placed over the top. As the moisture in the wet sand evaporates, it draws out any heat with it, keeping everything inside cool. Ingenious.

The fridge didn't take very long to put together using a couple of buckets. I put my vegetables inside and checked them for 'coolness' an hour later. They were slightly cool, but not much different from how they had been when they were sitting out in the open. I think the problem is that Nigeria has a slightly different climate from Sussex, and the rates of evaporation are probably a tad more intense in sub-Saharan Africa. Unless we have another heat wave I don't think the fridge will realise its potential.

After fridge maintenance it was time to bring out the gun and secure some protein for supper. I took the air rifle and donned my flat cap for luck. No sooner had I climbed over the gate than I saw a rabbit a good 160ft (48m) away. I crept and crawled until he was only 65ft (20m) away, stopping every time he pricked up his ears in alarm.

I got into position and went to take aim. The rabbit, thinking all was normal, had gone back to munching grass, and was effectively giving me the moon. With no clear target, I sucked on my hand, imitating the strange squeaking sound of a rabbit in distress. No sooner had the rabbit heard this familiar alarm than his ears pricked up once again, and in true sniper style (flat cap on backwards so I could see through the scope) I squeezed the trigger. A minute later I was walking home with a nice fat rabbit for supper.

At about 8pm, as I was about to gut the rabbit and pin out the pelt to add to my hearth rug, I figured out how I could use my marrow: I would de-bone the rabbit and bake it with potatoes, runner beans and stock inside the hollowed-out marrow! I went to the river to pick some large burdock leaves – the tree house equivalent of tin foil – to wrap the marrow in.

I browned the rabbit in a pan, par-boiled a few potatoes, chopped the runner beans and hollowed out the marrow. I alternated layers of meat and vegetables and topped up the marrow with vegetable stock. I then secured the lid of the marrow with small, whittled hazel stakes, wrapped the whole thing in burdock leaves, and then carefully placed it in the fire and covered it with hot embers.

BURDOCK (ARCTICUM MINUS)

DESCRIPTION

Widespread and common in woodland and on roadsides, burdock is a stiff, bushy plant reaching 3ft (91cm). Leaves are large and roughly heart-shaped. When in bud the egg-shaped purple flower heads look like thistles; these form spiky burs when the plant is fruiting. The stem is reddish-green.

USES **Burdock is one of the major players in the wild larder when it comes to sources of carbohydrate. The root of the plant is the closest wild equivalent to the potato. Harvest the root in autumn when the plant has stored up all its goodness for the coming winter. Unfortunately burdock's preference for hard, stony ground makes it difficult to dig up, but persevere and you will be rewarded. The root can be used in the kitchen in much the same way as the potato. The root can also be turned into a drink and represents one half of that foul drink of bygone days: dandelion and burdock – urgh!**

The leaves of the plant are some of the largest that grow in Britain and make a great wild substitute for kitchen towel. I use them for handling slimy eels, wrapping up food to go in the fire, and covering my underground oven, as well as for protecting perishables from flies.

The burs, or flower heads, are where the original concept of Velcro came from – as you will know if you have ever found them stuck to your clothes. This method is one of the most ingenious ways used by plants to distribute their seeds.

Forty-five minutes later, I unwrapped the burdock leaves and lifted the top off the steaming marrow – it smelt wonderful. I dished up a generous helping; even the cooking vessel was edible! The dish was perhaps too much for one person, but it will definitely be going in the recipe book for future use.

After supper I had to saw and chop a mountain of wood. Before I went away I had made sure there was wood for my first night back, but you can never have enough of the stuff.

It was great to spend a week with Clare and other good company after the solitude of woodland life. Sitting here, surrounded by my lamps with the kamikaze moths getting up to their usual tricks, I feel completely at home. I have everything I could possibly want, apart from my better half. Still, it is good to be back in the canopy. The silence is golden, the throne needs another new hole, and I am happy curling up in my nest amongst the branches.

Tuesday 21st July

One thing that always strikes me as odd upon waking is how much cooler it is inside the tree house compared to outside. Every morning, when I step out to get a brew on, I have generally been delighted by the temperature – but not the rain!

Down here, though, rain doesn't always stop play – there are two issues I need to address every day: food and fuel. Where food is concerned, I often over-pick my vegetables and so generally there are enough to last a couple of days, but meat is the deciding factor.

I cherish the time I spend reading in bed in the mornings and last thing at night. I think it is important not to establish too much of a routine down here, beyond providing my necessities. Establishing a routine is the start of a vicious circle that can make our existence mundane – the curse of modern-day life.

Today I was meant to weed and fix up the patch, but I decided I wasn't going to get cold and wet if I didn't have to – I didn't want to risk catching a cold. Instead, I busied myself under the shelter of the tree house doing all the small jobs that have been niggling away at me for the past month.

WEDNESDAY 22ND JULY

If you live in a tree, the last thing you want to hear when you wake up is the aggressive whining of multiple chainsaws nearby. It was like waking up in the middle of a nightmare. Fortunately it was just some fellas on the far side of the wood, clearing the way for some power lines – phew!

After they had left I went over to assess the damage and saw something that makes my blood boil: the workmen had clearly enjoyed a pleasant mid-morning snack and had left all their litter behind. Why do people do this? On my turf as well – I thought tree surgeons would have bloody well known better.

After that I heated up some water on the fire for a shower, and then sat and had a coffee while procrastinating over the long-overdue weeding of the patch. The sad thing is I struggled to try to think of more important jobs that might need addressing!

Before heading to the patch, I went to set up my Hawk Island No. 2 trap out in the field, in the hope of a lucky lunch. I crept to the edge of the wood. It was a very windy day so I hoped the pigeons wouldn't be as easily spooked as usual. A group of them were greedily pecking at clover, offering me an easy target. I put the trap down, swiftly ducked away, and returned a minute later with the shotgun locked and loaded.

I often find, when stalking anything with a shotgun, I get the shakes just before I raise the gun. I blame it on the loud bang I know is about to come. I shot one of the nearest pigeons, and the others scarpered quicker than a quick thing that moves quickly. I grabbed the trap, climbed over the fence, and picked up the pigeon. I plucked the breast feathers and then, using my knife, removed the plump breasts for lunch. I set up the trap, baited it, and then perched the remainder of the dead pigeon in a very life-like pose to work as a decoy. And then I crossed my fingers …

After returning from the patch with some salad for lunch, I skewered the pigeon breasts, cooked them over the fire and tucked into a tasty pigeon salad. After lunch I swept and cleaned inside the tree house. In the midst of my task, I heard the sound of voices in the distance, and walked out onto the balcony to get a better look.

Once again it was three of my landlords' sons. We had a cup of tea and a chat, and then the boys and I walked down to the maize field. I bade them farewell and then went to knuckle down (finally) to the thrills of weeding.

During this dull task I received a pleasant distraction: a phone call from a journalist at a London newspaper, who had been given my number by Tom, the Hungry Cyclist. She wants to write an article for next week about the tree house and my decision to quit the rat race. As I weeded away, she asked me loads of questions, which I answered as best I could.

After an hour-long interrogation over the phone I had finished the weeding. It hadn't been so bad after all, and I felt all the better for doing it. I walked back up to the wood and went to check the trap for pigeons. By this time the field was full of cows, which had unceremoniously kicked over and trampled the trap, and the decoy was nowhere to be seen. Of course – Frank! The cheeky bastard must have taken it – I don't think cows are all that keen on raw pigeon.

THURSDAY 23RD JULY

I woke up at about 8.30am with the strange feeling there was something I was supposed to be doing today, but couldn't quite put my finger on it. Half an hour later, I dug out my calendar up in the tree house, to see today's date marked with 'Foraging 10am' in green biro. Shit! There was no time for a shower. I grabbed all the gear I usually needed, locked up, and climbed down the ladder. I then wasted more valuable time having to go back up again three or four times for stuff I had forgotten.

I got there 20 minutes late, having had to stop at the butchers and pick up the day's rabbit order. I apologised for my tardiness and shifted the blame onto 'tractors' and 'small country lanes'. Today's group consisted mainly of WAG-types with wrap-around sunglasses and designer clothes – not what you would usually wear on a camping trip. The kids were energetic and poorly disciplined, but they did seem interested in foraging, especially when I showed them rosehip and explained that the seeds could be used as rudimentary itching powder.

Unfortunately I didn't notice that two brothers, the most mischievous of the bunch, had decided to try it out on each other. Five minutes later, both were close to tears. They had taken their shirts off and were scratching away at enormous red rashes that had appeared on their backs and chests. A very annoyed mother then stood in front of me with her arms folded in a 'look what you've done to my kids' sort of way. I explained that I hadn't encouraged them to do it and she admitted they did sometimes have a reaction like this to grass. I apologised profusely and did my best to resolve the situation. But, to be completely honest, it was their own bloody fault!

Back at the camp we made a few hedgerow delicacies and then I started the kids' favourite bit: processing the rabbits. As usual, I dished out bits of rabbit anatomy; then one of the brothers took the head and started kicking it about and laughing. I took him to one side and suggested that perhaps he should be more respectful to the dead animal that would be providing him with a meal later on. He laughed in my face and told me not to be so stupid.

So I decided on a different approach. 'Fine, but you have no one to blame but yourself when the evil king of dead rabbits pays you a visit in the middle of the night ...' 'What evil rabbit king?', he asked, wild eyed, and starting to get a bit concerned. His parents thought this was hilarious and carried on with the joke to wind him up even more. Job done.

After foraging I went down to the Seven Sisters, the big white cliffs that are one of the hallmarks of the British coastal landscape. I had brought my spinning rod on the off-chance that I might try for bass, but the wind was onshore, and I could barely cast more than a few feet into the sea.

However, the real reason for my visit was to stock up on some coastal wild greens. The tide was right in and the shingle beach was strewn with a variety of different seaweeds. I gathered dulse, bladderwrack and carragheen. Almost all of Britain's native seaweed is edible and rather good. I filled a carrier bag – it was surprisingly heavy! I also managed to get caught unawares by a freak wave and got very wet feet, but it was worth it.

I headed over to the estuary to gather sea purslane, samphire and sea beet. I sat with my legs dangling over the wooden piles as the tidal river ripped out to sea at speed and enjoyed the peaceful surroundings. It was short-lived: some tourist kept shouting to her mates and, judging by the looks on the faces of the other people around, I wasn't the only one to frown, scowl and mutter '*Honestly ...*' in hushed tones.

I got back to the wood at 5.30pm and pinned out the two rabbit pelts left over from foraging. I was really looking forward to supper, which was odd, because there was no meat involved.

Samphire is one of Britain's tastiest wild plants; it is so good it is regularly served alongside fish at most smart restaurants. I boiled some water in the kettle, filled the billycan, and chucked in a handful of washed samphire to boil for about eight minutes.

I have allowed myself two luxury items this week as I didn't have one last week: butter and Parmesan. I melted a generous knob of butter in a pan over the fire and ladled out the cooked samphire onto a plate. I coated the lush green stalks of samphire in butter and gave them a good twist of pepper. They were delicious; so much so, that I had another three helpings.

I lit the stove upstairs and stuck my shoes, stuffed with newspaper, underneath to dry overnight. I crawled into bed and began reading *Treasure Island* – what is it with tree houses, desert islands and pirates? Then I drifted off into a deep, blissful snooze for a good ten hours – probably more sleep than the disrespectful youth from foraging got, ha-ha!

COASTAL EDIBLE PLANTS

MARSH SAMPHIRE (SALICORNIA EUROPAEA)

DESCRIPTION **A succulent annual found on salt marshes, marsh samphire (also known as glasswort) measures up to 1ft (30cm). Stems are yellow-green, plump and fleshy. Flowers are tiny, white to reddish, and grow out of junctions in the stems from August to September. Its alternative common name, glasswort, refers to its previous use in the glass industry due to its high levels of soda.**

USES **Definitely one of the best wild greens, samphire is very popular and can often be found on restaurant menus to be served alongside fish. When harvesting the plant, take a pair of scissors and cut off the top three-quarters, leaving the root in place so the plant can continue to grow.**

As a vegetable, it is best steamed or boiled in water for three minutes. Drizzle with melted butter, a dash of cider vinegar, and a few twists of pepper, and dig in. It is best eaten with your fingers: samphire tends to have a woody stalk, which makes eating it all the more pleasurable – you just strip off the green flesh with your teeth.

It also pickles extremely well; the tops of the plant work best as they don't have much stalk. Chop them into pieces 1in (2.5cm) long, wash them thoroughly, put them in a jar and top up with pickling vinegar.

SEA BEET (BETA VULGARIS SUBSP. MARITIMA)

DESCRIPTION **A common perennial that bears a resemblance to its close relative spinach, but with larger, tougher, shinier leaves. It has insignificant clusters of green flowers that are borne on tall spikes from May to August.**

USES You would be hard pressed not to pick out the shiny green leaves of sea beet on a coastal walk. This plant is the great-great-grandfather of all our modern cultivated varieties of beets (beetroot, spinach, etc.), and has been widely consumed for hundreds, if not thousands, of years.

It should be treated just like spinach in the kitchen, but bear in mind it stands up to cooking better than its cousin. It is at its best in spring but can be used right up until December.

SEA PURSLANE (ATRIPLEX PORTULACOIDES)

DESCRIPTION This species grows in low-spreading mats at the edges of salt marshes and along the high-tide mark around the coast, especially in southern England and western Scotland. It has grey stems and paddle-shaped, succulent, silvery green leaves. The flower buds are pink and spikes of insignificant yellow flowers appear from July to October. It can be gathered year-round.

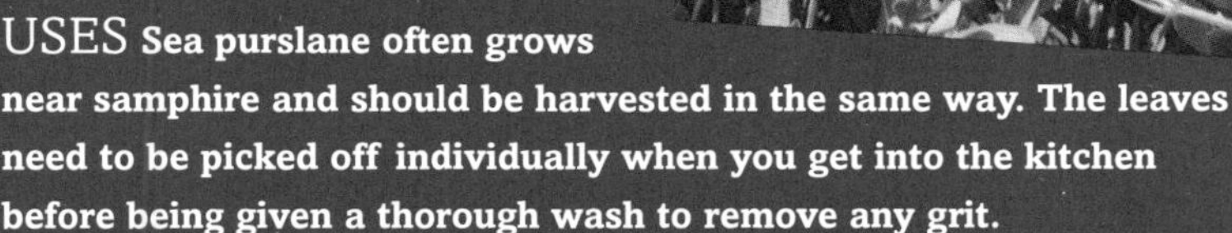

USES Sea purslane often grows near samphire and should be harvested in the same way. The leaves need to be picked off individually when you get into the kitchen before being given a thorough wash to remove any grit.

As a vegetable they are incredibly versatile. I favour mine pickled (the same method as samphire), but they are just as good boiled or steamed as a green vegetable. One of my favourite ways to cook sea purslane is to blanch the leaves for one minute, before frying them in butter and garlic, and serving on chunks of bread with a squeeze of lemon.

AMERICAN SIGNAL CRAYFISH (PACIFASTACUS LENIUSCULUS)

DESCRIPTION

Introduced into the UK in 1970 for the restaurant trade, the signal crayfish has taken over the territories of the native species, the white-clawed crayfish. Crayfish have five pairs of walking legs, the front pair having large pincers for catching prey. Signal crayfish are 6in (15cm) long and have bright red colouring on the undersides of their claws.

FRIDAY 24th JULY

Few things make me happier than waking up to the gentle pitter-patter of rain on my tin roof. A yawn, a stretch and a quick glance out of the window to confirm it, and I roll over for a few more hours of shuteye (it is usually light by 5.30am). If it's really rubbish (like today) I light the stove, get a brew on, read, and eat bread and quarters of orange.

As the morning wore on the weather improved a bit, so I set about processing the goods I had gathered from the coast. I cleaned and picked over the samphire, cut it into matchstick-sized lengths with some scissors, and placed it in clean jam jars. The jars were then filled with standard pickling vinegar and sealed. I've got about ten jars of the stuff. My latest tree house snack food has arrived! I did the same with sea purslane – I'm looking forward to having a nibble when they're ready. I hung up all the seaweed under the tree house to air dry so I can store it for use in soups and stews, and then spent the afternoon building a crayfish trap, even though I'm not sure there are any in the river. I set four nightlines, and when I checked them at 11.30pm, there were three eels – big ones too. At least now there is something in the fridge!

HOW TO MAKE A CRAYFISH TRAP

1 Why pay money for something you can make easily yourself? To make this trap you need some stiff plastic netting, fine wire, string and a pair of pliers or snips. Cut a piece of the netting 2½ft x 1½ft (76cm x 46cm) and tie it together with the wire to make a tube. Next, you need two cones with holes in the bottom to stick in either end of the tube; this involves a bit of nip and tuck with a piece of the netting.

Once you have the desired shape and size, with a hole big enough for a ravenous crayfish to slip through, tie it together with the wire. Fit each cone into the ends of the tube and tie on with more wire. The only thing left to do is to cut a flap in the underside of the tube for removing the crayfish; this you can tie shut with string.

2 To set the trap, put a couple of stones inside to weigh the whole thing down, tie a piece of smelly fish to the flap, and tie the flap shut with string. Tie a long piece of cord to the trap and drop it into the river near a likely crayfish hole: a spot with overhanging roots or slow-moving water is best. The trap should be checked every few hours or left overnight to perform best. It should work, provided your river has crayfish in it!

SATURDAY 25th JULY

I woke at around 10am to fantastic shorts weather. Today was about getting some more homebrew going. My recent efforts have been a disaster. Wild food guides include all the usual country wines and ales, but I really want to move away from the 'standard' and experiment a little. The nettles are not at their best anymore, so are off-limits until the fields or hedgerows are cut and a second crop materialises. The recipe for nettle beer is a good one so I want to use it but substitute the nettles with something else.

I thought about other green plants that I could use. Mint? No, it would probably taste like fizzy mouthwash. Horseradish leaves? No, probably a bit too hot and spicy. Yarrow? A possibility, as it has soothing properties and is good for colds. Finally I had it: meadowsweet!

I have already made meadowsweet cordial and I was pleased with the results. Meadowsweet flowers are the alternative once the elderflowers have vanished. I also use the leaves regularly as an infusion or herbal tea because of its medicinal qualities. It was these qualities that I thought might just make this the beer that brewers, and anyone who enjoys beer, have been searching for …

Meadowsweet is no stranger to alcohol. The plant has been used to flavour or sweeten mead (an alcoholic drink made from honey) for hundreds of years, and was given the name 'mead sweet'. Whether by default, or just because it often grows in grassy habitats, it has been re-christened 'meadowsweet'. Other than the fragrant, sweet-smelling flowers, which are used for cordial, the plant's medicinal value (as well as the flavouring) was the reason I wanted to coax it away from its former employer, mead, and offer it a position in the beer-making industry.

The plant contains high levels of salicylic acid, from which aspirin is synthesised, and the compound was first isolated from meadowsweet. This is why, when I have a mild headache, I make myself a mug of meadowsweet tea. My grand plan was to create a tasty beer that wouldn't give me a hangover. The chemistry behind it stands to reason – but there was only one way to find out.

I gathered the leaves and flowers from down by the river, and then set about making the beer using the same method as for nettle beer, adding the flower heads at the same time as the leaves. I will see what happens in two weeks' time – it should be an amusing test!

For lunch I took a bowl, some basic vinaigrette, and a knife and fork down to the patch. After lunch I had a quick fish to catch some bait for my crayfish trap. A small chub promptly became crayfish dinner – I wonder if I will get anything?

Meadowsweet Beer

100 sets of meadowsweet leaves

12 flower heads in full bloom

2½ gallons (12 litres) water

2lb 12oz (1.25kg) white granulated sugar

2oz (50g) cream of tartar

½oz (15g) brewer's or beer yeast

Brew in the same way as nettle beer (see p. 79).

Makes 2½ gallons (12 litres)

I made a good find in one of the fields this afternoon: a perfect white circle of a mushroom was sitting on a tuft of grass. Sure enough, it was a field mushroom – I hope some more pop up soon!

Monday 27th July

Awoke to the drumming of rain once again; the noise has become my equivalent of a 'snooze' button. I seem to remember the Met Office was predicting an Indian summer back in June. It was great when I was going about my daily chores in balmy 28°C heat: I was more smug than the Earl of Smug Manor in the village of Smugness, Smugshire SM18 UG5! I can't begin to imagine how people must have suffered in London in that heat.

This week, as I am still waiting for some wild fruit to appear, I have treated myself to some jam: traffic jam to be precise (a mixture of strawberry, marmalade and gooseberry). So this morning I lit Bertha, made up a couple of flatbreads stuffed with butter and jam, and ate them with endless cups of tea (coffee just doesn't feel right in the rain).

By 11am the rain had slowed and I put on my wet-weather gear to do a little exploring. No sooner had I walked a fair distance from the tree house than the heavens opened and the rain came down again. As there has been so much rain lately mushrooms have begun to spring up all over the place. So I decided to walk further afield, to some woods with outcrops of beech, oak and pine, to see if I could find something tasty for supper.

After a good four hours of stomping I returned home, very wet and completely mushroomless. What I had found I couldn't identify, save for a stinkhorn, which smelt worse than a kipper's armpit. I have found myself almost wishing that the seasons would move on. Autumn, with all its chestnuts, berries and fungi will have me spoilt. But I will also have to wave goodbye to the warmth, the shorts and the bare feet.

I cleaned the salt off one of the rabbit pelts. I do need more to get a good-sized carpet. Perhaps I should go on a killing spree, and smoke or pickle the meat, so I can get a rug in time for autumn?

I still haven't caught any crayfish. I would have thought that the American signal crayfish would be lurking in the river somewhere, and I have moved the trap to a few different spots, but all to no avail. I have read that banana can be useful for attracting male crayfish as it gives off the same scent as the female. It is a shame that bananas don't grow on trees, well, not around here anyway …

Thankfully I have always got the patch to rely on. At the moment I've got more runner beans than I can shake a stick at and plenty of potatoes too. I think I might try pickling some of the runner beans as my pickled samphire is going down a treat! I dug up a dozen potatoes for dinner tonight: I planned to make some gnocchi.

If I was going to have gnocchi, then I had to have pesto to go with it. The Parmesan has been sitting untouched in a box for almost a week. This stinger pesto wasn't as wild as the stuff I usually make when I take people foraging: to bulk it out I used the remains of the rocket from the patch – it would be pointless to let it go to waste.

The principal ingredient of gnocchi is potato, that much I knew. For guidance, I looked to my copy of the Larousse *Gastronomique*, which I have on my bookshelf in the tree house for inspiration. The recipes for gnocchi included eggs, nutmeg and cheese, none of which I had. I'd used up all the Parmesan making pesto. All I had was potatoes and flour.

My method was first to peel the potatoes, then boil them for about ten minutes, and drain. I mashed and seasoned them well and added flour until I had some dough with a good consistency. I made them into small parcels, which I boiled for a few minutes, and then I served them with a good splattering of pesto. It certainly made a nice change to my usual vegetarian specials …

Today I treated myself to a new wind-up radio with the money I made from foraging last week. The Ashes are in full swing. I am not a huge fan

Nettle Pesto

I have never been partial to pesto with the consistency of baby food – I like to have texture and therefore I go for a chunky, hand-chopped version. A lot of the kitchens I have worked in always blend it, which in my eyes is a cardinal sin, but they just don't have the time to do it by hand.

Ingredients

50 nettle tops

6–8 bulbs of wild garlic (finely chopped)

A handful of grated Parmesan

½ cup olive oil (add more if needed)

Juice of one lemon

Salt and pepper

1 Drop the nettles in boiling water for five minutes. Remove from the heat and drain off the water (you can use this as nettle tea if you wish – I hate the stuff – it smells of dog pee!).

2 Leave the nettles in a sieve to drain and cool. Once they are cool enough to touch, grab a handful and squeeze them so you remove all moisture.

3 Make the dried nettles into a ball, chop them finely and place in a bowl. You can also add a handful of hairy bittercress. Add all the other ingredients and mix well. If you like your pesto oily, which I do, add more oil. Add salt and pepper to taste: I find it pays to be generous.

of cricket (although it was the only sport at school I was ever any good at – skateboarding didn't really count), but the sound of the commentators bantering over the airwaves is synonymous with summer. And, I have decided I quite like *The Archers*, that most British of institutions. All hail Radio 4! I almost made the mistake of purchasing a wind-up radio without long wave, which would have meant no *Test Match Special*.

After my belly-bursting supper, I did some writing and listened to the radio. I then struggled through a bit more of *Walden* (I don't quite get it), and then switched to the childish delight of *Treasure Island* instead!

There were hoards of daddy-longlegs and moths tonight: I ended up over-exciting the moths by placing the hurricane lamps in a triangle to see what would happen – they went mental!

TUESDAY 28th JULY

Media frenzy! Today began like any other. I got up, made some coffee, had a shower, brushed my teeth, and packed up my stuff to go and teach foraging. It was quite chilly, with lots of dew in the field. I hope summer isn't running out.

This evening the article about the tree house is due to be published in the London *Evening Standard*. I was excited at the thought of commuters seeing pictures of the tree house and reading about my escape from the rat race. On the way to the foraging session my phone wouldn't stop ringing. By the time I got there I had ten missed calls and just as many voicemails – by 10am the media were already all over the story.

But first I had a lesson to teach and it went very well: nettle pesto, rabbit stew, various herbal teas, Jew's ear mushrooms, etc. I was really impressed with the kids: they made exceptional flatbreads, some of which were better than mine – it was a far cry from my last collection of campers!

I finished foraging at 2pm and then things kicked off: the local BBC news team wanted to come and film a report with a 'live-feed' to go on *South Today*. They wanted to come at 3.30pm so I had to race back and spruce the place up. Not that it was untidy – I just had to make sure everything looked as it should. I ended up getting a speeding ticket in the local village for going 35mph in a 30mph limit. I thought about charging it to the BBC on 'expenses' as technically it was their fault! As the tree house was fairly tidy, I made the bed, gave the floor a quick sweep, and made a fire to get the kettle on for a much needed cup of tea.

At 3.30pm on the dot a car, two vans and a truck with a satellite dish turned up at the top of the wood. The place became a hive of activity: as they weren't able to get a radio link to the tree house, they began running cables down instead. It was all a bit overwhelming. A chap from BBC Radio Kent also turned up to record a piece. I wasn't quite sure what to make of it, and to be honest I felt quite uncomfortable: my quiet little existence had suddenly become surrounded by vultures. My main worry was that they might give away the location of the tree house, which could potentially spoil everything. Once they agreed not to disclose the location I became a little more relaxed – this would all be over by tomorrow.

They were a very nice bunch so I made them a cup of tea. They filmed a brief interview with me and then went up to the vans to edit the footage before doing the live studio feed. So this is how they make the news! I was shocked by the speed of the turnaround; there really was no margin for error. It went live at 6.30pm and by 7.30pm the woods were quiet once more. Did it really happen? The only evidence is the mud that the crew churned up from laying the cables.

I made a basic supper of beans, potatoes and a few field mushrooms I had found while setting my nightlines (sustenance can appear at the strangest of times). I picked about ten, but half were infested with maggots. The mushrooms had a delicate nutty flavour. I fried them all up on top of Bertha, ate, and then turned on the radio. I read for an hour or so before checking the lines.

I got a call from Clare, who had picked up a copy of the *Evening Standard*, which she read to me over the phone. Apparently the article had also appeared in both of the capital's free evening papers – *The London Paper* and *London Lite*. One article even said I had quit my job as a high-flying City businessman, so it was a bit like a game of Chinese whispers – accurate research! Journalists *have* got lazy … Clare said it was quite strange to see all the commuters on the tube reading about the tree house. I would have loved to have seen that!

I checked the lines … nothing yet. It has been a bizarre and unexpected day. I wonder what will happen tomorrow?

Wednesday 29th July

The media circus continued today. At 10.30am the local ITV news team came down to have a poke around. I did an interview and gave them a tour of the tree house. I also showed them some eels from the freshwater fridge and the vegetable patch. Both news teams were eager to get shots of me sawing wood or sitting in the hammock – strange. I got a

strong feeling that my merry band of news reporters would have given anything to be somewhere else: They didn't really seem to like the countryside with all its trees, mud and insects …

After they left I had some lunch – runner beans grilled over the fire, wrapped in a flatbread with the occasional mouthful of pickled sea dulse. In the afternoon I was expecting a visitor down from the smoke. It was a guy called Al, another friend of Tom's, who had spent 4½ years cycling around the world. Perhaps I shouldn't be so willing to let strangers into my abode, but the truth was I was intrigued. When I met Al at the station, I could see he was prepared for anything – he had wellies strapped to his rucksack!

Before I took Al to the tree house we went to check for hedgehog fungi. Someone had announced on an online forum that he had found some, but I had the suspicion he was either wrong or a liar. There were none in the place I usually find them and, in fact, they are not even due for another couple of months.

Al was shocked at just how big the tree house is: 260sq. ft (24sq. m). Well, I wanted it to be big – I've got to live in it! We spent a long time chatting about this and that, and then we went to the birch grove to stock up with wood. Rain was forecast for later in the day and I didn't want to get caught with my trousers down.

Al seemed to have had a good chinwag with Tom before he came down, and produced a selection of 'housewarming' gifts out of his bag: a couple of books (*Pilgrim at Tinker Creek* and *Beachcombing at Miramar*), some real coffee, a stovetop espresso maker and, wait for it, a huge watermelon! It must have taken up half his bag.

He also gave me a copy of yesterday's *Evening Standard* – I hadn't expected the article to be a whole page, with some of my treasured recipes too! There were also a few pictures. I was really happy with the photo of the tree house – it looked awesome! It was so good I could hardly believe I'd built it myself.

After this the rain came, heavy and unrelenting. Cleverly, I decided that this was a good time to go and get supper. First we got the eels from the

Hedgehog Fungus (Hydnum repandum)

DESCRIPTION **Also known as wood hedgehog, this species is found in all types of woodland, particularly beech. The stem is short and white. The irregular cap is buffish-pink and leathery, and measures 2–4in (5–10cm) across. Underneath the cap, instead of gills, there are white spines. August–November.**

USES **This has to be one of my personal favourites in the whole mushroom kingdom. It is an ideal mushroom for beginners because it is so easy to identify: it is one of the few fungi to have spines instead of gills. Its firm texture makes it ideal for frying, grilling, freezing and even pickling. To prepare the mushroom, remove all the spines with the back of a knife (in younger specimens you can leave them on). This mushroom has a tendency to be slightly bitter, so slice it up and blanch in boiling water for one minute. They are best fried in a little butter, thyme and garlic, and spread over toast with a squeeze of lemon juice.**

freshwater fridge, and then we walked through the maize field to the patch, which, as if we weren't wet enough already, completely drenched us. Finally I took him to the field where I was consistently finding field mushrooms. There were more than ever so we picked our fill.

When we got back it was nearly 7pm, so I fired up Bertha, we changed into dry clothes, and I opened a bottle of elderflower champers. It was good, perhaps a bit sweet, but we drank it anyway. I smoked the eels, which we had with fried mushrooms, salad and potatoes. We stayed up late drinking tea while Al told me about his incredible journey around the world by bike.

THURSDAY 30th JULY

I had to wake at 8am, as I was due to receive a call from someone from Radio Sussex at around 8.40am. They played some of the audio from yesterday's BBC footage and then the presenter came on the line. He was astonishingly cheerful – how can people do that so early in the morning?

I briefly explained what I was up to, and then something unexpected happened. I know I live in a wood, and the mobile phone reception is not great at the best of times, but I wasn't ready for this. The presenter continued, 'Nick, for all our listeners out there who are on their way to work or sitting at their desk, could you paint us a picture of what you can see …' I opened my mouth to reply and 'bleep bleep' – that was it, my reception had gone.

Instead I turned my attention to one of Al's gifts: real coffee. I don't know why I have been using instant for the last few months, it's just wrong. I had no filter to pour the coffee through, so I used the old bushman's 'flick trick': I got a mug of cold water, dipped my hand into it, and then flicked cold water onto the surface of the hot coffee. The action of the cold water against the hot makes the granules sink to the bottom (don't ask me why, because I don't know). I then sat back and enjoyed one of the best cups of coffee I've had in a long while.

I asked Al what he fancied doing today. I like to know what my visitors are keen to experience for themselves, so they can take a little piece of my life home with them at the end of the day. He mentioned the word 'shotgun' a few times so we went in search of game.

We located a rabbit and I gave Al a brief lesson in stalking. However, on Al's approach the rabbit promptly disappeared – it was probably the sound of his wellies, or the bright blue fleece he was wearing! We gave up on stalking and instead I suggested fish for lunch, a fish that Al had no experience of: the perch. We paid £1 to park at the reservoir (a small price to pay for lunch) and as soon as we had sneaked down through the meadow to the jetty, I set up the rod.

We landed a fish on the first cast. Several more followed and

FAIRY RING CHAMPIGNON (MARASMIUS OREADES)

DESCRIPTION **Common in short grassland, this species typically forms rings. The cap is usually buff brown with a slight bump in the middle 1–2¾in (2.5–7cm) across. The top is smooth when wet but is hard and wrinkled when dry. Gills are free of the stem and produce white spores. April–December.**

USES **One of the few mushrooms available over the summer and the bane of anyone who keeps a meticulous lawn. They are surprisingly common and most easily identified by their scent: bitter almonds. I must urge you to consult a proper mushroom identification book as there are some impostors. Fairy rings are incredibly delicious, either fried, or cooked in soups and stews. Remove the tough stems before cooking and just use the caps. They also dry well: simply tie them up with thread and leave them in a warm, well-ventilated place.**

after ten minutes we had a good bag of perch. Al couldn't believe it was that easy. 'Now this is *my* kind of fishing!', he said, as he snapped off a few shots with his camera.

After fishing, we found a cluster of fairy ring champignons. People walked past and stared as we photographed and gathered the delicate little fungi – it seems people in Britain simply don't have the knowledge anymore to bag a free feast!

By happy accident a bunch of sorrel was growing a few feet from the fungi. The old saying 'Things that grow together, go together' certainly applied in this instance; in fact, I couldn't think of a better pairing.

Back at the tree house we got the fire up to speed again, only to be interrupted by a sudden downpour. So we worked under the shelter of the tree house instead. I scaled and filleted the perch, while Al got carried away sawing through all the oak limbs I had stashed in the wood pile. He called it 'gym training'; I didn't object – he produced a good stash of logs!

The fire reached cooking speed and we sat beside it as I put together my classic tree house version of *filet du perch* (complete with the odd bit of dirt and dead leaf – all good nutrition, sort of). I took the stalks off the mushrooms and fried them up in the pan with a twist of salt and pepper. When they were almost ready, as a final flourish I dropped in a handful of chopped sorrel and we ate straight out of the pan. It was the kind of meal that would have cost a fortune in London – minus the garnish of dirt and leaves, of course.

After lunch, I took Al back to the station. It was good to have someone to share my lifestyle with, to share the workload, and to swap stories and adventures. I am certainly getting to meet some interesting new people through being here.

FRIDAY 31st JULY

At midday I was expecting a visit from ZDF, a German television channel. I busied myself with cleaning: after a couple of days of wet weather, the inside of the tree house was covered with mud from wellies and bare feet, and various morsels of food that had sneaked out of the frying pan.

BERTHA

Be it clothes or shoes, I could always rely on Bertha to dry them out for me.

After a wet forage, firing up Bertha with birch was the best way to achieve warmth and a singing kettle (and to dry her out – notice the damp patch on the stove top from water that ran down the stovepipe, a constant problem).

The perfect woodland home: Bertha pumping smoke out of the stovepipe on a summer's evening.

The vegetable Patch

My landlords' pig, Bangers, giving me a hand turfing up the patch – probably one of the most exhausting jobs of the summer.

To keep unwanted animals away from my crops, I used a mix of hazel and willow to build the fences. The willow was coppiced from the trees in the background; removing them also gave the patch more sunlight – two birds, one stone!

Not finished yet – the boxed-in patch, complete with rustic entrance. I still had all the soil to dig over …

I built four runner bean wigwams out of hazel, two of which Bangers destroyed before I had the chance to put on a gate!

The nursery is finally brought down to take up residence at the patch: 15 runner beans, 8 broad beans, 3 sweet peas, 3 garden peas, 3 courgette, chicory, chives and rocket. The spinach and salads were sown directly into the ground.

Three weeks on and the patch was starting to produce plenty for the table. The dry spell in June meant watering twice a day.

HUNTING AND FISHING

A rabbit for the pot, shot with the air rifle; I stalked this one along the edge of the wood. By the end of September all the local rabbits were suffering from myxomatosis, another killer introduced by mankind.

A glut of pigeons – the result of a day's decoying with Tom. We shot 12 birds, all of which he kindly donated to me.

The first eel of the year! Caught on a nightline on 16 June. From this point on, the river was now able to provide me with a much needed variation in my source of protein.

Plucking a pheasant for supper on the rabbitskin rug. On the rare occasion I shot a pheasant, I always looked forward to the tasty evening meal ahead.

The one that didn't get away: a 3lb (1.4kg) brown trout from the river. I didn't just catch eels …

MUSHROOMS AND WILD PLANTS

The biggest horse mushroom I have ever found. Its smaller cousin, the field mushroom, was a regular on my tree house menu.

Fairy ring champignon: one of the tastiest of the summer mushrooms. As the name suggests, these grow in large rings, which meant there was always plenty to take home for tea.

I had to wait until October for the cauliflower fungus to appear. This one kept me well fed for at least a week.

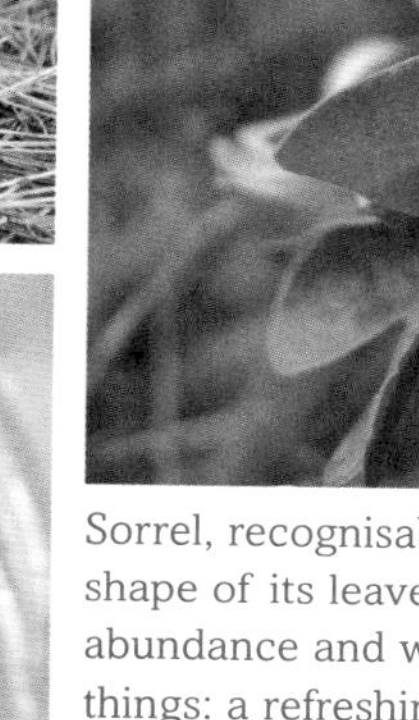

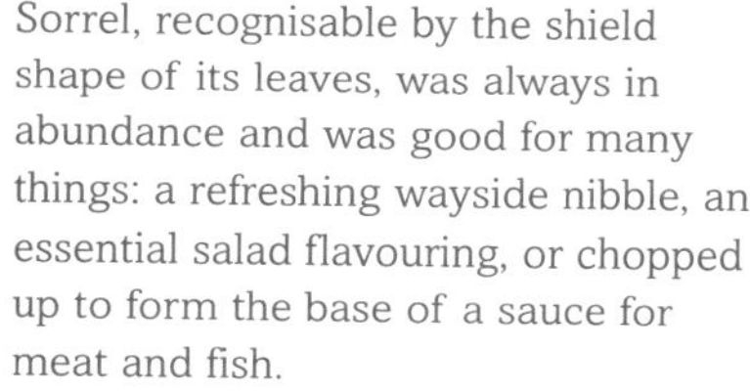

Sorrel, recognisable by the shield shape of its leaves, was always in abundance and was good for many things: a refreshing wayside nibble, an essential salad flavouring, or chopped up to form the base of a sauce for meat and fish.

I didn't expect to rely on hop shoots as a staple, but they formed part of virtually every meal I ate for the first two months. The hedgerows had so many I was even able to put aside some for pickling.

Fresh samphire, with the Seven Sisters in the background. Samphire is my favourite of all wild foods; it is also outstanding when pickled, and was a useful snack throughout the summer.

FOOD AND DRINK

A new way to cook rabbit. Some of my courgettes grew too big, so I filled one with fried pieces of rabbit, hazelnuts, spinach, potato and a little stock, and baked it in the embers.

If I was lucky enough to shoot a pigeon, I wouldn't waste a bit. I would pluck the bird and roast it on the fire for supper: a tree-house favourite by a long stretch.

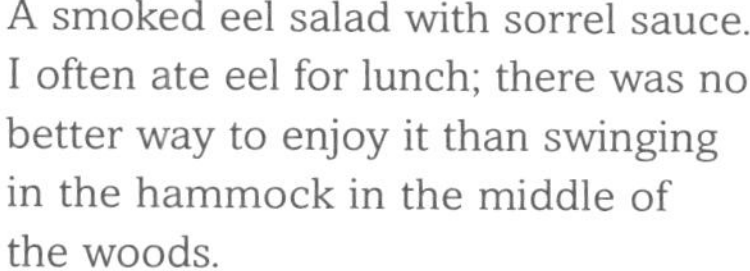

A smoked eel salad with sorrel sauce. I often ate eel for lunch; there was no better way to enjoy it than swinging in the hammock in the middle of the woods.

Roast pigeon salad with pickled hop shoots and patch lettuce – a standard lunchtime meal.

Having guests was a good opportunity to try out some of the tree-house brew. Tucking into Birch Sap Wine 2009 – it wasn't quite ready.

Meadowsweet Beer

My experimental meadowsweet beer under way: I put a mixture of leaves and flower heads on to boil for 15 minutes.

Draining the beer through muslin into my brewer's bucket to cool off, before adding the sugar and yeast.

A week to ten days later the brew, a 6.4% corker, was ready for bottling up on the balcony. I couldn't resist trying a little at this stage. I always did – just to make sure it wasn't a disaster, like my weedkiller nettle beer!

FRIENDS

An evening in the outdoor living room, seen from the tree house balcony. The sound of laughter mixed with the warm glow of the hurricane lamps was so comforting after a week spent alone.

Clare, after finishing the clay oven – my favourite guest of all.

The friends from my trip to Scotland at the tree house – good times.

Building the Coracle

1 Rather than bending hazel and willow to make a circular frame or 'gunwales', I opted for a rectangular-shaped frame made from stout lengths of hazel. To me it was more of a 'boat' shape. I pegged the gunwales in the same way as my bench. I notched the ends of the hazel lengths, drilled a hole through each, and hammered in a whittled hazel peg until it just came through the bottom.

2 As this wasn't a conventional coracle design, I was able to play around with the way it was fixed together. I began by using some pre-bent hazel that had been left in a jig overnight. I drilled holes at 6in (15.2cm) intervals down each side of the gunwales, into which I fitted the bent hazel rods. The hazel rods at the front were smaller so that the coracle was shallower at the front and deeper at the back. To try to get the bottom of the coracle as flat as possible to give it more of a square profile, I fixed bungees around the centre of the hazel rods to encourage them to bend into place, and left them for 24 hours.

3 The next stage was to fix three hazel rods lengthways to form a lattice, which would create a stronger frame. I began with the middle strut and then placed one on each side. Each strut was tucked on the inside of the front of the frame (the bow), bent over the hazel rods, and tucked inside the back of the frame (the stern).

4 Finding the correct spot for the seat was a question of trial and error: I put a few thick lengths of hazel across the top of the coracle, sat on them and shifted them about until I found what I felt was a good balance. I then cut four straight lengths and screwed them onto the top of the frame.

5 Traditionally, coracles were covered in large animal hides. With no suitably large animals to hand, I used thick canvas in the largest width I could get, which was 5ft (1.5m). I bought 8ft (2.4m), which cost about £15. The canvas fitted widthways at a stretch! I used my staple gun to pin the canvas taut over the coracle gunwales. First I stapled across one side, starting from the centre and working outwards. I then went round to the other side, pulled the canvas as taut as possible, and repeated the process from the middle outwards. I used the same method for the front and back.

6 The finished coracle ready for its waterproof coating. So far I had spent roughly eight hours working on it.

7 To make the coracle waterproof, I bought a tub of bitumen emulsion – the kind of stuff used to waterproof garage roofs – from my local DIY shop. I gave the coracle four coats just to be safe, although three are sufficient. I left it to dry for about six hours between each coat.

CORACLE VOYAGE

Under cloudy skies: the official expedition photographer's portrait of the daring duo.

Not the first time I've climbed a tree for supper: plucking a chicken of the woods, 20ft (6.1m) up, off its host.

The final leg of the journey: Tom leading the coracle donkey-fashion past the village of Alfriston. The coracle carried all our gear most of the way; she made a great trailer and would help to keep the kayak straight as you paddled – always a bonus.

Surely we should be here! The map was somewhat deceiving – after thinking we had gone miles, often we found it was an awful lot less. Church spires were the most useful way of finding our position – they were all we could see over the riverbank.

Coracle portage: every time there was an obstacle I would adopt the turtle position and head for the next section of open water.

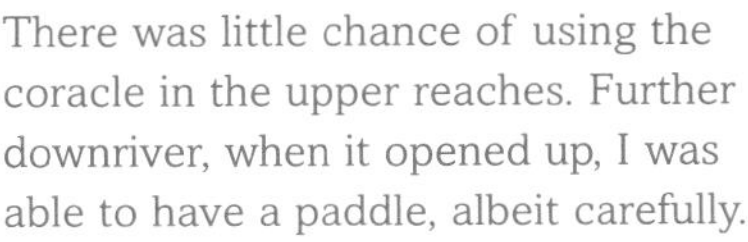

There was little chance of using the coracle in the upper reaches. Further downriver, when it opened up, I was able to have a paddle, albeit carefully.

So close and yet so far. Staring wistfully towards the coast – had it not been for the tides we could have made it.

THIS IS THE LIFE!

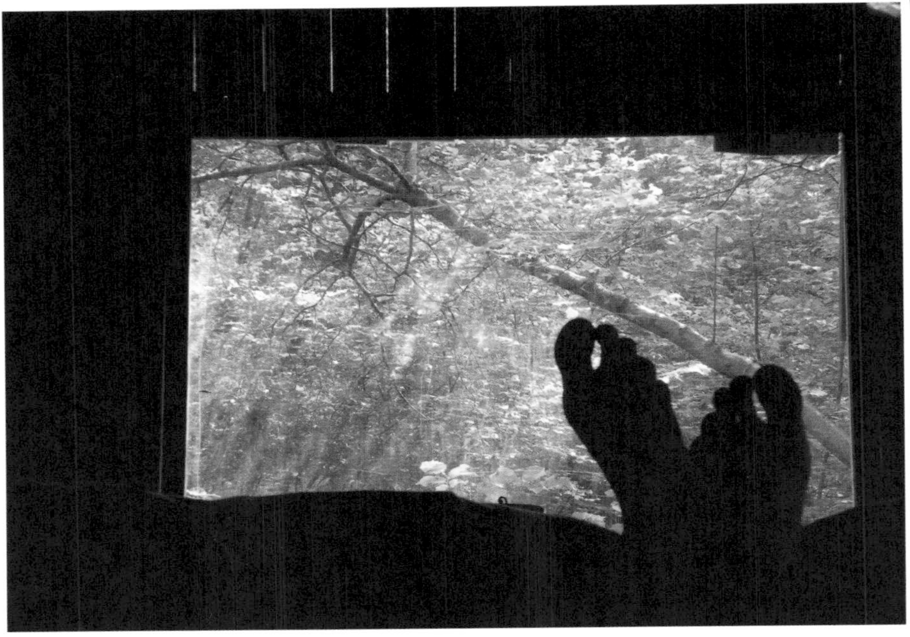

A room with a view. I don't think I will ever forget the view from bed in the morning – that alone made the whole experience worthwhile.

If I had no luck with the gun, the river wasn't such a bad place to spend a few hours …

I tried out my new espresso machine; I wasn't sure how it worked. At first it was a bit like giving a Neanderthal a Rubik's Cube but I got there in the end. Initially I put it straight onto the flames, but the handle caught fire, so I realised it might work better if I put a heavy frying pan underneath. I had heard that it made strong coffee and after a few cups I was absolutely wired – now that's the way to take coffee!

I had not washed properly since Tuesday morning so I had a shower. Being clean and jacked up on caffeine made me feel on top of the world, not a bad place to be before filming. On the dot of midday, with typical Germanic efficiency, the phone rang.

'Zee Germans' were not actually German at all, but a fantastic couple of English types, and I warmed to them immediately. They were very impressed with my set-up and I was surprised when they gave me two carrier bags full of bits as a thank-you present for having them down.

My haul included: one coconut and orange cake, a big bar of chocolate, a packet of Hobnobs, two bottles of red wine, a jar of tikka masala curry sauce, and a jar of apricot and tomato tagine sauce. They did some filming and I made them some tea. I showed them around, did some interviews and got a great photo of the cameraman filming the throne. Imagine having someone coming into your house and filming your toilet! It was more than a little surreal ...

They left at around 4pm, and I made some dough for the weekend. I then had a few hours to start work on a boat paddle. Since I first moved here and saw the river, I have been thinking about building some sort of boat, and navigating the river all the way to the coast. I love the idea of seeing Sussex from the river's point of view. It will also be a good way of finding future fishing spots, as well as being a very different kind of journey that will give me a few days in the wild that won't centre around the tree house. My vessel will be one of the most ancient of watercraft: the coracle. Now I've just got to build one!

HOW TO MAKE A PADDLE

The wood I chose was a sweet chestnut branch, about thigh-thickness, that had bent and split; the outer inch looked like shallow guttering and had come away from the rest of the wood.

I used the saw, hatchet and hammer to split the edges off to give me a paddle shape. From what I have read, paddling a coracle uses a figure-of-eight stroke, so the curve had to go! After a couple of hours' whittling, it was well on its way to being finished.

Clare called at about 7pm to say she was at the station and I was a happy chap once more. It has been a busy week, made even more hectic by the media attention. All very exciting, but it did leave me little time to get on with life and activities down here. My 'To Do' list hasn't got many ticks on it!

From what little feedback I have had, it seems people think I am trying to cut myself off and live a solitary life. But this isn't an experiment in becoming a hermit. I live a relatively normal life like most people do – I just happen to be living in an unconventional house and eating a slightly different diet. There have been some interesting comments posted online that Clare had printed off at work and brought down for me to read. Amongst the many things people had written, some positive and some negative, there was one that caught my eye: 'It is funny that while we strive for a more simple existence like this, people in the third world aspire to live more like us.'

AUGUST

SATURDAY 1st AUGUST ☼/☂

The weather today was forecast to be good in the morning and wet in the evening. Clare and I had three guests coming down for the night. In the morning Clare went to Brighton with her sister and I got on with my daily chores.

So that we would be warm and comfortable later on, I restocked the wood store while the branches were still dry. I have still not yet mastered the oven and managed to produce a completely successful tree house loaf. When I have made a loaf, it has gone stale in about 24 hours, and I can't eat the bread fast enough to avoid much of it going to waste.

I moved some smouldering logs from the fire to heat up the oven, leaving the door half off to help draw up the flames. I then got on with sanding and finishing the paddle for my coracle. I am pleased with it, although it is a bit on the heavy side; but there is only so much wood I can shave off.

While I was sanding away I sensed some movement over by the oven. I turned to look and saw a very distressed and bewildered toad hopping out of the entrance to what had, until a few minutes ago, been his very own dark, damp hovel – he was actually smoking! The clay oven had become the proverbial Toad Hall for the local amphibian population; I hoped he was the only one in there – looking at the inferno within, the others wouldn't stand a chance.

When the oven looked ready, I put the bread in, sealed the entrance, and turned my attention to my 'To Do' list. I went up onto the roof of the tree house to saw the top off one of the support/roofing posts. The post was in the same corner as my bookshelves and during the recent downpours water has been trickling in and gradually soaking my prized book collection – not what I want. As I was sitting on the roof I heard voices approaching. Jamie and Nicole had been to the tree house for supper, but had not yet stayed the night. They had so much stuff it was hilarious: tent, duvet, pillows and sleeping bags. They were only coming for a night, not a week!

I climbed down to greet them and they handed over a bag of gifts: I seem to have become something of a charity case. The first thing I pulled out was a carrot and orange cake, so we had tea and cake by the fire.

I checked on the oven – the bread was baking, but very slowly. Unfortunately Jamie and Nicole also brought the rain with them. Jamie is the least outdoorsy person I know, and he started to have doubts: 'I don't know if we'll stay if it's going to keep raining', he said. Nicole swiftly told him not to be such a big girl's blouse – I always suspected it was she who wore the trousers in that relationship.

So Jamie then begged me to help him set up his tent. This always happens – just because I live in the woods, people automatically assume I know how to put up every single type of tent! In this case, I did know, as I have one exactly the same under the bed upstairs in case of emergency. While we put up the tent, Nicole roasted mushrooms on a stick over the fire, not the slightest bit bothered by the glorious British weather.

In the midst of the deluge two screaming girls came running through the trees towards us. Clare had picked up our friend KP from the station on her way back from Brighton. KP had brought a copy of *Reader's Digest* so I could see my column for the first time.

I stepped out into the rain and went to check the bread, which was finally done – it had taken about two hours to bake. Nicole used my smoker to try out a smoked egg recipe: tea leaves, carrots, sugar and Chinese five spice are used instead of sawdust. We boiled the egg for three minutes and smoked it for two. We sat around a plate dipping freshly baked smoky bread into the equally smoky runny yolks of the eggs.

I pulled out my party piece – the radio – and we all took turns winding it up (making sure we didn't break it this time!). We sat under the shelter of the tree house, in hammocks and hammock chairs, talking and drinking while the rain continued to fall. A happy and relaxing night was just what I needed after the week I have had.

SUNDAY 2ND AUGUST

It has been ages since I've read the Sunday papers, let alone had any delivered. At 8.30am I walked to the top of the wood to meet a BBC Radio van and the man inside gave me a stack that included every single Sunday newspaper – my guests were delighted!

He also gave me a big walkie-talkie/radio-type thing, a set of headphones, and a microphone. As a relative newcomer to Radio 4 I was still finding my feet with regard to the content of radio programmes. All I had been told was that I had to choose some stories that interested me and talk about them with a few other people in an 'on-air, round-table discussion'.

When I got back I lit the fire and had an espresso, as last night's shenanigans had left me feeling a bit ropey. Everyone was still fast asleep. I read through the papers and drank some more coffee. I found some interesting stories and chose a couple that I could relate to: one concerned the Met Office's 'Indian summer' prediction; the other was about container vegetable gardening in towns and cities.

I was sharing a discussion on the 'Broadcasting House' programme with Aggie (from 'How Clean is Your House?'), a GP from Cardiff, and host Paddy O'Connell. It went well, although I was a bit nervous to start with. Aggie offered to come and clean the tree house – well, actually, I asked her. Afterwards I was exhausted. I slept for two hours, and woke to a very clean camp, with all the washing and tidying done. After everyone had gone Clare and I read the papers in the sunshine, drinking tea and eating the rest of the cake. A top-notch Sunday afternoon!

My landlords called to say they were off on holiday and to remind me that I had agreed to look after their animals. The farmyard consists of six chickens, one pig, five horses, six cats and a flock of sheep. The best part is that it looks like I will be getting 3–4 eggs a day for three weeks – a quick-fix solution to my protein problem!

Monday 3rd August

It was a beautiful morning. I had a complete flake-out today and did very little other than make plans for the coracle. On my way to water the patch I tried a few blackberries – still very tart! I am pleased to see fruit arriving, and mushrooms too. I also found a chicken of the woods fungus at an early stage of growth on a big oak tree: I am looking forward to that one.

Using the advice I had picked up from the coppicers at the South of England Show, and a fantastic old book, *The Complete Practical Book of Country Crafts*, by Jack Hill, I began splitting down some lengths of hazel for the top of the coracle frame or, in nautical terms, the gunwales. The work was slow; I had to get my hatchet into the

split and turn it to the left or right, and this would split the wood one way or the other. The trick was to use a combination of the two to ensure the wood split straight down the middle.

I banged some wooden stakes into the ground in a 'U'-shape to act as a jig, and then bent some thin lengths of hazel into it; this should help the lengths bend and set into the correct shape over the next 24 hours. These will form the hull of the coracle. Unfortunately the lengths I had split for the gunwales cracked when I tried to bend them, despite steaming the wood over the kettle first to try to relax the fibres. It was clear I needed a different approach. I had a rough idea of how to make a coracle so I decided to give it my own interpretation.

I used some seasoned hazel I had cut down in spring for pegs and put together a sturdy frame of thick hazel lengths. I had to coppice some fresh hazel with a natural curve for the front and the back. This new frame will now act as the gunwales. I packed up my tools and had a shower as another guest was on his way. This place is fast becoming a halfway house.

Chuck is a friend from university and is now a teacher at my old school. As it is the school holidays he is one of the few people I know who is free during the week. He arrived at about 4pm and we sat on the balcony and had a cup of tea while Chuck filled me in with news of my alma mater.

I had nothing for supper, but I knew Chuck was no stranger to a shotgun, so he took charge of the weaponry and we went for a walk in search of food. Chuck was a dab hand and managed to clip a very fast pigeon (he wasn't quite quick enough), but we were really after rabbits. Our walk took us past the patch and I stopped to fill my bag with runner beans, spinach and my first two red onions. They weren't huge, not much bigger than a golf ball, but they had a rich, sweet, pungent smell. I have never grown onions before but I will certainly do so in the future.

We walked up to the field where I had found all the field mushrooms; there were no new ones, but we did come across some more fairy ring champignons, which I added to the vegetables in the bag. Near the middle of the field there is a copse of oak trees surrounded by brambles. Chuck spotted two rabbits near the hedge line. He crept up slowly and raised his head, which put the rabbits on full alert. Chuck fired off both barrels in quick succession at the retreating rabbits, taking down the second just short of its burrow. The rabbit was a good size, big enough for both of us.

I kept the pelt for my rug and pinned it out on a board with some nails. We snacked on the hunter's prize, the liver, cooked on a hazel skewer over the fire. I split the rabbit down the middle, following the spine, and made a basting liquid with wild garlic, olive oil, lemon juice and the remains of a jar of Dijon mustard. We roasted the sides of rabbit over some hot embers while we fried up the onions, mushrooms and vegetables in a pan.

We ate up in the tree house at the table. Chuck was surprised by my level of self-sufficiency. I haven't really thought about it too much, but indeed, everything on the plate came from within a mile of where we were sitting, and was as fresh as it could possibly be; it was a true 'locavore' diet with zero emission status (save that of the shotgun going off).

After supper, Chuck reached into his bag and presented me with yet another gift: a bottle of ten-year-old Laphroaig whisky. I am a fan of whisky, but the peaty stuff like this one is an acquired taste – however, it was a warming after-dinner dram all the same. I pulled out a bottle of my own Tree House Elderflower Champagne, June 2009 vintage. It is improving with age and was not quite as sweet as the last bottle, but it was primed and ready to explode as ever. Following a thorough tasting session and a few games of cards we hit the sack at about 2am.

Tuesday 4th August

This morning I had to pick my mother up from the airport at 7am; she has been staying with my brother in New York for the last two weeks. After just four hours' sleep I was exhausted, but I had no one to blame but myself. When I got back Chuck was still fast asleep in the corner of the tree house. The trip to the airport had been worth it though: my mother had brought me a bottle of punchy chilli sauce. I climbed back into my soft bed and slept for a few hours. I woke up at 11am feeling refreshed.

For breakfast we ate Al's watermelon; I wanted to share it because it was far too big for me to eat by myself. I ceremoniously sliced it in half with a full swing of the machete – and half of it fell on the ground, cut side down, and was immediately covered in woodland debris. Gallantly I claimed that half and gave it a good wash in the sink. It has been ages since I last had a watermelon and it was so good! I have always shied away from them because I find the black seeds a pain, but this one didn't have any. I wrapped the leftovers in a burdock leaf for later.

My boat trip is due to kick off on 12 August and I needed to crack on with the coracle build. Chuck offered to give me a hand. I took the lengths of hazel out of the jig – they had bent into shape quite nicely – and we began work on the hull.

As well as the bottle of single malt Chuck had another gift up his sleeve. We got in his car and drove over to a village not far away. Chuck pulled up outside the local butcher and turned to me: 'Right, we're going to go in there and you can choose whatever cut you fancy from whatever animal you want – my treat!'

For a humble hunter-gatherer like me the butcher's shop was the height of convenience. It was almost too much to cope with. I couldn't begin to imagine the sensory overload it would have given Stone Age man.

We stood in the corner of the shop whispering away and asking the butcher the odd question. I quite liked the idea of chicken hearts again and I thought Chuck might enjoy them. The butcher said they had only a dozen or so – I supposed that could make a good starter. I wondered what other offal they had. 'What's the strangest thing you've got in here?' I asked. 'Well, you two at the moment', came the reply.

In the end I left it to Chuck to decide on the meat course. He chose veal chops. When I heard the price I was instantly reminded of the reason I had gone 'native' in the first place: two fairly modest veal chops cost £18.99 – more than two weeks' worth of my tree house budget!

For dinner we had mashed potato, courgettes sliced lengthways, and whole runner beans griddled over the fire along with the pricey chops. Simply seasoned, and cooked over hot embers, they were divine. I had been craving a slice of beef ever since the cows had moved in next door. After supper, we settled into some ale, Laphroaig, coffee and cards. Chuck taught me how to play 'Beggar My Neighbour'; the first game lasted an hour before I claimed victory. With an early start the next day I celebrated by going to sleep.

Wednesday 5th August

I had to teach foraging this morning, so I skipped a shower, washed my face, shaved, drank coffee and brushed my teeth, and made it there by 10am. It was a good group today, mainly adults. I did my usual menu, but high summer on the South Downs has become a bit stale: The fruit isn't quite ready – there are dozens of damsons ripening in the hedgerows but they are too tart to eat at the moment. Some of the group had read the newspaper article about the tree house and bombarded me with questions.

After foraging, I went back to the tree and continued work on the coracle – it is starting to look like a proper boat! Later I went to my parents' house to use the computer and update the blog. When I returned to the tree house once more I had a wee dram before crawling into bed to read.

I've got about five books on the go at the moment. I suppose it's my equivalent of that annoying TV habit: channel surfing. I tend to pick one up – a travel book, for instance – decide I'm not really in the mood, and reach for a novel instead. It is a bit more complex than pushing a button, with fewer options to choose from, but on the upside it gives me a chance to flex the old cranium!

Thursday 6th August

I got stuck into the coracle build first thing and spent most of the morning tying together all the crossovers of the hazel lengths with jute twine. My hands became really painful after a while: quite raw and very sore. I made toast from one of my loaves and ate half a lemon because I had run out of oranges – it gave me a face like Kenneth Williams getting into a hot bath. Ouch!

Once I finished the framework, I decided to call on a man who knows more about coracles than I do: Richard J. Taylor builds them for a living. I found his number on his website and asked him for any tips regarding the covering and waterproofing of the vessel. He was friendly and extremely helpful, and he asked me to send him a photo of my finished 'Sussex' coracle.

Using the information gleaned from my coracle 'guru', I went to a fabric shop to buy some canvas, which came in at £15. I then went to the DIY shop to buy some bitumen emulsion for waterproofing the canvas once it had been fitted.

My trip to the shops cost me £25, not much money for a boat, but more than I could really afford. The mosquitoes were out in force in the afternoon. My hopes for mosquito 'immunity' seem unlikely ever to come to fruition, so after an hour of slapping myself every minute or so, I reached for the repellent and watched the mosquitoes think twice before preparing to dine.

I worked on the seat of the coracle and it took some time to find the centre of gravity. I soon realised that the practicality of a vessel like this one on the narrow Sussex waterways will be limited – it felt mighty unstable! With the seat sorted, I moved on to the canvas. The covering went well, made easier with the use of a staple gun. The canvas just about covered the width – with hindsight, it might have been a good idea to find out the width the canvas came in before I started building. I mean, you wouldn't build a garage only to find out your car didn't fit in, would you?

Chuck called me later that day to say thanks for the stay and to find out how the coracle was coming along. I mentioned my concerns about stability and whether or not it would be able to go the distance on the river. Chuck said the school had a few kayaks that were gathering dust in one of the sports equipment storage rooms, which I was welcome to borrow. I might take him up on the offer – back-up is always useful.

I was tucking into a vegetarian special outside when the humidity was broken by a spell of heavy rain – impeccable timing!

Friday 7th August

I picked the kayaks up from Chuck at about 10am. Instead of the ancient, dilapidated boats I had been expecting, they are actually quite state-of-the-art, and the paddles are in good nick too, but there was no sign of any splash decks. Tom has offered to come on the coracle adventure in the role of expedition photographer, so I needed a kayak for him and a back-up one for me, in case anything happens to the coracle.

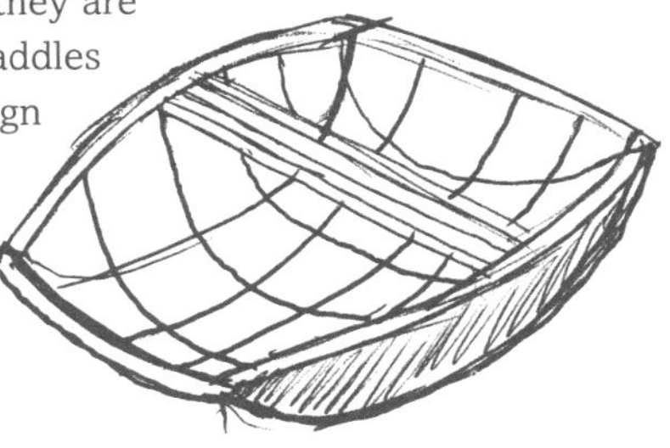

Back in the woods I began the final stage in the covering. I was unsure whether the staples would be sufficient to hold the canvas in place so, for insurance purposes, I sewed the canvas to the gunwales using weatherproof twine and a big thick needle fashioned from a piece of coat hanger.

I finished my stint as a seamstress and was quite happy with the results (sewing has never been one of my strong points). I had a break and a cup of yarrow tea – it was a hot day. After a bit of downtime I moved on to the final stage of the coracle: waterproofing.

Bitumen emulsion is basically a runnier version of tar, and very unforgiving if you happen to get any on yourself. I put on the first coat and left it to dry for a minimum of four hours. I managed to get about as much of the bitumen emulsion on myself as I had on the canvas. I didn't have any white spirit so I used the next-best thing, paraffin. It did the trick – I just kept well away from the fire for the rest of the afternoon!

I will let the first coat dry overnight. It should take three coats to make it watertight; I'm going to do four just to be on the safe side.

Saturday 8th August

Foraging again today: it was another good group and I had slightly different ingredients. Dan, the camp owner, had provided four pigeons and two rabbits (a couple more pelts for my rug). He also threw in a giant puffball – the one mushroom that is still on my wild fungi wish list. Try as I might I have never found one. Dan has a secret spot that keeps him well stocked throughout the summer, but like most mushroom foragers, he keeps his hunting ground a closely guarded secret.

GIANT PUFFBALL (LYCOPERDON GIGANTEA)

DESCRIPTION **Found in woods, field edges, near hedges and quite often amongst patches of nettles, the giant puffball, as its name suggests, is a large, white, round fungus that can measure anything from 6in (15cm) to 30in (75cm) in diameter. Older specimens may be yellow or green. July–November.**

USES **I have been given a few giant puffballs in my time but I have never found one personally – and it is not for want of trying. It seems that this is a fungus that will only be found when it wants to be, so there is little point in going out looking for them. They are at their best when the flesh is still pure white, and the entire puffball is edible.**

Due to its size, there are a number of culinary possibilities. The first is to slice it into ½in (1cm) thick steaks and fry it in a griddle pan. Alternatively you can hollow out the puffball in the same way you would a pumpkin and fill it with meat, vegetables, herbs and a little stock, wrap it in foil, and bake it in the oven for about an hour. You can also chop them into small squares. They look very like marshmallows, so treat them the same: roll the chunks in melted butter and minced garlic, put them on the end of a stick and cook them over the hot embers of a fire.

I de-boned the rabbits, took the breasts off the pigeons and cut the puffball, which was about the size of a football, into slices. I got the campers to make a giant batch of stinger pesto and then we had a very smart lunch: pan-fried pigeon and rabbit, served on a slice of toasted puffball, with dollops of stinger pesto. I surprised myself today, and the group were shocked at how sophisticated wild food can be.

I put a second coat on the coracle in the afternoon: cue more scrubbing with paraffin, followed by a much needed shower. I pinned out the rabbit pelts for the rug. I have quite a few now – it looks like I have a fur trader's workshop underneath the tree house!

Clare came over at about 6pm and we went to a country pub to meet up with a few friends for a beer or two. It was nice to go out for the evening; although I have remained pretty sociable at weekends, I haven't been 'out' for quite a while.

That's something else I've been thinking about. The distinction between weekdays and weekends has become increasingly blurred. Weekends are now very like any other day, except I am more likely to have visitors. Another funny thing is that I used to hate working at weekends; now I spend most Saturday mornings teaching foraging, which I thoroughly enjoy. Then again, foraging doesn't feel like work – I do it every day anyway!

Sunday 9th August

I hadn't seen my friend Charlie since he quit the City and his glum existence as a recruitment consultant. He has now started to train as a pilot: something he has always wanted to do. Today my plan was to test the water, as it were, and take on the first stage of the river by kayak. Charlie and I have talked about doing the river journey for the last two years, but have never been able to arrange the time off work together.

Although quite intelligent and switched on when it comes to work, Charlie does also have the tendency to be a bit of a muppet, and is one of those people you can get to do just about anything with enough coaxing. We had become firm friends at university through our mutual love of fishing: he is the only person I know who has fished as much as, if not more than, me, and we spent three happy years exploring Northumbria's waters in search of trout, salmon and virtually anything else that swam.

Charlie turned up at around midday, and was lost for words when he saw the tree house. Clare and I watched as he checked out my living arrangements. 'Mate, you've got so much stuff in there … for doing stuff.' He sounded really surprised. 'Yes, well, I do live here', came my reply.

We dropped Charlie's car off downriver. Then Clare gave us a lift up to the start point with the kayaks and paddles, waved us goodbye, and left us to

it. We manhandled the kayaks down the riverbank and set off under the bridge. We both had a waterproof splash bag containing the essentials: water, camera, phone and wallet (just in case).

The kickoff was superb. We had talked about doing this for so long and here we were casting off on a scorching summer's Sunday. The reconnaissance was a good idea. We found that the river was full of obstacles, certainly no place for a coracle: shallow runs peppered with sharp rocks, branches, overhanging bushes, and even the odd bit of barbed wire spanning the river to denote a land boundary.

Every so often we would get grounded on a shallow section and have to get out and drag the kayaks to deeper water. Charlie didn't disappoint and managed to capsize on several occasions. Fallen trees, that had collected a huge amount of flotsam, clogged the river around every corner. All we could do was try to find the path of least resistance or take the kayaks up the bank and walk them round.

I was certainly a lot better at controlling my vessel than Charlie, probably because I'm not as tall as him – he could hardly get his big legs into the kayak for a start! This led to a bit of friendly competition, and we started to see who could give the other the biggest soaking with the paddle, charge the other one into strands of overhanging blackberry and rosehip (painful), and, above all, capsize the other one's boat.

After passing the first checkpoint, a bridge just outside a village, the river broadened and the flow slowed down. We took a break from our continual paddling and drifted, admiring the surrounding landscape and glorious weather. As we came around a bend the river branched off and I saw a beautiful old mill house surrounded by weeping willows. I also saw a very grumpy-looking woman heading in our direction. First she tried to make out that we were scaring her cows, but they looked about as laid-back as a hippy in a hammock. Then she tried another tactic: 'You know this is private property, don't you?' Charlie and I both knew full well she didn't own the river, and once she realised she was fighting a losing battle, she called us some rude names and then stormed off in a huff.

As we slid further down the river it became shallow and narrow again. The odd dog-walker offered some local knowledge about what was coming up and we continued to push through. The river was rich in fish; we saw a few chub and watched small trout flash past, startled by the sight of our big red kayaks. We disturbed a fisherman from time to time, but they all said they didn't mind (I'm sure they did really – I would have done). We had a few 'extreme' moments flying down the little weirs that popped up every so often. These 'white-knuckle' rides almost always resulted in us filling the kayaks with water, due to the missing splash decks.

Eventually, after four hours of paddling and plenty of scratches from stray, overhanging rosehip thorns, we reached a convenient place to stop. As luck would have it we were right by a small country pub. We dragged the kayaks up the bank into the beer garden and celebrated with a few pints of Harveys. The beer certainly helped ward off the chill I was getting from sitting in a wet rash vest and board shorts.

I spotted some horseradish growing down by the riverbank, so we went and dug up one of the roots. On the drive back to the tree house Charlie bought some cream and sirloin steaks for supper. I made up some flatbreads, prepared some fresh horseradish sauce, and fried up some red onions from the patch – superb sustenance after burning off all that energy!

It was about time to sample my meadowsweet beer. I pulled out a couple of bottles and some pint glasses and put them on the table.

There was a satisfying 'pfffssszzz …' as I unscrewed the cap, but it was nowhere near as explosive as the nettle beer. As we needed to give the beer's medicinal value a proper test-run it was essential to get stuck in. Charlie, I decided, would make the perfect guinea pig. It tasted like cider and was thoroughly drinkable.

HORSERADISH (AMORACIA RUSTICANA)

DESCRIPTION **A kitchen-garden plant, 1–3ft (30–91cm) high, widely naturalised on waste ground throughout England and Wales. Stems are hairless and the dark green leaves have wavy, slightly toothed edges. White flowers appear on long spikes, May–September.**

USES **In mid-summer the big 'donkey's ear'-style leaves of horseradish can be seen growing in most country lanes, even by the side of main roads. Although young leaves can be used in salads for a bit of a kick, the real prize is underground. You can buy long, straight, cultivated horseradish roots in the supermarket, but they are no match for their wild ancestor. Wild horseradish is devilishly strong and the misshapen, knobbly root is not always that easy to extract from the ground in one piece, but you won't need that much!**

Once you have dug up the root (make sure you have the landowner's consent), it will need a good scrubbing to remove any dirt, and the root will need peeling. To make a simple horseradish sauce you have to grate the root finely. This is the dangerous bit – if cutting onions makes you cry then grating horseradish will really turn on the waterworks! For the sauce, mix together the grated root, a bit of mustard, double cream and sugar, and season well with salt and pepper – and have the roast beef ready!

With the stove going, we played cards and drank, we talked and drank, and then we played some more cards and drank a bit more. It was potent stuff and I think by the time we went to bed, we were more than a little tipsy – it would certainly be clear in the morning, whether or not I had managed to create hangover-free grog.

Monday 10th August

Much to my disappointment, the meadowsweet beer wasn't as effective as I had hoped. On the upside, I didn't have a headache, but all the other hangover symptoms were there. I suppose I can call it a partial success.

I woke to find a lantern still on – stupid! I went downstairs to find Charlie trying to make a fire using freshly cut wood. I watched him struggle for a bit longer before pointing out his mistake. I had hoped he would figure it out for himself, but his hangover was as bad as mine.

After a much needed cup of coffee I took Charlie down to my recreational fishing spot to catch some carp. Charlie loves his carp fishing, and after a couple of hours and some invigorating battles with some good-sized fish, our hangovers had melted away to nothing. Charlie left after the fishing so I did a bit of housework and put a final coat on the coracle.

The *Sunday Times* Home section had asked if they could come and do a feature on the tree house. I was a bit confused as to why, but I suppose it is a home. A journalist and photographer turned up at about 2pm with yet more goodies: three bottles of Hobgoblin Ale, some cookies and, most surprisingly, loo paper – I haven't moved on to leaves just yet!

They took lots of shots of the tree house and really liked what I had achieved. The photographer had all sorts of interesting kit and, being something of an amateur snapper myself, I took the opportunity to pick his brain. The article is due to be in next Sunday's edition. I will have to get Clare to pick me up a copy.

I have been taking note of all the creepy-crawlies that hang out with me every night. The moths continue to behave like mindless, suicidal idiots. I am finding daddy-longlegs, the ones without wings, everywhere I look – they especially like the eaves of the tree house where they gather by the dozen; it must be the warmth. My favourite, and the least annoying, are the shield bugs. Mine are brown with a little orange dot on the centre of their backs. I do enjoy their company and they seem comparatively intelligent – until I switch on the head torch.

Tuesday 11th August

I had a gloriously chilled morning. I made coffee, ate an orange and read. Then I had a shower, mainly to get rid of the lingering smell of river water from Sunday's trip. After shaving, I began to write a list of food supplies for the boat trip: rice, oil, vinaigrette, six mixed stock cubes, two lemons, salt and pepper, sugar, tea, coffee, four red onions, two bunches of runner beans, and a bag of spinach. These are just basics; the rest of it will have to be left to chance. I shall wait and see what Tom brings down.

The plan is simple: we have three days (all Tom has time for) to travel from the point I left off with Charlie, make our way down the river through Sussex, switch rivers to the River Cuckmere, and hit salt water at the Seven Sisters – ambitious to say the least! I would take the coracle and Tom would paddle one kayak and drag the other one behind him as the support vehicle.

I thought I should give the coracle a test-run, so I took it down to the river. It sat very well in the water until I attempted to get in it, at which point all hell broke loose, and pretty soon I was in the drink. It was very unstable, paddling was very difficult, and I went absolutely nowhere apart from round in circles. It looks like the coracle will now have to be the supply boat, and I will try to use it where I can, otherwise we won't get very far …

Tom wasn't due down until 10pm so I packed, cleaned up a knife as a gift for his next big adventure up the Mekong, and then I set up a vegetable hotpot with stock and rice, and went on a wander to do some foraging. I found lots of tawny grisette mushrooms growing in the birch wood. When I got back I checked my identification books just to be sure. Three guides correctly identified the mushrooms as tawny grisettes, but one identified them as death caps. I was sure it was a hideous misprint, but to err on the side of caution, I got rid of the mushrooms.

When Tom arrived at about 10.30pm, we had some food, discussed the route and then went straight to bed ready for an early start.

WEDNESDAY 12th AUGUST

The alarm clock was set to one of the worst possible tones – you know, the ones that get you out of bed in a hurry, just to make the noise go away. Nowadays 8am seems like an ungodly hour whereas, for a normal worker, it is obviously quite civilised. We wrapped up our belongings – clothing, sleeping matter, camera and food – in a few bin-bags. After Sunday's performance in the kayaks, I wasn't taking any chances.

> **'You weren't there, man! You weren't there ...'**
>
> TOM KEVILL-DAVIES, SUSSEX, 2009

Tom had brought the ingredients for a partial fry-up, just the kind of fodder to fuel the early stages of negotiation of the Sussex waterways, and definitely a meal for which I was truly grateful. We began our adventure where Charlie and I had left off, as the passage from the tree house would be virtually impossible for the coracle.

We lowered the coracle into the water and doused it with a little cider brandy (the river and the two of us were also doused – you can't scrimp on luck or goodwill on a mission like this). We loaded the coracle with our belongings and then went to pull in the kayaks. As we did so, a posse of cows wandered up to the bank, led by a bull with the largest testicles I had ever seen. As he started to scuff the ground he lifted up his tail and emptied his bowels in a stream that would have easily knocked you to the ground had you been standing in its path. Clearly he was not happy. With increasingly threatening noises emanating from the huge bull, I suddenly realised the big red kayaks probably had something to do with it. Swiftly kayaks and gear were stowed and we were well on our way ... well, almost – Tom managed to capsize in 2ft (61cm) of water after only 100yds (91m). 'Bugger. First round's on me!' I wasn't going to disagree ...

After 15 minutes of gentle paddling through an overgrown passage of water, we hit our first shallow patch. This meant jumping out of the kayaks and manhandling the coracle, loaded with 70lb (32kg) of gear, over large rocks and shingle that could end both its life and the entire expedition very quickly. The whole unloading/reloading and in/out process was something I was expecting, but perhaps not the frequency with which it occurred: weirs, fallen trees and vegetation all provided obstacles to be overcome. There was even a cow carcass at one point, which brought on much gagging and plenty of hurried paddling.

There was a strange kind of beauty involved in travelling through these closed-in Sussex waterways, never knowing what was around the next corner, and being unable to view the surrounding countryside added to the mystery of the whole escapade. Banks of Himalayan balsam and Japanese knotweed, and trees intertwined with a jungle-like tangle of hops, made our surroundings seem more like Siam than Sussex – however, the temperature soon dispelled any allusions.

The trees lining the bank were our main focus of interest as we paddled along the enclosed river. I scanned every oak tree we passed for a bright smudge of orange that would mean a good feed. Eventually, after rounding a bend, there it was – a chicken of the woods fungus, attached to a tree trunk 20ft (6m) up. Never one to miss out on a free meal, I was up the tree in a flash, while Tom sat in his kayak, bewildered at my sudden show of primate behaviour. I descended with a good-sized fungus and placed it lovingly into the coracle.

As we continued downstream the river widened. The space was refreshing and allowed for a faster pace, but inevitably we reached another weir. This was getting tiresome. As we went through the now painfully familiar routine, a puff of smoke appeared above a nearby field, followed by a loud 'whoooo-whoooo'. The Bluebell Railway was following our descent and reminded us of the reason for this very expedition. This was countryside as it should be, in all its glorious rusticity. I was half expecting the children

CHICKEN OF THE WOODS (SULPHUR POLYPORE)

DESCRIPTION **Also known as sulphur polypore, a fan-shaped bracket fungus that usually grows in tiers, often on oak, sweet chestnut and yew (never pick them from yew as this renders them poisonous). Deep orange-yellow above, with sulphur yellow undersides that fade to pale yellow with age. May–September.**

USES **As fungi go, this is the strangest in flavour and texture. It is virtually the same as chicken – hence its name. Again, it is a great mushroom for beginners as it is so easy to identify. Its bright orange and yellow colouring makes it stand out on tree trunks amongst the green foliage. Only young specimens are worth using; as they get older they dry out and become chalky and inedible. To get your hands on one, be prepared to work for it; quite often it will involve a certain amount of tree climbing.**

You can use it as a substitute for chicken – either pan-fried or as part of a casserole; however, it must be cooked. A word of warning: this mushroom doesn't agree with everyone – there are rare cases of people having stomach upsets after eating chicken of the woods, but nothing more serious than that. If in doubt, try a small bit and see how you feel over the next hour.

from *Swallows and Amazons* to pass by in a sailing boat, shouting 'golly gosh!' and 'simply smashing with lashings of ginger beer!' – but sadly they didn't appear.

Lunchtime had come and gone with no food for us and we continued paddling with rumbling stomachs. In the distance we heard gunshots, and plenty of them. As we drew closer I climbed up the bank to see what was going on. At the edge of a wheat field a couple of fellows were decoying for pigeons. This is a technique that involves placing a dozen plastic pigeons on the ground in a 'V'-formation facing into the wind to emulate the pattern of a group of feeding pigeons. Pigeons flying above assume there is food available and fly down to join the decoys. I was half tempted to ask for a few pigeons, but rather than risk being shot or giving away their position, I climbed back into the kayak. Suddenly, out of nowhere, something came crashing through the trees; there was a flash of grey, followed by a splash, and up popped a freshly dispatched pigeon. Food for free is a glorious concept and we hadn't even fired the gun! We found two more pigeons that had met a similar fate and immediately had the basis for a good evening meal.

Our original plan of making it to our target near to Barcombe Mills turned out to be a gross overestimate. By 6pm we were nearing the village of Newick with sore, tired arms and cramped legs. As we got close to the weir, I went ahead to do a recce of the approaching obstacle: it was a 45-degree chute leading into a swirling pool with a narrow exit. I paddled up to it and then, after seeing it was something that would involve a 'walk around', turned the kayak to paddle back to Tom and the coracle. The river, however, had other ideas. 'No, no, no … NOOOOOO!'

The swift current by the weir had taken hold of the kayak and sucked me down backwards as I tried to paddle upstream. It was actually quite fun, one of those rare, unexpected moments of danger when you know there won't be a disaster of epic proportions – a bit like peeing into the wind.

After the excitement of the weir, and half a kayakful of water had been bailed out, we continued on our way … well, I did. Tom dragged his kayak up over the weir so he could shoot the rapids one more time, and fill his kayak with water all over again.

It was an absolute relief to climb out of the kayaks; we patted down soggy skin and wrinkly fingers with a towel, and we dressed in dry clothes. We hung our hammocks and ponchos in a small wood on a hill, overlooking the river. Below us, black-and-white cows stood chewing grass, a kestrel hung in the air looking for mice, and pigeons clapped over the fields of barley. The evening sunlight shone straight through the trees and lit up the smoke as we got the fire going. The temperature was perfect; this was Sussex in all its glory and exactly the reason why I had left London.

Looking at our rations for the evening we were spoilt for choice. The three pigeons were plucked and de-breasted (the chicken of the woods we would save for the following night) and we put on a billycan of rice and runner beans to add bulk to our meaty feast. The pigeon breasts were liberally doused in salt and pepper, flash-fried in a hot pan for three minutes each side and left to rest. Then we made the sauce using some sorrel we found in a field by the river.

SORREL SAUCE

The fields and hedgerows of Britain are home to one of the wild larder's greatest assets – and in profusion, I hasten to add. Sorrel is one of the most versatile of the wild greens: its bright green, shield-shaped leaves have an intense citrus kick which adds interest to any dish, be it a simple salad or a piquant sauce for game or fish. Tom and I had come across patches of sorrel between strategically laid cowpats and gathered enough to make a sauce for the pigeon breasts.

INGREDIENTS

- A handful or bunch of young sorrel leaves
- The zest of half a lemon
- 3 tbsp olive oil
- A good pinch of salt and pepper

1 Stack the sorrel leaves on top of one another and finely chop them so you end up with thin slivers. Chop the lemon zest into small pieces.

2 Put the chopped sorrel and zest into a small bowl and add the olive oil, salt and pepper. Give it a good stir and leave to sit for ten minutes to allow the flavours to combine.

3 This piquant sauce is best used drizzled over meat or fish. For best results, use it as a dip for chunks of pan-fried pigeon breast.

We each took up a fork, speared a breast, and dipped away at the sorrel sauce. Few things have tasted better than those pigeon breasts. Food for me is all about who, when and where – I doubt even Claridges could have offered me a better dish at that moment. Out in the Sussex countryside, sitting around a fire and eating the freshest free food cooked in the most simple of ways, was the place to be.

After our tasting menu of country morsels, my mind drifted over the day's events, and one incident in particular: 'Right, Tom, the village is just up the road, and I believe the first round is on you!' So off we strode into the twilight, across the meadows and past the cows, to water ourselves before the final bell of last orders rang out across the village green.

THURSDAY 13th AUGUST

Try as I might, I just couldn't sleep last night. I like to sleep on my front, which is a little uncomfortable in a hammock. So at about midnight I moved onto the floor by the fire and finally nodded off.

At 4am the rain started, gently at first, but it steadily grew into a proper downpour. I got into the hammock under the poncho and tried to get back to sleep. It was impossible – the rain was running down the hammock lines and slowly soaking my sleeping bag. Even Tom, with his swanky new set-up, got drenched too. The rain continued for four hours and everything, save what was under the coracle, got wet.

It was not a great start to day two. My body ached from the day of paddling and the last thing I wanted to do was go through it all again. I reviewed the map, and the distance we had covered yesterday, and then I looked at how far we had to go today. Rather than merely ambitious, it was inconceivable! It was time to regroup and assess the situation.

The section of river below us was a popular fishing stretch. I didn't want to upset any anglers if I could help it – most of them are armed with catapults to fire out bait and the two of us would make easy targets for a disgruntled fisherman. Everything needed to dry out, our next destination was out of reach, and so it was time to call for back-up.

This was supposed to be a fun break from the tree house rather than a gruelling expedition – I wanted to enjoy it and I'm sure Tom did too. Fortunately the sun came out at 8am and it turned into a lovely warm day. We took our chance to hang everything up in the sun and then I called a proper support vehicle to come and take us over to the Cuckmere.

Somehow we managed to fit both kayaks and the coracle onto the tiny roof rack of my mother's car. She happened to be heading down to Cuckmere Haven for the day to meet some friends, so it was all very convenient. Neither Tom nor I could resist stopping at our favourite cider barn to pick up some mead to enjoy later in the evening. We didn't have that far to paddle so our day was more about having fun and looking for food, rather than clocking up the miles. We got dropped off at the Cuckmere and we loaded up the boats before heading downstream to set up camp. Charlie's parents used to own a pub in a nearby village, and a local landowner had been a regular. I had given him a call a few days ago and he was more than happy to let us stay on his land as long as we cleared up afterwards.

Most of the trees around our designated camping area were unsuitable for hammocks – hawthorn. To avoid a prickly night I chose a spot with a willow that looked hammock-friendly. I had already decided I was going to sleep on the floor under my poncho, but Tom insisted on setting up his hammock rather than lower himself to my style of shelter. The first two limbs he attached it to seemed sturdy enough, but as soon as he got in the hammock there was a creak followed by a loud 'crrrraaack …' After a bit of rearranging Tom finally found one that held, but for how long?

We found some large rocks for the fireplace, which we placed over some cowpats that had been dropped in our corner of the field, and then went on a walk to collect a mountain of firewood for the night. It was scarce

at first, but luckily we came across a large fallen ash that met all our firewood needs.

Once we had set up camp we moved on to a spot of recreational fishing. I thought we could catch a pike for supper. I knew there were pike in this stretch of river, but my previous catches had mainly been in the dead of winter. At the moment the river was so clogged up with weed there seemed little hope of using a spinner.

We spent the afternoon fishing but caught nothing. I did see a perfect-sized pike shoot out of the water to get a closer look at my lure, but after catching sight of me, it disappeared into the thick weed, and flatly refused to show further interest. The morning's rainfall seemed a distant memory: the hot sun made it perfect swimming weather, so we messed about in the coracle for a while, testing its limitations – I soon discovered it definitely wasn't the sort you can stand up in.

At 5pm we went in search of free food for our evening meal. I knew what sort of hedgerow greens we could expect – this was the same area where I taught foraging. We gathered some sorrel, nettles, dandelion leaves, chickweed and some hedge garlic. As we passed a smallholding we saw a box with a sign saying 'Eggs: £1 for half a dozen'. Well, technically we had found them in the hedgerow, so we left the money and took the eggs so we could have an omelette in the morning before the final push.

Back at camp we put together a hedgerow salad and doused it liberally with vinaigrette. Tom got the fire going and prepared a pot of rice and beans, while I sliced up the chicken of the woods on the only convenient chopping surface, the blade of one of the kayak paddles. We fried up the mushroom in my small frying pan. It had been about a year since I last had some and Tom had never tried it. Chicken of the woods really does have a smell and texture similar to chicken.

After a filling supper we had a couple of glasses of mead as the sun dropped behind the downs. I got out the wind-up radio and we took turns to charge it up. We talked about book writing and the fact that we had both fallen into the same line of business. We drank some more mead – it was strong stuff and, coupled with a full belly, the two of us began to feel sleepy. Tom got into his hammock and was out like a light. It took me a while to nod off. I lay under the stars, listening to the crickets and the occasional snore from Tom.

FRIDAY 14th AUGUST

As soon as I woke up I was dying for the loo. It was 8am. If we wanted to run downstream with the tide then we had to leave soon. Not far away was the lock where the river became tidal. There had obviously been some recent building activity because, next to the lock, was the welcome sight of a portaloo.

I don't think I have ever been so pleased to see one in all my life. I raced over to the lock and climbed up the ladder to cross over the walkway, and then I had to negotiate a few gates. Finally I grabbed some dock leaves from the hedge by the loo and ducked inside. I needn't have bothered – there was even a full roll of toilet paper on the holder. Bliss.

When I got back Tom had the fire going and was busy knocking up a six-egg omelette. I picked some sorrel, tore it up for essential flavouring and tossed it in the pan. After breakfast we struck camp and left without a trace. We loaded up the coracle and the tide was already on its way out: time to get going. Low tide was at midday and we had roughly three hours to make the coast.

The river seemed much more overgrown than I remembered and in parts it was not much wider than the kayak. The thick weed made it tough work to push on but we had no time to lose. As we came around a bend, a smell suddenly materialised out of nowhere that made me gag – there in the water was the carcass of a dead swan teeming with maggots. I managed to get around it using the smallest, quickest strokes possible so I didn't disturb it. I didn't have to bother warning Tom – he heard the heaving soon enough …

As we passed the village of Alfriston the river gradually opened up, and the vegetation around us began changing too. We started to see evidence of coastal plant life – sea beet and the occasional frond of seaweed. Even the fish changed and we saw mullet swimming along the slick, muddy riverbank searching for food. We took turns trying to knock them out using our paddles as spears but without success. The valley before us opened up as we continued with the flow of the tide. I kept checking the long fronds of weed to see whether the tide had turned. It was 11.30am, and there was still some distance to cover.

We stopped for a rest in the shadow of the White Horse. This section of the river became very shallow and we had to manhandle the coracle over the rocks with all the gear still in it. There seemed to be a small puddle forming in the bottom, but I wasn't going to worry about it just yet …

On we paddled, stopping momentarily to stock up on samphire, which coated the mudflats either side of the river. Then it happened. The weed had started to point the other way – the tide had turned.

The last mile was a real effort and we took it in turns to tow the coracle. Eventually we reached our exit point and the car park of the Golden Galleon pub. It was not a bad place to finish – there was little hope of reaching open water, as the incoming tide was far too strong. The coracle did contain quite an impressive puddle by the time we took it out of the water. The canvas had worn through in places and needed a good patching up.

It had been a wonderful journey full of surprises, and I had seen another side to Sussex I hadn't really thought about before – the way of the river …

SUNDAY 16th AUGUST

It is great to be back in the branches; although I enjoyed my taste of nomadic self-sufficiency, it has made me appreciate my tree house settlement. Here I have everything I need, and I know when and where to obtain my food.

Ten thousand years ago, during the Mesolithic Period, bands of hunter-gatherers would have moved around the landscape in much the same way as Tom and me (although probably without the wind-up radio and digital camera), perhaps even with a homemade boat of sorts. It must have been incredibly hard work and now I can fully appreciate how the dawn of farming changed things. Farming first started in the Middle East at the beginning of the Neolithic Period, 6,000 years ago, but the practice didn't reach Britain's shores until 4,000 years ago. The domestication of crops and animals gave our ancestors the chance to live a more sedentary existence, and the first concept of a home was established.

With this in mind, I am having a bit of an identity crisis. On the one hand, I hunt and gather for a certain proportion of my food – a Mesolithic way

of life – but then on the other hand, I also have a permanent dwelling and vegetable patch where I grow my own crops – a Neolithic style of living. I think I'm particularly confused as I have just started experimenting with animal husbandry – my landlords' menagerie.

Perhaps I have been thinking too much about things: these days we take farming and domestication for granted, but what must the hunter-gatherers have thought of the first farmers and their 'alien' concept? No doubt a bit of trading took place between the two cultures: a haunch of venison for a load of wheat, etc. But surely the farmers were better off because they could still live from the land – the hunters didn't have the knowledge to grow crops to fill the seasonal gap. Anyway, enough anthropological debate – I have animals to feed!

At 8am I fed all the animals and let out the chickens; I just have to keep an eye on the other livestock (the horses, sheep, etc.). When it gets dark I have to come back and put the chickens to bed, and lock them in for the night so the foxes don't have a midnight feast.

Breakfast was quite the occasion: the chickens kindly supplied me with four eggs so I had a huge omelette packed with spinach and slivers of red onion. If I am going to get four eggs every day, I'm going to have to think of things to do with them. Pickled eggs? Could make a good snack.

I spent the afternoon unpacking from the boat trip. After some time lazing in the hammock reading a little fishing literature, *The Accidental Angler* by Charles Rangeley-Wilson, I started to think about supper. I liked the idea of pigeon (as always), but fate was the final decision maker, and my nourishment for the evening turned out to be rabbit – or so I thought. On closer inspection the rabbit appeared to be suffering from myxomatosis: a lethal disease for a rabbit that causes a most unpleasant, slow death. The swift dispatch had been a favour to the beast, but I am not one for eating diseased animals.

As I wandered past hedgerows ripe with fat blackberries and tangled with mature hops, a pigeon flew lazily out of left field. At that moment I was in the middle of a hedgerow pee. I managed to get both hands on the gun and 'bang'! The pigeon crumpled in mid-air amidst a flurry of feathers and floated to the ground. I found a few field mushrooms on the way home, and picked some courgettes and runner beans for a vegetable medley. Great nosh.

I went up to my landlords' farm at about 9pm to find all chickens present and correct on their perches. It was quite odd to look inside the coop with the torch and see four surprised chickens staring back at me.

Apparently the tree house made the front cover of the *Sunday Times* Home section under the headline 'Special Branch'! Unfortunately there was rather a cheesy picture of yours truly obscuring most of my lovely house.

MONDAY 17TH AUGUST

I woke at 7.30am to go and tend to my animal duties. I fed the chickens first and they rewarded me with three eggs. After feeding the cats I went to see Bangers. The big pig was flat out on the grass and at first I thought she might have keeled over and died – that would have been a great start, although I suppose I would have got first dibs on some choice cuts. But with the faintest shake of the bucket of feed she was up, bounding across the field – the food lasted all of a minute.

The little pony that shares the field with Bangers has such a big quiff falling over its eyes I was not sure it could see me. It must have done though, because it started chasing me, and making funny noises, until I had given it the food.

After feeding time I had a relaxed morning. Breakfast was an omelette, with some fairy ring champignons and sorrel that I found in Bangers' field, washed down with espresso. It was possibly the best tree house breakfast to date; the eggs have made a serious impact on the first meal of the day.

I began making shotgun key rings to sell at a stall I have been asked to do at a foraging day in October; the organisers saw the tree house article in

CEP (BOLETUS EDULIS)

DESCRIPTION **Also known as the penny bun, and in Italy the porcini, the cep is found in woodland, often associated with oak or beech. The brown cap is smooth and dry, measuring 2–6in (5–15cm) in diameter. Underneath the cap the pores are spongy in appearance, and are white at first, then turning yellow. The light brown stem is short and bulbous, and the flesh is white and firm. August–November.**

USES **The cep is one of the most sought-after mushrooms and worth a few bob. They are part of the *Boletus* family, which is distinguished by sponge-like pores instead of gills. They make fantastic eating and can be used in an enormous variety of ways. As they tend to deteriorate soon after picking, they are usually dried. Once dried, they can be reconstituted in soups and stews, or ground into a powder as a flavouring.**

Unfortunately we aren't the only species to be partial to the cep's wonderful flavour: grubs, maggots and slugs often get to them before us, so always make sure they are free from infestation when you cut them in half.

the *Sunday Times* and asked if I would be interested. I have made the key rings out of a small length of hazel with the metal end of a cartridge nailed to it – a great way of recycling my spent cartridges but, more importantly, each one represents an animal I have shot and eaten.

The *Sunday Times* article has generated a second flurry of media interest and I have been getting a few requests. Today I had an interview with an Irish radio station. As I listened to the presenter I had to do my best to keep Father Ted out of my head. And then he said, 'Now, Nick, I have to say, you sound quite posh!' I paused – what on earth was I supposed to say? 'You sound quite Irish …' Needless to say, the conversation didn't last much longer after that.

I found a cep growing next to the tree house today: the king of mushrooms on my doorstep! A bloody slug had had a go at most of it, so on the off-chance that there might be more lurking in the wood, I went for a wander. There were no ceps but there were lots of sickeners at the top of the wood between some larch trees. These ones had bright red caps and, as the name suggests, are best left alone. Mushrooms are the chink in my foraging armour. I have been gradually learning more about them over the last five years, but they are not a foodstuff to be messed with – the slightest carelessness can land you in serious trouble and might even kill you.

Today I got an invite to go on a television programme for UKTV Food. I will have to find something interesting to feed to the presenter Tom Parker-Bowles.

TUESDAY 18th AUGUST 27°C!

After two months of owning a copy of *Walden; or Life in the Woods* by Henry David Thoreau I still don't get what he is going on about, but I do know it certainly isn't about living in the woods. Had I been planning a revolution or something it might have been useful, but as I'm not, I took him at his word – 'Simplify, simplify, simplify ...' – and used some pages of this worthy tome (which inspired the likes of Marx and Gandhi) to light a fire. After drinking a cup of tea with water boiled using some of America's finest literature, I too felt the bristles of inspiration – hunger-wise.

I collected three eggs from the chickens this morning – one of them is not doing its job properly.

Ceps are meant to be dotting the landscape at this time of year so for today's breakfast I went further afield to find some. I found several under an oak tree in a field quite a long way from the wood. In fact, I think they are actually bay bolete, a species almost as tasty as the cep, and perfectly edible. I used a couple for breakfast, but I am going to try drying the rest, grinding them into powder, and using them for more challenging culinary pursuits.

After breakfast I had to do some admin; I filled in the form to renew my passport, and I read and signed my book contract ready to send back to the publishers. My bank card stopped working a week ago so I really need that advance! To try to rectify my financial situation, and prevent any more ludicrous bank charges, I went to the bank to try to increase my overdraft. I had to run through a questionnaire on my income and

outgoings with a personal banker. She asked what my job was so I showed her the book contract as proof that I had money coming in. 'Oh! You're the man who lives in a tree! I've been following it in *Reader's Digest*!' As I had a fan, I had hoped the bank would be kind and process my request, but no, of course not. In future I might start keeping my cash under the mattress …

Dan and his fiancée were due for supper. I had planned to go out and shoot the main course, but Dan told me not to bother. He brought some pork chops from one of his recently dispatched Gloucester Old Spots and some *lardo* (belly fat, which you just slice thinly and eat – Italian style). He also brought some plums, parsley, cucumber, mint and grapes, all from his own back yard.

I boiled up the remaining samphire from the boat trip and we had a feast! We talked about his plans for the campsite next year and about his previous life as a journalist. He also offered to lend me some solar panels! I declined in the end, because the idea of having electricity in the tree house just didn't feel right, and also because I would be terrified of breaking them – a lot of debris falls on the tree house roof! They left at 11pm, and I tidied, did some writing, had a cup of tea and went to bed.

Wednesday 19th August 27°C!

I woke to something big landing on the roof and shot out of bed with a 'What, what?' Outside it was beautiful and I walked out onto the balcony in my birthday suit. After a quick trip to the loo (quick being the operative word when you are starkers and there are mosquitoes around), I chucked on shorts and a T-shirt and went to sort out the animals. I then had to nip to my mother's house to use the computer and update the blog.

I devoted the rest of the day to food experimentation. Over the last few days I had saved up seven eggs so I could pickle them to use as snack food. My plan was to hard-boil them, peel them, smoke them for two minutes and then pickle them in cider vinegar with rosemary, peppercorns and grated wild horseradish. I looked through my copy of *The Best of Mrs Beeton's Jams, Pickles & Preserves*, which has consistently proved to be my first port of call for any preserving. I changed the recipe slightly to fit my ingredients. One egg wouldn't fit in the jar, so I ate it whole.

Then I moved on to the ceps I found yesterday. I've got a recipe in mind for them but I needed to dry them first. I had two choices: slice them and thread them together to hang over Bertha; or set them up on wire racks over a smoky oak fire. I opted for the latter to add a hint of smokiness to the drying process.

Next I tried using the smoke to 'finish' my rabbit pelts. I had a stack of them drying under the tree house, covered with a mosquito net to stop the flies laying eggs on them. To limit any damage, I tried one skin at first for about an hour. The skin dried extremely well but did get quite brittle, although as I am not making clothes with it this isn't really a problem. I put the other skins around and over the fire and left them for an hour. After smoking, I got some pliers, removed all the nails and took the pelts off the boards. What a quick-fix curing process!

HOW TO DRY MUSHROOMS

First I cut the mushrooms into ¼in (5mm) slices and built up a smouldering fire. Then I moved two tree stumps into position either side of the fire, placed a grill between them 2–3ft (61–91cm) above the fire, and arranged some boards around it to control the breeze and create more of a chamber. Every time the fire burst into flame I doused it with a little water to keep it smoky. After 3–4 hours I had a decent batch of smoky, air-dried porcini slices.

Jeff the pheasant has been gone for a long time. I have been taking care not to shoot any pheasants with white rings around their necks. Today I finally saw him again and not in the best circumstances. On the other side of the wood, I came across his dead body. He hadn't been dead long and the thick white ring around his neck looked almost angelic. I was sad. Jeff had been a familiar face throughout the tree house build, and although we exchanged few words, he had been pleasant, pheasant company.

I went to get the shovel, dug a hole, and placed him at the bottom. I threw him a handful of rice, just as I had done before, and filled in the hole. I think what frustrated me was that this was not of my own doing. I had always thought that if push came to shove, Jeff would end up in the pot. But like so many things with this way of life, it was out of my hands. Mother Nature holds the cards and pulls the strings – not me.

Later on I picked Clare up from the station and dropped her off at her parents' house. She has moved back there to save some money before starting a job in Biarritz for six months. When she got in the car she said I smelt nice – like smoked salmon. Great. So I smell of cured fish!

Her parents have a fine collection of apple trees in their garden. I took my chance, grabbed the patio umbrella, and began poking the trees. Apples rained down and I kept going until I had filled my rucksack. Cider anyone?

THURSDAY 20th AUGUST

I found an interesting passage in *Robinson Crusoe* today: 'In a word, the nature and experience of things dictated to me upon just reflection, that all the good things of this world, are no farther good to us, than they are for our use.'

This struck a chord in me, and made perfect sense – perhaps I can become less of a hoarder. I remembered that after the first pages of Henry David Thoreau's *Walden* ended up in the fire, there was a line that caught my eye: 'Simplify, simplify, simplify …'

I decided to skim through what was left of *Walden* and found there were many parallels to my own experience over the last few months, even down to the squirrel racing across my roof in the mornings. It is a shame I struggled to make sense of the book to begin with – it does get better! However, although my present living arrangements may be similar to his, I'm not sure if we sat together over tea and roast squirrel, we would see eye to eye.

I suppose it is feasible to compare *Crusoe* and *Walden*: each came to spend time in nature for different reasons. The thing I find strange is that Thoreau *wanted* to live in solitude, while Crusoe had it forced upon him. Also, the latter was extremely resourceful and built a comfortable existence, whereas Thoreau settled for a basic lifestyle and lacked the ambition to improve his surroundings.

As a source of inspiration for me and my tree house dwelling, it is a surprise that I have found Defoe's fictional masterpiece more compelling and useful as a resource than a real person's actual account. Perhaps if Thoreau had read *Robinson Crusoe*, a book published 135 years prior to *Walden*, he may have strived for a more ambitious, comfortable existence.

FRIDAY 21ST AUGUST ☼ 26°C!

The blackberries are in full flourish at last! I had them for breakfast on my way to sort out the animals this morning. I even managed to pick the only remaining raspberries that the birds hadn't got at. It was a fine example of 'ambulant consumption' – a theme made popular in Richard Mabey's 1972 classic, *Food for Free*. I collected four eggs, but the omelette had to wait.

I spent the morning walking around picking as many blackberries as I could. I have always strived to turn wild food into something special, so this week's luxury item is a big tub of extra-thick double cream. I want to make that most indulgent of desserts, blackberry fool.

It couldn't have been a better day to lounge around the fireplace. *Test Match Special* was covering the Ashes and I listened as Broad and Trott gave the Aussies what for. It was a real caning! My only problem was having to wind up the radio every so often, and it developed a habit of running out just as the excitement reached a crescendo.

By mid-afternoon I was ready to eat some more blackberries so I began to make my fool. As a test, I picked a few leaves of mint, wrapped one around a blackberry, and popped it in my mouth. It was delicious, so I made some minted sugar to go in the fool.

SUNDAY 23RD AUGUST ☼ 26°C!

Today was spent out and about rock climbing and swimming at a nearby reservoir. I returned to the tree house at 6pm to find an unexpected batch

BRAMBLE (RUBUS FRUTICOSUS)

DESCRIPTION A very common shrub of hedges, woods and waste ground. Arching stems, up to 10ft (3m), have sharp prickles. Flowers are pink or white with five petals, and appear May–August. The fruit, or blackberry, ripens from green to black and is available from August to October.

USES There probably isn't much I can tell you about the blackberry that you don't already know, except that there are around 400 micro-species in Britain alone, each slightly different in size, taste and juiciness. The blackberry is the first thing most people tend to harvest from the wild larder, often as children. It is a chance to gorge on the closest thing to free sweets! The berries can be eaten as they are, made into puddings, tarts, fools – the list is endless. My personal favourite is the fool. Don't pick blackberries after 10 October – according to folklore that is when the devil comes and pees on every bush in the country.

of gifts! I am always concerned about unknown intruders. I love having people to visit, but this was different.

There were a dozen eggs, a punnet of plums, four cooking apples, eight eating apples and a selection of herbs tied in a bunch. No note, no phone call – who on earth? It was such a kind gesture I was eager to find out who the visitor was. All the people I thought it might have been came up a blank. I have a real mystery on my hands.

BLACKBERRY FOOL

Please note I didn't have much weighing equipment so here I used a pint glass.

INGREDIENTS

Juice and zest of 1 lemon

½ pint (300ml) white granulated sugar

2 sprigs mint

1 pint (600ml) blackberries

1 pint (600ml) extra-thick double cream

Serves 2 (or one big helping!)

1 First, zest the lemon (you can squeeze the juice straight into the pan). Pound the sugar and mint leaves in a pestle and mortar until the sugar has turned green.

2 In a pan over a fire (or hob), heat the blackberries and allow them to break down naturally until they begin to release some of their juice. Add the sugar, lemon juice and zest, and stir until warmed through. Put the mixture to one side until it is completely cool.

3 Place a few fresh berries in the bottom of a suitable vessel and add some of the blackberry mixture. Add a good dollop of cream and press down into the glass. Add another layer of berries and the mixture, and then a final layer of cream. Decorate with mint flowers or leaves and blackberries.

4 Eat at once. Or, if you have a fridge, put it in there for an hour and enjoy in sunny weather! A good addition is elderberries, which should be around at the same time of year.

MONDAY 24th AUGUST

There are many strange and unrestricted eccentricities lurking in the deepest corners of the countryside, and this is probably why I love it so much. Within the confines of the cliffs and beaches of Britain, weird shit is *always* afoot. Tonight, for example, I am on the balcony with the sound of bagpipes drifting across on the evening breeze – in Sussex?

Today was interesting. I woke up as usual at 8am and went to feed the animals and water the patch; my summer harvest is now slowly tailing off. I had received a tip-off about ceps from one of the campers I taught foraging to – he was clearly not a mushroom hunter himself, or he would have kept his mouth shut. I made a beeline to the place where I spent the first 14 years of my life, Ashdown Forest. Back then, in my eyes, wild fungi were not as highly prized as they are today; the bizarre fruiting bodies were simply part and parcel of the changing seasons.

I parked a stone's throw away from my old family home, and I immediately noticed something unusual: a chap with long, black pigtails was pulling something that looked like an animal hide around a rope lashed to a tree. Curiosity got the better of me and I walked over to say hello. As it turned out, his Native American appearance was misleading and his name was actually Steve. However, even if his name didn't live up to his hairstyle, his accommodation did – he lived nearby in a teepee. It was good to meet someone else living in a similar situation to me, and we exchanged banter on the pros and cons of living an outdoor lifestyle.

I watched him stretching and working a complete fox hide – head, tail and legs – back and forth over the rope. This was 'brain tanning'. The idea is to boil up the brain from the animal for its essential oils, and then you work it into the lattice of the skin, using the rope. The oils prevent the skin sticking back together and becoming stiff. Steve told me that this skin was nearly done, having had about ten hours of work. He was going to finish it by smoking and then rubbing it with cedar berry and other fragrant oils. I sniffed the hide – it did smell pretty foul.

I explained to Steve what I was up to and he showed quite a bit of interest, and after a bit of conversation about yurts, deer and wild food, we exchanged details. Apparently rabbit skins can be cured in a day using egg whites as an alternative to brains. I may have to call upon his expertise if I decide I need more pelts to make a hat or a waistcoat.

I left him to continue his work and he gave me his own cep tip: he said he had once found a 6½lb (3kg) beast of a mushroom just over the road. This spot was sounding better and better. Excited at the prospect of a record haul, I raced off into the woods. After a couple of hours, though, all I had found were a few tiny, slug-ridden impostors.

Having had no luck with the ceps I had another think about my alternative currency – barter. I am already paying rent for the wood by bartering, but I wanted to see what else could still be bartered in the country, and how many people would consider it an acceptable form of currency.

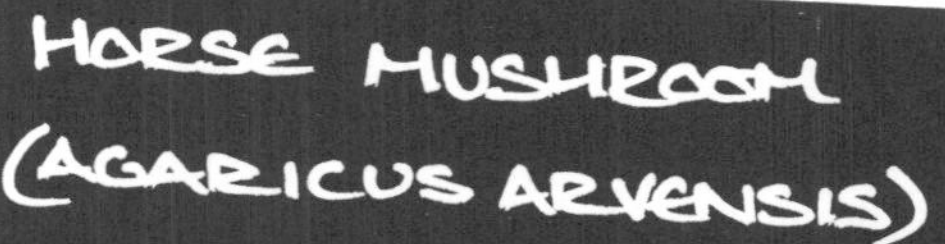

DESCRIPTION **A traditional grassland species, the horse mushroom resembles the field mushroom, but is larger with greyish gills and smells of almonds. The cap can measure up to 1ft (30cm) across when fully grown. August–November.**

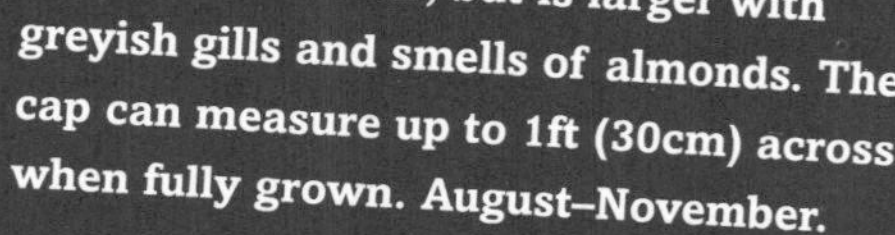

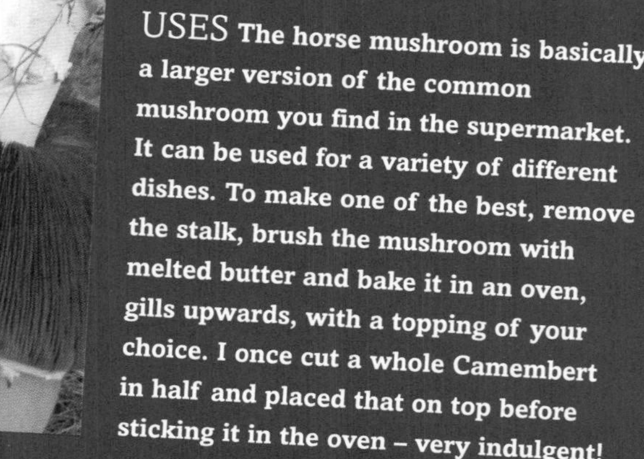

USES **The horse mushroom is basically a larger version of the common mushroom you find in the supermarket. It can be used for a variety of different dishes. To make one of the best, remove the stalk, brush the mushroom with melted butter and bake it in an oven, gills upwards, with a topping of your choice. I once cut a whole Camembert in half and placed that on top before sticking it in the oven – very indulgent!**

I went to see James, a local dairy farmer. I can see his farm from the woods and I have watched his tractors cutting silage in the fields next door. When I called him to introduce myself, I explained my project, and how I was eager to offer a bit of graft in return for a dribble of milk. His answer was not what I expected: 'With all the Health and Safety garb today, it would take more time to train you to work – sod it! You can have the milk for free.' As I didn't want it to seem like I was on the take, I said I would use the milk to make some cheese for him in return – that was, after all, why I wanted the milk in the first place.

James was as good as his word. I got to the farm and found a load of barns chock full of the standard black-and-white Sussex milk machines. The smell blew me away at first – that many cows' arses in a confined space! I tried not to gag. A few deep breaths and a couple of minutes of acclimatisation put to rest any involuntary reflexes.

The farm is a fine example of what makes Sussex tick. Although James didn't have the time to give me a tour he told me to help myself to the fresh, unpasturised milk. James also said that the farm supplies a leading supermarket chain, and I was pleased that, once again, I was bypassing the corporate stranglehold of the supermarkets and going straight to the source. I had a taste of the milk as I filled up my bottle – it was fresher than fresh and a moment of pure dairy fantasy!

As my mushroom forage had been disappointing so far, I went home via some fields that were home to some horses, and a few scattered oak trees. I was on the lookout for chicken of the woods, the fungus that favours the oak, and the horse mushroom that is found in pastures. I walked up to the nearest oak and straightaway I found my supper in the form of a single fungus: an enormous horse mushroom that was bigger than my face!

I was expecting my mother for supper, so I asked her to bring down a bottle of white wine, butter and some Parmesan, and knocked together a damn fine mushroom risotto.

TUESDAY 25th AUGUST

This morning I taught foraging. As the summer has worn on, the wild larder has finally started to change. Following my success with the blackberry fool, I planned to incorporate this into the lesson. I also added another ingredient that was locally abundant – elderberries.

ELDER (SAMBUCUS NIGRA)

DESCRIPTION A common shrub found in woods, hedgerows and waysides (up to 33ft/10m), with corky bark and scaly twigs. Leaflets are dark green and slightly toothed, and grow in groups of 5–7. Sprays of small, sweet-smelling white flowers appear in June and July. Clusters of small, reddish-black berries appear from August to October.

USES Elderberries do contain minute traces of cyanide. I always enjoy telling my foragers this and saying we will be eating them, just to see the look of horror on their faces. Only then do I tell them that we will be cooking them first, which renders them safe to eat. You should never eat the berries raw; one or two are fine but don't gorge!

The berries used to be extremely popular for making elderberry wine and Kent was once planted with orchards of elder for that very reason. These days it is used more often in jam and jelly making. Elderberries are rich in flavonoids and vitamins A and C, and as a cordial are quite effective at fighting off colds and coughs. The elder tree is steeped in folklore: elder trees were often planted adjacent to dwellings in the belief they would offer protection against dark forces. Elder leaves are traditionally hung above doorways on May's eve to bring protection and good luck.

I took the group through their herbal teas, stinger pesto, rabbit stew, pan-fried squirrel and, as my *pièce de résistance,* the fool. I always enjoy rustling up these feasts with the campers. Cooking for others has always been something I enjoy. Cooking for myself at the tree house is fine, but if there is no one to share it with, sometimes I get a bit lazy with my inventiveness.

I thought the tree house was going to blow away tonight – with me in it!

Wednesday 26th August WIND

Today began like any other but something told me it was going to end up being hectic – the quiet ones always do. I went up to the farm to feed the animals. The chickens are always quite feisty when I let them out in the mornings. The big cockerel, Kochin, has a set routine. He comes out of the coop, ruffles his feathers, and immediately pounces on the nearest hen in an unromantic attempt at procreation. Today it was my turn.

> **'A dessert without cheese is like a beautiful woman with only one eye ...'**
>
> JEAN ANTHELME BRILLAT-SAVARIN

When I opened the coop door, rather than move to the side to let the chickens shoot out, I was looking over at Bangers to make sure she was okay (she was very still, but probably bluffing as usual). Kochin landed at my feet and, deciding I was a bit too close for comfort, began kicking, flapping and pecking at my exposed leg. I ran towards the hens, hoping he would turn his advances to them, and fortunately he did.

Today my plan was to try my hand at cheese making. I had always been put off by the word 'rennet' in cheese-making recipes – having to use something that sounds like it comes from a chemist just isn't right to me.

The recipe I chose was so simple I felt foolish for not having tried it before. Rather than a moulding, blue-veined stinker, this one would produce a fresh, pure cheese called queso blanco, also known as halloumi or paneer, depending upon where you are in the world. After my experience collecting the milk to make this cheese, I have christened it 'Sussex Heave'.

Sussex Heave

The only piece of 'specialist' equipment you will need is a thermometer.

Ingredients

3¼ pints (1.8 litres) milk

1¾fl. oz (50ml) cider vinegar

1½ tsp salt

1 Heat the milk for 20–25 minutes, making sure the temperature does not go above 85°C/185°F. Give it a good stir occasionally to make sure the heat is evenly distributed. Slowly add the cider vinegar and stir. Remove from heat and allow to sit for ten minutes.

2 By now you should have a collection of curds and whey. Using a big slotted spoon, take out all the curds and put them into a sieve over a bowl to drain.

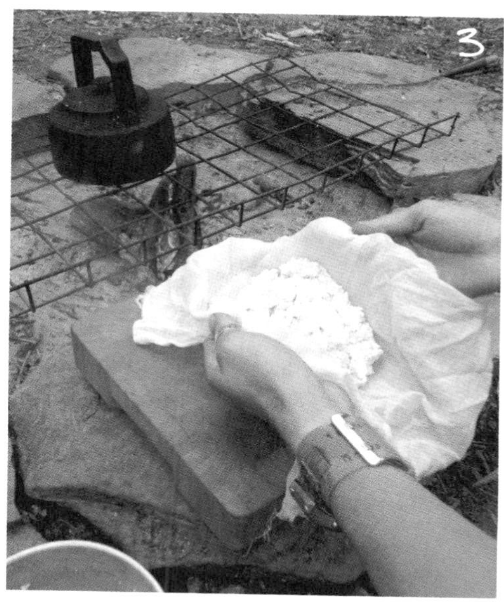

3 Once drained, empty the bowl of any excess whey, and tip in the curds. Add the salt and stir vigorously. At this stage, feel free to add any extras: chilli flakes, chopped black olives, basil, sun-dried tomatoes, etc. Tip the curds into some muslin.

4 Tie the curds up tightly in the muslin and leave to hang over a bowl for 1 hour to drain off any excess moisture.

5 To compress the cheese, place it in a press or mould. Leave for 3–4 hours. I used two round containers, one inside the other, with a heavy brick on top.

6 Eat as it comes or fry in a hot pan until golden brown, with a good squeeze of lemon juice! It will keep in a fridge for up to a week.

While I was compressing the cheese, to fill the time, I made another batch of meadowsweet beer. The meadowsweet flowers have largely disappeared, so I could only use the leaves. With a brew under way, I was still waiting for the cheese, so I took most of the eggs I had been left by my mystery visitor and made another batch of smoked, pickled eggs.

By the time I had dropped the last egg into the pickling jar, the cheese was ready to try. I was starving! The cheese was definitely worth the effort – I must have eaten half of it in one sitting. I fried slices until they were golden brown and doused them in lemon juice and pepper.

Then I took the shotgun out to get supper. Drizzle began to fall at about 6pm. The rabbits didn't seem to mind the weather and were out in force. As I walked across the field near the copse that was often a useful spot for rabbits, I spied one by a bunch of thistles. I fired and it disappeared – damn. I took two paces forwards and another rabbit, a big fat jack, sprinted towards the nearest holly bush for cover. I fired the second barrel just as he shot behind the bush – double damn!

I know I'm not the most skilled marksman in the world. My usual approach when I go out with the gun is to keep everything crossed and hope for the best. So imagine my surprise when I walked up to the holly bush and found one big dead rabbit! I then thought, if I had been that lucky by the holly bush, what about the thistles? And, lo and behold – another rabbit. Perhaps all the practice is finally paying off. To cap it all, on the way home by the side of the wood, I managed to bag a third rabbit.

I sat under the tree house in my drenched clothes, but I couldn't have been happier – my most successful shoot yet. I paunched all three rabbits, and skinned and de-boned one for supper. The German TV crew had brought me a jar of curry sauce, so I thought I might as well try a rabbit Rogan Josh.

I lit Bertha and stacked her high with a few chunky pieces of oak and ash. I thought it would be a good idea to go and sort out the animals before settling in for the night, so I walked over to the farm in the pouring rain. Then I experienced another first: someone drove past, stopped, reversed,

and offered me a lift to the nearest village. That wasn't where I was headed, but it was still very kind …

It was pitch black as I walked back through the wood, and the only thing I could see through the mist of rain and howling wind was the faint glow of the hurricane lamp hanging on the tree house balcony. It was a welcoming sight. As I walked into the tree house I was amazed by the difference in temperature between inside and out. I wasted no time stripping off my wet things, drying myself off with a towel, and putting on a new set of clothes. I fed Bertha a few more logs and started making my rabbit curry. For the first time since I've been living here the weather is not quite so friendly. Perhaps this is it – the first signs of autumn.

According to the news on Radio 4, the inclement weather and high winds are the result of the back end of a hurricane. It is certainly windy! The tree house is basically an extension of the tree it sits around. It moves in the same way – it is a living, breathing house. I am warm and comfortable, eating rabbit curry and filling in my diary, while it rains outside. I still can't believe that I made this wonderful creaking place!

THURSDAY 27th AUGUST ☼ WIND ⇒

The weather had cheered up a bit by the time I went to feed the animals this morning. On my way back through the wood something landed on my shoulder: a single sweet chestnut leaf, a delicate mixture of yellow and brown. As I held it in my hand, studying it closely in disbelief, I looked up at the trees. In between the dark green of the oak and hazel leaves, the sweet chestnuts were on the turn – it was almost like, in that very moment, autumn had begun.

At 2pm I took another group of happy campers on a forage across the downs. If I thought it was windy back at the tree house, it was almost up to hurricane speed on the downs!

In the evening I met Charlie (my kayaking companion), George and Charlie B (who came down for supper some time ago with George) at the Cat Inn for a few pints. I finally found out the identity of my mystery benefactor – it was Charlie B!

After we left the pub Charlie, on leave from flight school, asked if he could come and stay at the tree house. I thought, why not? We played cards for a bit and cracked open a bottle of red wine. It is still bloody windy!

FRIDAY 28th AUGUST

I woke up at 9am feeling a little delicate, and I was late feeding the animals. I didn't see why Charlie should get a lie-in while I didn't (and I fancied some early-morning entertainment) so I dragged him along with me.

We went to see the chickens first. I told Charlie he needed to stand in front of the coop to help 'divert the chickens' towards their food. Charlie wasn't the least bit suspicious. Down jumped Kochin the cockerel and the attack began! A chase ensued as Charlie sprinted for the safety of the fence, at which point Kochin gave up and went to bother the hens instead.

After that I drove Charlie home. He lives near an Army surplus shop, and now I was solvent again (my advance has just hit the bank account) I wanted to buy some clothes to help me through the changing seasons: I spent £15.99 on a padded lumberjack shirt that looked insanely warm; and £25 on an Army-issue Golock, a knife that is a bit like a small machete with a heavy blade.

Later on I went to stay with Clare. For some bizarre reason, she didn't fancy staying at the tree house – perhaps the wind had something to do with it?

SATURDAY 29th AUGUST

I had an interesting foraging group today, a really friendly bunch. The list of amusing questions I am getting is growing longer: today a three-year-old boy asked me if I ate many parrots in the tree house!

As the wind had dropped Clare agreed to come and stay at the tree house for the night. We decided to make pizzas for supper in the clay oven. We went to the patch and picked some red onions, the first of my tomatoes, and a few baby leeks that were more like spring onions. On the way back I plucked a few field mushrooms from my usual spot by the river.

Clare had brought some mozzarella and prosciutto as her essential toppings. I made the dough and pulled out the nettle pesto to flick onto the finished

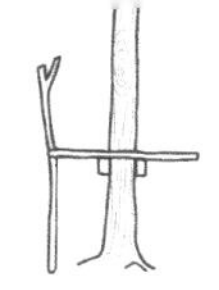

pizzas. Once the clay oven had heated up, I gave my spade a thorough scrub with disinfectant so we could use it to cook the pizzas on. We were both impressed with how quickly the pizzas cooked and, more importantly, how incredible they tasted! We managed to put away about three to four medium pizzas before declaring ourselves full. Yet another string to add to the clay oven's bow …

SUNDAY 30th AUGUST

This morning, while Clare slept on in bed, I installed some bird feeders. The wood has a diverse range of birdlife, but by far the most common is the tit family: blue tits, great tits, long-tailed tits, even the occasional coal tit. They have provided me with pleasant birdsong over the last four months and I wanted to repay them. I got two bird feeders, one for the front of the tree house that would be visible from the balcony, and the other for the back so I could sit in bed and watch them through the window.

Each one was packed full of peanuts and hoisted up a tree with twine. This time the peanuts were their luxury item – not mine! After less than ten minutes the birds descended: blue tits and great tits were the first to get stuck in, and a raucous ruckus of avian squabbling ensued. From what I could make out the larger great tit was the bully and the only way the blue tits could get a look-in was to draft in reinforcements. A new form of tree house entertainment has been born!

Some more friends from London (Caz, Ed, George, Huftown, Chief, Nick and Weaze) were coming down for a rustic retreat, so Clare and I got on

with all the necessary preparations. We decided to make pizzas after last night's success and I forfeited my week's luxury item for a leg of lamb to cook in the underground oven.

I went down to the patch to get all the vegetables. All the salad is finished, the runner beans and courgettes are tailing off, so all that is really left are the tomatoes, a huge glut of spinach, leeks, potatoes and red onions. I do hope it is enough to see me through the next two months – mind you, the wild larder is fairly well stocked at the moment.

As I walked past the river, I gathered a load of burdock leaves for the underground oven and dug up a few more wild garlic bulbs for essential flavouring. When I got back to the tree house, Clare was humming along to the radio (which had, much to my dismay, been tuned into Radio 1) and sweeping out the tree house. I cleaned out the accumulated ash from Bertha, took it over to the throne and dumped it down the hole. I decided it was best to have the throne looking, and smelling, its best.

Next we went out into the fields and walked along the hedgerows picking blackberries and elderberries to make a big fool for pudding. I showed Clare how to make it and got on with preparations for the main course. As I had built over my old pit with the clay oven I had to dig a new one. Then I collected a stack of oak limbs for fuel and set about de-boning the lamb.

I stuffed the lamb with wild garlic bulbs, mint, and rosemary from my hanging baskets. I rubbed it with oil, and salt and pepper, before wrapping it up in burdock leaves. All that remained to be done was the pizza dough, which was just as well as our guests were due to arrive in an hour!

To add to the outdoor ambiance, I had purchased two flaming torches, which ran on paraffin. I filled them up and dug the bamboo holders into the ground. George, Ed and Caz were the first to arrive, but sadly they were not staying the night. They all brought me presents: olive oil from Caz; Jamaican jerk and piri-piri seasoning from Ed; while George returned a small Coleman cooler that I had taken up to Norfolk when I went to stay with him back in 1993 – er, thanks, George! The others arrived in dribs and drabs over the next hour.

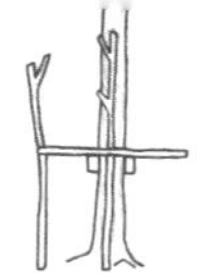

We had a great night. Clare and I kicked back after our busy day of cleaning and catering. Once it got dark we got creative and used one of my new torches to do 'sky writing', using Nick's camera on a 30-second delay. Nick gave the girls fairy wings, himself a wizard's hat and wand, and Weaze a bow and arrow.

The torches ran out halfway through the evening, so I re-filled and re-lit them. Five minutes later George, who was sitting comfortably in the hammock chair, calmly announced that one of them had been on fire for the last couple of minutes. Thanks again, George! After George, Ed and Caz had left, we retired upstairs and set up inflatable mattresses. We chatted until the last of us fell asleep some time in the early hours.

MONDAY 31st AUGUST

The tree house held up fine with all six of us inside. Huftown was the first up and looked how I felt – terrible! And he had to captain a cricket side for the day – rather him than me!

When everyone was up and about, we decided it was too hot to do anything except sit in the shade of the wood and chat with mugs of meadowsweet tea. So that's exactly what we did – the perfect bank holiday.

SEPTEMBER

TUESDAY 1ST SEPTEMBER

Not only was today the first day of September, it also felt like the first proper day of autumn. I wandered the fields in search of ceps and a gust of wind tore a flurry of orange birch leaves off the trees and scattered them down around me.

On my way to the farm to sort out the animals for the last time I saw something by the side of the road that hadn't been there last night. The badger had probably been run over some time during the last twelve hours and so it was pretty fresh. It certainly smelt all right, despite the presence of the normal musky badger odour, so the meat was unlikely to be rotten. Judging by his misshapen head, the badger must have been hit in a head-on collision, so its innards would not have split and tainted the meat.

I am not in the habit of scraping up road-kill for consumption; I would much rather obtain it by my own hand, so I can be sure of its freshness and provenance. But there comes a time when, if you wish to try something new and exotic, you have to go the extra mile.

Badger meat has been on my wish list for some time, but as they are protected and killing one is a criminal offence, I would never dream of attempting to shoot one myself. I am also extremely fond of badgers: one of my favourite countryside moments was when I watched ten of them rolling around outside their burrow for a good half an hour (downwind, of course). So although this venture into the wild larder was going to be a difficult one, curiosity got the better of me.

I picked up the badger by its leg and noticed that rigor mortis had already set in. As I walked along the road, cars passed and the faces inside sported a variety of shocked and bemused looks. Rather than skin and gut the badger at the tree house, I decided it would be more sensible to take it to my parents' house, where I would have access to more hygienic facilities.

Badgers have received an awful lot of bad press over the years for being known carriers of tuberculosis. Most farmers point the finger at badgers for giving TB to their cattle, whereas others believe cows infect badgers. I had my TB vaccination some years ago, so I hoped if there was a risk, I would still be covered. For back-up, I decided to call the only person I

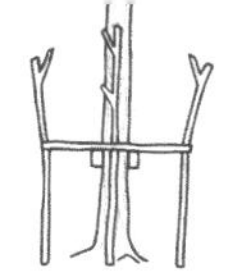

knew who had previous experience with badger – Fergus Drennan, forager extraordinaire and road-kill chef. If anyone could give me some pointers, he was my man. Strangely, his most valuable piece of advice was the last thing on my mind: 'Have you got a girlfriend? Because it takes about three days to get rid of the smell of badger meat off your hands – make sure you wear some gloves!'

Fortunately I was not seeing Clare until the end of the week, but nevertheless I took his advice, and reached for a particularly fetching pair of pink rubber gloves.

I decided the way to deal with the butchery was to treat it like any other wild animal. It has the same anatomical layout as a squirrel or rabbit, so why should it be any different – apart from the fact it was twice the size of both of them put together …?

The first job was to remove the head and feet. It was hard work hammering the blade of the machete through the bone, and the thing that put me off (other than the fact I was taking apart a badger) was the number of ticks hiding in the badger's fur, none of which I fancied playing host to – this pelt was not for keeping.

When I had finally popped out the hind legs from the skin, what I had in front of me no longer resembled a cuddly badger – it looked more like a skinned bear. I removed the guts and jointed the badger up in the same way as I would a rabbit, then I put it in a bucket and gave it a thorough clean using the outside tap. The hardest things to remove from the meat were the fiddly bits of badger hair that stuck to practically everything.

That evening I was due to go to the end-of-summer barbecue that Dan was holding for everyone who had helped out at his camp. I thought it would be a good opportunity to get a general overview on the culinary versatility of badger. But rather than just frying up lumps of seasoned badger meat, I took advantage of my mother's kitchen, and turned the meat into burgers.

I had to de-bone the badger first and remove any fatty lumps or pieces of gristle. Fergus had been right – the smell was quite overwhelming, but probably not as bad as it would have been in the breeding season.

Badger Burgers

Ingredients

1 red onion

2 garlic cloves

Meat from one badger (de-boned) or 1lb (450g) minced beef

1 tbsp ketchup

1 tsp Worcester sauce

½ tsp Tabasco sauce

1 tbsp mustard

A pinch of salt and pepper

Makes 12 mini-burgers

1 Mince the onion and garlic in a food processor, and remove. Then do the same with the badger meat. Cooked badger looks much like steak – see photo above.

2 Combine all ingredients in a bowl and form into patties for the barbecue or pan.

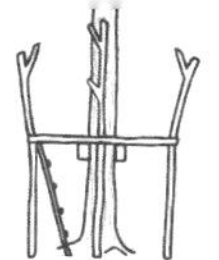

Before I made anything I fried up a chunk of badger fillet to get a taste for the animal. I tried to make sure it was still slightly pink in the middle, but only a touch. I was quite taken aback: it tasted like a cross between beef and venison, and was really quite special! But I told myself I mustn't acquire a taste for the species.

The barbecue was held by the yurts at the campsite. Charlie, whom I had last seen when I set Kochin the cockerel on him, came with me for the festivities. We turned up with badger burgers and cider, intent on a bit of a party. I gave the burgers to Dan and asked him to guess the meat – it didn't take him long; I suppose he already knew I was partial to squirrel.

> 'Everyone and their mums is packin' round 'ere'
>
> DS ANDY CARTWRIGHT, HOT FUZZ

The general feedback was really quite positive. Plenty of people tried it and 90% said they would happily eat it again. Pleased that I had made some converts, I was suddenly afraid I had put the local badger population, in this part of rural Sussex known for its gun-toting locals, in peril.

WEDNESDAY 2ND SEPTEMBER

After waking up in a yurt on the South Downs, I found myself walking out of London Victoria station just before rush hour. The contrast could not have been more dramatic.

Somehow London does feel different, probably because I don't live there, which is nice, but in some ways I slightly miss the excitement, the hustle and bustle – something I had previously despised. Viewing Britain's capital from a country dweller's perspective is like looking through rose-tinted spectacles; you see the nice bits – the smart buildings, the glitzy lights, the happy shoppers, and the suited city workers outside the wine bars and pubs, laughing and enjoying that all-important après-work pint.

Then I remember the cost of such indulgence – the daily grind of a mundane job, and the painful transport system – and the nostalgia disappears. People seem to be in London for two reasons, work and play, and little in between, except perhaps the museums. I've always liked the museums …

I stayed with my brother, who has just moved back to London after two years in New York. He was certainly pleased to be back in London, a place that he definitely calls home. But, unlike me, he is all about business; I don't think I have ever known anyone as driven and focused as him. We are two very different peas from the same pod …

Thursday 3rd September 

I had a meeting at my publishers today to meet a few people, judge a cake competition, upload all my photos from the previous four months, and to photocopy my diary.

Since I have been living in the woods, there are two things I have guarded closely: my diary and my camera. Without these I would have no record of my experience. There have been a few instances in the tree house when I have woken in the middle of the night, drenched in sweat and filled with panic, because I have dreamt that my diary has disappeared into thin air. At this point, I scrabble around under my pillow until I can feel the familiar leather-bound cover, and then fall back to sleep. My camera is equally important – I probably look after it better than I do myself.

Publishing is certainly a female-dominated business – without women it would crumble into obscurity. I rather liked it. It is a different world compared to those of set design and cheffing, where every workshop and every kitchen is filled with testosterone-charged monkeys, all trying to screw one another over so they can assume the position of alpha male within the company hierarchy. My next appointment was with UKTV Food. I had planned to bring up something special for the presenter, Tom Parker-Bowles, and I had put aside some of my badger burger mix for that very purpose.

I had emptied half my tree house larder of pickles and preserves for a 'show and tell' piece. Fortunately I didn't have to lug them from Kensington to Camden on public transport – the studio sent a car to pick me up. As I sat in the back seat of the electric eco-friendly cab, I felt quite the celebrity, but I told myself that this would probably be a one-time occasion, and it was best not to get used to it.

When I arrived I was immediately ushered into make-up. The make-up girl told me I looked knackered and stank of wood smoke. I felt I needed to explain: 'That's probably because I live in a wood.' Ahhh, you poor thing', she replied. I then pointed out this was by choice and she finally shut up.

I met Michael Caines, a wonderfully talented Michelin-starred chef, and Rachel Allen, one of the presenters and a teacher at the Ballymaloe

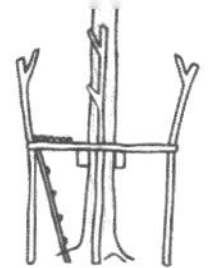

cookery school in Ireland. I had read Tom Parker-Bowles' first book, *A Year of Eating Dangerously*, just before my time in the Cook Islands. It would be fair to say that his wonderful descriptions of food haunted me for the whole time I was there.

I did my interview, which took no more than five minutes; we sampled the badger, which he quite enjoyed, some meadowsweet beer, pickled eggs and nettle pesto. Afterwards I had a plate of kedgeree, which had been cooked for filming, for my supper. I received a small bonus too: a selection of vegetables that was left over from the day's filming. I grabbed the celery, said my thank-yous, and went on my way. They provided me with a car back to Victoria station, and by 9pm I was walking through the woods in the moonlight, back to the tree house.

I fired up Bertha and sat at the table in my coat while the tree house heated up. On the shelf next to my books I spotted a half full bottle of whisky left over from the bank holiday weekend. I poured myself a dram, leant back in the chair, and mulled over the day's events. It had been an experience, but I was glad to be home. I could hear the cows in the field, the owls were calling, and in the distance I could hear the faint ring of church bells. I didn't turn on the radio. It has been a while since I sat back and listened to the mellow sounds of the countryside.

Friday 4th September

With the changing seasons I feel there is still so much I need to do before my time in the woods is over. Summer seems to have come and gone in the blink of an eye. In my childhood the summer seemed to last forever, but now it is winter that seems to linger on.

This afternoon I had a visit from a journalist for an online English website for Italians. Today's goody bag included some honey, a mango and a pack of Jaffa Cakes. I'm afraid that in my opinion the Jaffa Cake is a ridiculous excuse for a biscuit: a piece of foamy cardboard, coated in crusty brown paint, with a slice of cold 'orange'-flavoured phlegm in the middle – I hate Jaffa Cakes! But I did say thank you.

'I was born a day-dreamer and I confess it without shame.'

IAN NIALL, *THE NEW POACHER'S HANDBOOK*

Saturday 5th September

Unless you're a stripper, a waiter or a barman, not many guys get involved with hen parties. However, today a hen party decided to come foraging, and I was their lucky teacher. 'Hey, you're the survival guy from Shipwrecked!', shouted one of the more outspoken hens. I was quite surprised she recognised me, but she seemed happy with her minute slice of reality TV, and as long as the hens were happy, so was I.

We went out foraging for blackberries, elderberries, nettles and yarrow for our food, and I showed them a few other useful and not so useful wild plants. I also took my opportunity to gather some hawthorn berries, as they were just about ready to be turned into something a little more useful.

When we got back to camp, the ladies cracked open the bubbly and got stuck in. They were an entertaining bunch! I listened as they regaled each other with stories about men. By the end I couldn't help but agree what bastards men are, but at the same time I kept touching the knife on my belt to reaffirm my male status.

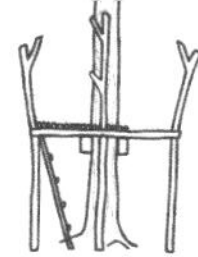

HAWTHORN FRUIT LEATHERS

Hawthorn is unusually high in pectin, the ingredient that helps jams and jellies set. With the addition of a little water it is possible to make a Stone Age snack that will last for up to three years!

INGREDIENTS

2lb (900g) hawthorn berries
½ pint (300ml) water
3 tbsp honey
Juice of 1 lemon

1 Pick the hawthorn berries and give them a good wash. Put them in a bowl, add a little water, and start to squash them up by hand. This is a messy business – be warned!

2 You are after a slimy consistency, not too watery, so add a little water at a time. Add the honey and lemon juice.

3 When you have achieved the right consistency, push the mixture through a sieve into a rectangular dish or mould where it can set.

4 Once set (this takes about 30 minutes), turn out the mould; you should be left with a hard hawthorn jelly.

5 Cut it into thin slices with a sharp knife and then lay them out to dry. You can either leave them in the sun or put them in the oven on a very low heat for 4 hours.

6 Once dried, you have the wild equivalent of those fruit bars that cost a fortune in health food shops! They taste slightly like apple and are best enjoyed on their own or chopped finely and scattered over puddings.

I put some of the hens to work skinning and gutting a rabbit (cue much high-pitched screaming), and they also made some pesto, flatbreads, and a blackberry and elderberry fool. We then turned the hawthorn berries into fruit leathers (there were a lot left over, which saves me having to go foraging for more later).

I spent the afternoon reading and snoozing at the tree house in a hammock. Clare came down in the evening and we continued being lazy together.

SUNDAY 6th SEPTEMBER

Clare and I spent today working down at the tree house. We both sat at the table inside tapping away on laptops – for once, modern technology had taken over. She was working on a design project and I was working on a talk and a slide show I am due to be delivering tomorrow at a local school.

This talk had come about through my foraging: the headmaster of the school was part of a group I took out back in May. He is eager for me to talk to the children about the tree house and the lifestyle of a 21st-Century hunter-gatherer.

I spent the evening bellowing out my speech to the birds and bees, and any other woodland creature within earshot. My talk will be accompanied by a slide show of the tree house build and all the mod cons. I am a bit nervous about talking in front of 200 small humans – is that weird?

There do seem to be far fewer insects these days. The mozzies have packed their bags and buggered off – good riddance! But why have they all disappeared all of a sudden: what do they know, that I don't?

MONDAY 7th SEPTEMBER

I was woken at some point during the early hours by some sort of bird 'dispute': a barrage of angry chirping that must have lasted at least ten minutes. Perhaps the tits are angry I haven't filled up the bird feeders.

The school asked if I wanted to stay for supper after my talk, but I finished with school dinners a long time ago, and I have no intention of returning to them. It was getting dark as I returned to the wood, so it was too late to

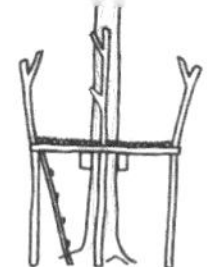

go out shooting. I'm fed up with last-minute veggie meals. I need to get some hunting and fishing in. And I must make some blackberry jam.

TUESDAY 8th SEPTEMBER

'We wunt be druv.' This ancient Sussex motto reflects the county's natural antipathy to being pushed around, particularly by figures of self-appointed authority or outsiders. It also fits well with what I have been trying to achieve down here.

My original motive for spending six months living a simplistic lifestyle in the woods was the desire to rid myself of the unnecessary costs of modern-day life, which were being dictated to me by a higher authority. Was it really essential for me to pay for things like rent, electricity and gas bills, Council Tax and, above all, food? The simple answer is yes, it is, if I wanted to remain part of modern-day society.

Those who do not wish to conform are pushed to the edge of society. The people who create their own communities or eco-settlements in a bid to live off the land, manage it sustainably, and harness the power of the elements for basic electrical needs, are regarded as non-conformists, weirdos and outcasts. It also seems that society tries to penalise these people, when in fact they are just trying to live a cheaper, more sensible lifestyle, which is more considerate towards the environment. For instance, even though a person might own his land, he may not be granted permission to build himself the sort of home that would save him money, and have a negligible impact on the environment.

John Zerzan, a leading figure of the Primitivism movement, believes that humans began their downhill slide with the domestication of plants and animals. His theories are based on an assessment of human prehistory, which reveals that for an incredible two million years our ancestors existed as hunter-gatherers. Zerzan is one of many who now believe that this form of existence is the only truly successful human adaptation to this planet. However much I support the lifestyle, I know the world is now too over-populated to return to a hunter-gatherer state. Presently the world population stands at 6.8 billion, up 83 million from last year!

I have enjoyed taking a step back from technology, albeit I do still use a phone, and occasionally the computer. I believe the Luddites were right when they voiced their objections to the mechanisation of British industry over two centuries ago. Technology, for all its fantastic advances, is also an insidious thing. Today people live their lives vicariously through the

TREEHOUSE BLACKBERRY AND ELDERBERRY JAM

A jam thermometer is an essential piece of kit for this recipe, so you can find the crucial setting point for the jam, which is 108°C (226°F). The saucer test is also a useful back-up for finding out whether or not your jam will set. Put a teaspoon of the jam on a saucer (if you happen to have a freezer at your disposal, put the saucer in there for ten minutes) and leave it for a few minutes, before nudging it with a spoon. If it wrinkles, your jam will set.

INGREDIENTS

2lb (900g) blackberries

2lb (900g) elderberries

Juice of 2 lemons

4 sprigs mint

½ pint (300ml) water

3lb (1.4kg) white granulated sugar

1 In a large saucepan or pickling pan, simmer all the fruit, mint and lemon juice, with the water until soft. At this stage some people prefer to remove the pips by pressing the fruit through a sieve. I think the pips provide the essential body of the jam, so I don't bother. It is worth removing the sprigs of mint, but this can be done by hand.

2 Add the sugar to the pan and simmer rapidly, stirring occasionally until the setting temperature has been reached. If you are worried about the jam setting, add a little more lemon juice – citrus fruit is naturally high in pectin, the ingredient that helps jam to set.

3 Pot up the jam in warm sterilised jars, and seal immediately.

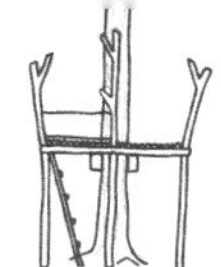

medium of television and the media; people eat their meals around the television rather than the table, and children play computer games and interact in a virtual world, rather than simply play with each other in the great outdoors. On the other hand, the Internet has allowed me to share my experience here through my blog, and has given me access to much of the information I needed to get me started on my project.

Another day, another rant; this 'hammock time' can wreak havoc with the brain sometimes.

Wednesday 9th September

I have been thinking more about the whole technology vs simplicity debate and I believe there are strengths on both sides. Like many things in life a healthy balance is probably best. And me? I am a hunter-gatherer who lives in a tree and uses the Internet. Say no more.

It was a day to indulge – in jam making, that is. I wanted to take advantage of more than one of the fruits on offer so I grabbed my basket and spent a couple of hours searching the hedgerows for blackberries and elderberries.

The blackberries have been out for some time, but my craving for something delicious to put on my bread has not diminished. I am not sure why I put it off for so long.

After making the jam, I was already looking forward to tomorrow's breakfast, so I baked a fresh loaf of bread in the clay oven especially for the occasion.

Thursday 10th September

I did another talk about hunting today at the school. I used a few gory pictures involving rabbits and badgers being skinned, gutted and jointed, because I think it is important that kids understand that meat doesn't come from packets, but does in fact come from real animals.

What happens if there is an apocalypse? The Mayan calendar runs out on 21 December 2012. The end of the world is unlikely, but there is talk that there could be a new world order or perhaps even a return to a more basic lifestyle. It *could* happen. The Roman Empire disappeared virtually overnight and the Mayans – well, they vanished too, leaving only magnificent ruins behind. Could climate change and the recent economic collapse be a taste of things to come?

I feel I have been delving into serious questions about the future of mankind this week – it is all getting a bit too heavy. I think I will take out the rod for a few hours and, with any luck, bring something home for tea.

FRIDAY 11th SEPTEMBER WIND

Summer has gone again! I woke to a slightly chilly tree house, and when I looked out of the window, I could see the first hazel leaves on the turn. I lit the downstairs fire and put the kettle on to boil. I brought down my toasting grill, the loaf of bread, and my latest creation – the jam. I sliced the bread carefully and, after making coffee, toasted it over the remaining embers of the fire. Good toast, bit smoky though …

I am starting to find I'm getting a bit fed up with the majority of my food being 'smoked'. I have always loved smoked food, but not all day every day. Thank goodness I have a pan! My clothes smell of smoke, my food is smoked, and even my skin has its own special smoky aroma.

The jam was fantastic! I ended up having five slices of toast. The future of breakfasts now looks promising, and I have enough jam to last me well over six months: 12 jars!

Today was a 'me' day: I read, listened to the radio, and fixed up the coracle. I also began the rather fiddly business of sewing together my rabbit skin rug. I used the large needle and twine that I had used for the coracle. My efforts were passable, but Clare could have done a much better job. I laid it down in front of Bertha and it had the desired effect of making the tree house look even more cosy than it does already.

It was very windy and the creaking in the tree house reached fever pitch. I read a couple of books in the hammock, and then I did some work on an oak table. The legs are made from a cunningly shaped oak limb, which broke off into three branches, and the top is a section of an oak tree. I bolted the pieces together using coach screws, and then shaved down the legs with my knife as I had done for the tree house banisters.

I had a call from Clare to say we were going to the Cat Inn for supper with some friends we hadn't seen for a long time. I had duck, red cabbage and mashed potato – amazing. I wish there were more ducks about my wood.

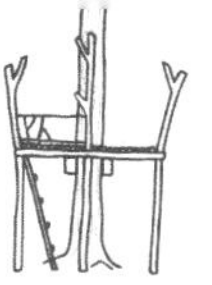

When I got up to visit the loo, I walked past a table and heard someone say my name. It was a group of staff from the school where I'd just done my talk. I said hello and asked if they were enjoying the food. One of them asked, 'Shouldn't you be in a tree?' My answer was concise: 'Well, I'm not a hermit – at least not yet.'

Saturday 12th September

I wonder if today was the last day of summer; it was beautiful. It was also Clare's grandparents' 60th wedding anniversary and the whole family gathered together to celebrate. I helped Clare's mother with the food and we sat out in the garden for lunch.

I went back to the tree house in the afternoon to continue working on the oak table. But I can't stop thinking about marriage. I have been pondering the subject for some time, ever since I moved down here. Clare and I have been together now for almost five years, and we have lived together for four of those. We love each other and we are happy. The reality of asking Clare to marry me is a nerve-wracking one. But I think, in the not too distant future, I do – sorry, I will.

SUNDAY 13th SEPTEMBER

The corner of the tree house under my bookshelves has been looking bare for some time. Clare and I had a small butcher's trolley in our last flat, so I went home to my mother's house to pick it up. She also gave me a chilli plant, something I have tried to grow down at the patch, but I failed miserably. I was looking forward to some fresh heat. I love chillies – they get the endorphins going!

I went out shooting this afternoon, hoping for a pigeon or even a pheasant. There were lots of rabbits, but I didn't feel like rabbit tonight, so instead I went to the patch to dig up some potatoes. Half a dozen tomatoes were ready, plus a couple of onions, and some spinach and courgettes. I had a very Italian voluntary vegetarian supper: gnocchi with two-month-old stinger pesto (it gets better with age!), and a tomato and onion salad.

Autumn is well under way now: the patch is tailing off, the leaves are turning, and the evenings are drawing in (dusk came in at 7.30pm). I used to like autumn as a child, with piles of leaves to jump in and kick (just after my father had slaved for hours to collect them all), stoves bubbling away with comforting stew, and welcoming log fires in the sitting room.

I don't appreciate it now. It seems so sad, like watching a close friend wasting away. The fields, meadows and woods are slowly dying and there is nothing I can do to stop it.

Never before have the seasons had such an impact on my life: shorts have been exchanged for trousers, the hammock has come down, the unpatched eaves of the tree house need sorting out, and the wood pile needs supplementing. SAD is amplified in the countryside; I do feel down. It is at times like this the tree house comes into its own, and makes me realise what a comforting, warm home it is.

The stove is fired up, I've got a hot toddy on the go, I am sitting on the rabbitskin rug listening to Classic FM, and I'm reading a good book. And I don't have to go to work in the morning – but I do have to face the morning chill under my bucket shower!

MONDAY 14th SEPTEMBER

I spoke to a friend today who works for a hedge fund. He has just been offered a new job with a big pay packet. It is hard to believe someone I sat

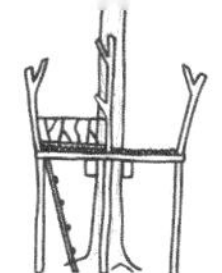

next to at school is earning so much money. Actually, he was in the 'A' stream and I was in the 'B' stream – explains a lot!

We all need money to get by; even I have to pay my phone bill every month. But at what point did money take over people's lives? Strip a person who works with their hands – a skilled labourer like a carpenter, a blacksmith or a woodsman – of all their money and possessions, and they could build a new life for themselves. Take the money and possessions from a businessman and they have nothing. My friend is a bit like that: the sort of person who will throw money at a common household problem and hope it will be sorted out, rather than trying to fix it by himself.

As a general comparison, are the people at Tinker's Bubble (an eco-community) better off than a stockbroker in London? Probably, and happier too – for themselves and the environment. They probably laughed their eco-asses off when they heard about the recession – while the stockbroker was crying his eyes out up in the City!

I have become an avid Radio 4 listener; am I getting old? I love the banter of Just a Minute, Excess Baggage, etc. I have found myself turning off the news. It's always depressing and focuses on government issues, money, death and despair. It doesn't do an awful lot to improve the mood …

TUESDAY 15th SEPTEMBER

I like foxes; they are the pirates of the countryside: sly, cunning and proper scavengers. I saw one in the field on my way back from shooting last night and knew exactly what he had been eating – the remains of a pheasant I had just shot. The foolish bird had gone up to roost too early and I shot him as he flew up into an oak tree.

I met my editor today. I had set six nightlines for a possible lunch and only caught one small eel – good thing she didn't stay for food! It rained a lot so we drank coffee on the balcony and discussed the book.

I spent the afternoon getting together some wood to build a cider press. With all the apples around at the moment it would be foolish to miss the chance to make my favourite tipple. I returned to one of the builders' yards I had frequented during the build back in May. One of the chaps in the workshop recognised me: 'You still living in that tree?' Of course I am – I've got nowhere else to go!

HOW TO MAKE

1 A cider press costs about £100, but I made one for next to nothing. I built a sturdy frame using 2in x 4in (5cm x 10cm) recycled timber and bolted it together with long coach screws. I screwed five small pieces of timber onto the bottom of the frame to hold a tray. I did have to make sure the juice from the apples wouldn't come into contact with the wood – most timber is treated and the weatherproofing contains traces of arsenic – so I used a clean plastic tray with a few holes in one end to siphon off the juice into a bucket.

2 Once I had made the press, my first job was to get a piece of untreated timber and mash all the apples into pulp. Roughly half a bucket full of apples yielded one 'cheese' (a cheese is the word used to describe the mashed-up apple folded up in a tea towel or muslin). I placed the cheeses one on top of the other inside the tray.

3 The device I used for the actual pressing was a car jack; this fitted between the top of the frame and the cheeses of mashed-up apple. I then placed a wooden chock on top of the cheeses and tightened the car jack. Gradually I increased the pressure and the juice began to flow.

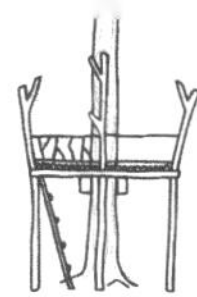

A CIDER PRESS

4 After four presses, each using three cheeses, I ended up with 14 pints (8 litres) of pure English apple juice. Unfortunately the final push on the last press was too much for my knocked-together frame, and an ear-splitting 'crrraaack' spelled the end of my pressing activities.

In traditional cider making, nothing is added to the juice: the naturally occurring yeasts are left to work their magic and ferment the sugar in the juice into alcohol. After reading up on the subject, I decided to add the recommended two campden tablets (used to prevent any bacteria growth) per gallon (4.5 litres) and I prepared ⅕oz (5g) of beer yeast in a little warm water to help kick-start fermentation.

I took a measurement with the hydrometer, which came out at 1.055, so when fermentation was complete I ended up with a cider of about 7.00%. However, I was not able to enjoy my cider in the tree house: it took at least three months before I was able to bottle it.

I had a fine meal this evening: pan-fried pheasant breast with mashed potato and spinach, coated in a rich jus made from some stock, a tablespoon of my jam, and a quarter bottle of red wine I found under the sink downstairs.

It is nice not to have any commitments for a while, so I can get stuck back into day-to-day life down here. I also have to start preparing for autumn: any weaknesses in the tree house will soon become apparent …

2am: Screech owls are having an orgy above the tree house – I do wish they would find another tree to mess about in.

WEDNESDAY 16th SEPTEMBER

I have started to embrace these unpleasant 'start-of-autumn' days – after all, what can I do about them? This morning I went to Clare's parents' house to gather all the windfall apples. Clare's mother has already collected four bucket-loads over the last couple of weeks, but I gave the tree a final shake to get the last few down and then went back to the tree house to make my cider press.

The tradition of 'wassailing' to bless the orchards in the hope of a good crop has been going on since the 1500s. 'Wassail', which comes from the old English phrase 'waes haeil', means 'be healthy'. Traditionally groups of men would gather in orchards to toast the trees' good health, so they could hope for a bumper harvest the following year. Judging by the number of apples, Clare's mum must have done her wassailing last year!

SUSSEX 'HOWLING' VERSE

Stand fast root, bear well top,
Pray God send us a good howling crop,
Every twig, apples big,
Every bough, apples enow,
Hats full, caps full, full quarter sacks full,
Holla boys holla, Wassail!

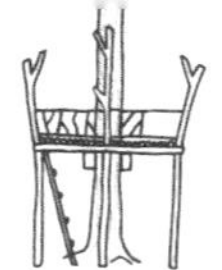

Thursday 17th September

As part of my rent-paying duties, I spent the day with one of my landlords' sons, doing a few jobs around the farm. I met him at the top of the wood at 11am and on the walk down we saw a dead mole by the side of the path. He joked and asked if I was going to have it for lunch – er, no. I don't think it would be worth the effort, but I should add it to the wish list anyway. The moleskin would make a wonderful pair of gloves!

We dug a few holes to put in some sleeves for fence posts and cleared out the stream running through the wood, before breaking for tea. After that we walked down the fence line on the far side of the wood, replacing any broken posts with hazel lengths. My workmate left at about 4pm and I continued my day of energetic work with wood collecting and chopping. I find I have to go further afield to collect wood these days: I have used up most of what was around the tree house. Perhaps I should have done it the other way around …

Friday 18th September

I made Clare a ring from hazel for her birthday this morning. It took a few attempts – the first three broke while I was sanding them down. I was pleased with the final result, until I realised it looked a bit like a wooden hula hoop; but then I thought, that's okay – Clare loves hula hoops!

I went for a fish at 3pm down at the river. Two days ago I saw a fat trout above the bridge; he swam lazily near the surface, rising to grab the occasional snack. I had the shotgun with me at the time and considered blasting it out of the water. Then I thought better of it as the gunfire would shred it to pieces. I fished for a couple of hours with little joy and eventually gave up.

Wondering what to have for supper I remembered that last week, in a nearby village, I had seen a couple of chicken of the woods perched high in an oak tree by the road. I took the car over to the village to assess the situation.

The fungi were still there, but a little higher than I remembered. There were very few low branches to haul myself up on, so I parked the car directly under the tree and climbed up off the roof. Bemused passers-by watched as bits of mushroom and leaves began to fall out of the tree – followed by me! The thin branch I was standing on gave way and I fell, face first, onto the roof of the car – the dent is quite impressive! The worst part was that after all the pain, effort and indignity, the mushrooms were dry, chalky and well past their best. I drove back to the wood in a huff, with a skinned knee and a bruised head. It would have been hilarious had I not landed on my face …

When I got back I took out the gun, hoping for a bit more success, and was rewarded for my persistence. A solitary mallard was paddling around in the river as I approached the bridge. As soon as he spotted me he took off, only to be shot out of the air a couple of moments later. Fantastic – I love duck!

After a slap-up binge of pan-fried duck legs, I salted the breasts for tomorrow. I also cleaned the gun and sharpened my knife. Then I dug out the chess set to try to play chess against myself. The only problem was, I couldn't remember the rules.

SATURDAY 19th SEPTEMBER

As our friends from our trip to Scotland were coming today Clare came down early to help me spruce the place up. She refused to do the washing up when I found a dead mouse floating in the run-off bucket under the sink, and she gave me a strict telling off regarding my hygiene regime. What can I do? I live in a wood – I'm surrounded by mice!

Our guests arrived at 3pm bearing gifts: Jim and Clare brought nose cups and spray-on plasters; Emma and Justin brought four plantains, African spice, a ceramic pot for jam and dried bird's eye chillies. They all loved the set-up. Emma's comment was a corker: 'Your bed is just like – a bed!' We sampled my meadowsweet beer, and after a cupful everyone felt a bit woozy, so it must be stronger than the last lot! Then we all went for a walk to gather blackberries and elderberries for jam making.

It was great to have a 'Scotland' reunion. It felt quite hectic and the tree house was clogged up with more bedding than a shop that sells beds – and bedding. We had a few in-depth discussions and debates, and finished with a few amusing rounds of charades.

They had brought a beef joint, which I set up on a spit over the fire, and the night continued into the small hours. Once again the tree house slept all six of us without a hitch. The girls weren't best pleased with all three of us boys snoring our heads off though!

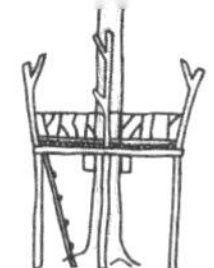

Sunday 20th September

Everyone woke at around 9am all dying for the loo. Justin and Emma's mattress had been blocking the door overnight – no one could get out! I fired up the oven and Jim baked a loaf of wholemeal bread to try out the jam we made yesterday evening. The girls had brought some bottled pectin to ensure the jam would set – it set all right, like a bloody rock! I think I was a bit over-zealous with the measurements. The oven performed so well the bread was baked in half an hour. I must try doing a roast in it.

At midday we went over to the reservoir for a walk. The water was so low that, as we walked over a footbridge, I could see a huge pike chasing a little fish – I might have to venture up with the rod.

Monday 21st September

I spent most of the day crouching on the balcony with the air rifle, playing soldiers. There were quite a few marrows that I certainly wasn't planning to eat so I cut them in half, carved angry faces in them, and set them up on blocks of wood about the place. I then moved from target to target executing each vegetable time and time again. I didn't really have anything else to do – there was no need to go out looking for supper today.

It was Clare's birthday and in the afternoon I headed up to London for a small gathering of friends at a restaurant. I gave Clare her wooden ring – she loved it! It was a bit too small and she got it stuck on her finger, which, after a couple of hours, started to swell up and turn blue! It might need a bit more sanding …

After a tasty meal at a little Italian restaurant near Smithfield Market we crashed at Justin and Emma's. Before bed we watched a movie, something I haven't done for ages.

Tuesday 22nd September

This morning I made my way over to Fulham to my brother's office to use his computer. Then I dashed back to Covent Garden to see my agent – the bus this time, no TV company car; I had a few meetings lined up with some TV folk.

We had a good chat about various ideas of theirs and some proposals I had put together. I held back a bit on the details and gave them only the bits tailored to my skill set. The last thing I want is for my ideas to be pinched and presented by someone else.

Once again, when I got home, rather than waste money on a taxi, I walked back to the wood from the station cross-country. It took about an hour and it was almost dark, but after the close confines of the city, it was quite liberating.

As I approached the tree house I heard a scarily loud growl and bark. Whatever it was, it was big and a bit too close for comfort! I shot up the ladder, quick as a wink, and fumbled with the keys to the door, desperate to get inside and arm myself with whatever came to hand first – which turned out to be a Wellington boot! Another bark was followed by a scuffle in the bushes – foxes. They seemed intent on doing each other some serious damage and the fight continued on and off for a good 20 minutes. I poured myself a mug of meadowsweet beer and sat on the balcony to watch. A spot of free entertainment was the least they could do after scaring the shit out of me. I assumed Frank was one of the contenders, but I couldn't be sure. They weren't even bothered by the torch!

WEDNESDAY 23RD SEPTEMBER

Today went quite quickly. I woke at 9am and lay in bed watching the tits fighting over the bird feeder – the blues against the greats – a real turf war! The animals in the wood have really got the fighting spirit at the moment.

In the afternoon I went shooting. I hid behind a hedge and picked off a pigeon that flew over my shoulder: a surprisingly good shot – I think I am getting better with the gun. The hedgerow was covered in hops; I thought they might look good hanging off the beams in the tree house, in the same way they are strung up in country pubs. While I was picking the hops, a line of six geese flew overhead well within range – bugger! I was on one side of the hedge and my gun was on the other. Roast goose would have been delicious – but I'm not convinced I would have been able to get it through the door of the clay oven …

I have sorted out a mini surf break to Cornwall for this weekend. Although I have missed surfing this summer, this trip is actually a bit of a smoke screen – I'm going to propose to Clare. I want to spend the rest of my life with her and, in the future, it would be great to have a couple of mini

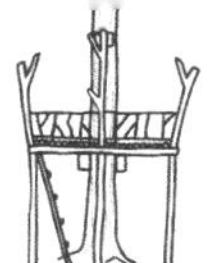

versions of the two of us. It wasn't a hard decision to make. I did toy with the idea of proposing to her on the tree house balcony, but then I thought it might be nice to get away for a few days, and provide the future Mrs Weston with somewhere a bit more luxurious than a two-star tree house. The place I have chosen in Cornwall is above the very beach where we first kissed ten years ago – and I get to have a paddle in the Atlantic, dude!

All I need now is the ring. In the past I have heard two things from Clare concerning rings: white gold and diamond. That should tell me all I need to know. I don't think an engagement ring made of wood would make the grade; besides, I've already done that.

On the way back from the patch tonight I came across some flashing blue lights by the side of the wood: someone had managed to flip their car on a perfectly straight bit of road. When the driver opened the boot to unload his shopping it all fell out! At least no one was hurt. I stood and watched from behind a tree not far away, while an ever-observant policeman looked on.

Thursday 24th September

I am very disappointed: it turns out the meadowsweet beer I made and bottled recently is not as astounding as I previously thought. When we tested it last weekend there were no side effects. After drinking 2 pints (1 litre) of it in the space of an hour today it messed with my belly in a big way. Despite the beer doing what it would say on the proverbial label, half an hour after consumption, the runs set in. Mostly running to the loo, followed by an uncomfortable minute or two. I didn't feel unwell; my stomach just made a series of uncomfortable groans, which I soon learned was the start of a two-minute countdown. What a shame. Best in small doses!

My book advance hit my account today – the bank must have been shocked and a little frustrated they couldn't charge me anymore! After clearing some outstanding debts, I made a valuable investment: a Nikon D3000 digital SLR camera, a great bit of kit! I have spent a while trying to figure out how it works and I still don't understand. The difference in quality is astounding!

Tomorrow I am going pigeon decoying. With any luck I will have pigeons coming out of my ears – nothing that some good old-fashioned smoking can't cure. It's about time as I need a new snack food – my jars of pickled samphire are running low.

At 11pm I went downstairs to cut a few more logs to feed Bertha. As I got outside a worrying thing happened: for the first time since April, in the light of the head torch I could see my own breath – goodbye summer, hello winter!

Friday 25th September

I woke early (7am) to a misty morning, and popped down to the fields to take a few photos as the haze lifted with the rising sun.

At 9am I met Tom, a true Sussex gent, and we set off to go decoying. We went up to a ridge, about ½ mile (800m) away from the wood, and I revelled in the 360-degree view of the surrounding Sussex countryside.

We pitched the hide, a frame of hazel covered with camouflage netting, in front of a bowl in the newly cut maize field. There was plenty of fodder

for the greedy pigeons, except that most of the other fields had also been cut, so the birds would be spread out.

Decoying is a wonderful way to pass the day. I find it hard to understand why people pay large sums of money to spend a day blasting away at pheasants, when a day's pigeon shooting comes for free – if you can get permission. I am sure many a pheasant shooter would agree that the woodpigeon presents a far more sporting challenge than a dopey high-flying pheasant. Pigeons fly at a ridiculous rate, more so on a windy day; moreover, their eyesight is phenomenally good, and they can spot you a mile away.

As I was to learn, there is a lot more to decoying than simply plonking a bunch of plastic pigeons in a field. The fake pigeons are mounted on short lengths of coat hanger wire, so they 'nod' in the breeze. The decoys must face the wind in a 'V'-formation, which needs to be sharper in high wind and flatter (almost horseshoe-shaped) in light wind. The idea is that this mimics the behaviour of a group of pigeons feeding on the ground, in the hope that it will attract real pigeons to feed alongside the decoys. Today, as there was barely any wind, we opted for the horseshoe arrangement.

I completely missed my first four shots. But on the fifth, and probably most difficult 'over the hedge' shot, I was successful. This was followed by another six pigeons before it got quieter and Tom fell off his stool backwards into the hedge!

We sat and ate cheese and pickle sandwiches, thoughtfully provided by Tom, while he entertained me with stories of poaching and ferreting in his youth. He also helped me realise that my left eye is stronger than my right, which explains why I am so cack-handed with a gun, and why I have never been able to look through binoculars properly …

Tom promised me the entire bag. Usually, if he doesn't need to top up his freezer, he swaps the pigeons with a butcher friend in return for select cuts. So bartering is still alive and well in Sussex! We continued to shoot until 3.30pm and we had a good bag of 12 birds.

Back at the tree house I started to de-breast the birds – the flies had already begun laying eggs on them. As I plucked and gouged, I thought just how lucky Frank and his mates were to be getting all this free pigeon. I had worked hard today and had a sore shoulder to prove it. The foxes are my rubbish bins – none of us will go hungry tonight!

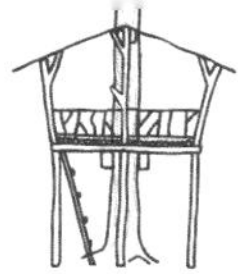

Saturday 26th September

With my proposal to Clare imminent I went ring shopping in Brighton with her rather pregnant sister Emma for back-up. I had spoken to Clare's parents and asked permission for their daughter's hand (not that I am a stickler for tradition, but some things are just polite), at which point Clare's mum began to cry – I assumed they were tears of happiness! They both agreed, so that was the first hurdle; the next is that Clare will be equally accepting …

The streets of Brighton were crawling with armed policemen because of the forthcoming Labour Party Conference. At each shop we visited, the ring we had selected was passed to Emma to try on for size, the vendors assuming, because of her rather large bump, that we were having a shotgun wedding. 'No, it's not for me, it's for my sister', she had to keep saying. Eventually I found the perfect ring that fitted Clare's criteria, and was within budget, although I did have to haggle. I didn't think you could haggle over the price of an engagement ring – but it turns out you can.

Shopping trip over, Clare and I strapped our surfboards to the roof of her car. Clare's parents wished me luck and we set off. The six-hour drive is always an exciting one; the highlight for me is passing Stonehenge on the A303, a topic I studied in depth for my archaeology degree. Clare always gets the same old chat every time we go past, about how and why it was built, the three stages of the build, the two earlier henges that stood in its place, and the origin of the stones used in the circle we see today. After so many years she no longer pretends to listen politely and just claps her hands over her ears and says 'la-la-la-la-la-la' until I've finished. I'm just trying to keep it fresh in my memory, dear …

On the way down, Jamie called to say that two friends, John and Katie, had just got engaged in Paris. Of all the weekends to choose! I passed on the news to Clare, who, completely unaware of my plans, went off on one about how 'we're still too young' and 'they've just run out of things to talk to each other about' – great, this all sounds extremely positive!

My friend Nick's parents have kindly allowed Clare and me to use their house in Polzeath for the weekend. I did offer them rent but they told me to stop being so ridiculous – they were also in on my plan. When we arrived at the house, there was a bottle of champagne and a card on the table. As Clare reached for the card I began to panic – would it give the game away? But it simply said 'enjoy your stay'. To celebrate being back in Cornwall we went for last orders at the local pub. I ordered a stiff drink; I needed something to calm my nerves …

SUNDAY 27th SEPTEMBER

Proposal day! I woke up early, already nervous, and we went to check the surf. It was perfect for both of us to enjoy: 3ft (1m) and clean. Before donning our wetsuits we went to the shop to get a few essentials. Clare suggested we buy some Prosecco, but I was already reaching for a £40 bottle of Veuve Cliquot. Neither of us had ever bought *proper* champagne.

'What are you doing? That's bloody expensive!', said Clare in disbelief. I thought on my feet: 'It's my birthday tomorrow', which it is. Clare gave in to my extravagance, but I was worried she might have twigged about what was going on. We spent the next few hours bobbing up and down in the Atlantic and riding whichever waves came our way. It was great to be out in the surf and it certainly was a welcome distraction.

Clare and I first met ten years ago on Daymer Bay between the Cornish Riviera villages of Polzeath and Rock, during the hedonistic summers of beach parties, body boarding and underage alcohol consumption. I thought that, as this was a place that was historically significant in our relationship, it would be the perfect spot to propose.

We hiked up Brae Hill in glorious September sunshine and found a spot with the best views up the Camel Estuary and out to the Atlantic. As Clare was taking pictures of the view I asked if she wanted some champagne. Instead of going for the bottle I reached nervously into the bag to grab the ring box, and, sliding onto one knee, tapped her on the shoulder. 'Will you marry me, Clare Buckle?' The look of utter surprise on her face made it clear she had suspected nothing – she isn't that good an actress. 'Are you serious?! Is that real?!' She did say yes in the end!

We sat in the sun and guzzled champagne, and talked about the future – it was the perfect moment and the perfect place. The talk very quickly turned to wedding venues, dresses and bridesmaids. After about half an hour, Clare gave into temptation, and went for her phone to start telling the world.

MONDAY 28th SEPTEMBER

My birthday! Well, I picked the right day to pop the question; the weather outside today was grey and miserable. The surf had also dropped to piddly little waves that were not worth bothering with. I had originally planned to propose on my birthday – that way I would never forget the date and risk forgetting anniversaries!

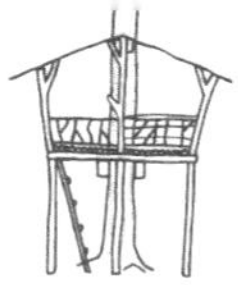

My fiancée (!) and I went to Port Isaac today. We went to the fishmonger's and got oysters, mussels and tiger prawns for a very reasonable £10! In the evening we cooked up a seafood feast back at the house: grilled oysters with garlic and Parmesan, *moules marinière* and grilled tiger prawns.

I am now 28 years old, engaged, and I have a column and a book deal. At last I feel I am on track, after years of beating my head against the wall trying to start a writing career. Who would have thought a tree house could have been the start of all this? I wonder how the tree house is? I am beginning to miss it …

OCTOBER

THURSDAY 1st OCTOBER

WIND

After all the excitement of the last few days, I am back in the trees feeling rejuvenated. Having had my fill of Cornish surf and seafood, I am ready to embrace the onslaught of autumn, and make the most of my final month in the woods.

Each gust of wind releases bursts of orange and gold leaves around me, and the warmth of the fire in the chill of the morning is both evident and welcoming. I fully expect Bertha to be in constant use, mainly to keep the tree house at 'room' temperature.

Previously I was saddened by the loss of summer and the disappearance of the swallows. Now I am happy with the chestnuts, rosehips, mushrooms and, above all, the official start of the shooting season! For the last five months I have been turning a blind eye to the rules of engagement when it comes to game, which, I must admit, I have not been happy about. My only justification is that I am 100% reliant on wild meat – not many people can use that as an excuse. Although it would have been acceptable to stick to rabbits, pigeons, squirrel and fish, sometimes I had a craving for something a little different. I was selective about my choice of bird: I shot only older, cock pheasants and left the hens well alone, so they could continue breeding with the fitter, younger males. Why did I stick to the rules regarding the fishing season and not the shooting season? For the simple reason that I prefer meat to fish. Now I can freely hunt game, a huge weight has been lifted off my shoulders. But the guilt of misbehaving remains.

With the turn in the weather, it was time to patch up my summer 'ventilation' holes. There are two areas that need addressing: the top of the walls where they meet the roof, and the hole in the ceiling that the oak tree runs through. I searched through the remnants of my scrap timber to patch up the sides, but had none left for the roof hole. My landlords have sheep and keep hold of their wool, for no practical reason as far as I can make out. They have kindly donated a large bagful for me to use to fill in the gaps. I hope that the lanolin in the wool, which prevents sheep sucking up water like a sponge, will keep the rain off.

When I opened the bag and pulled out some of the wool out fell a rather ominous-looking spider – I moved back quickly. I have always suffered

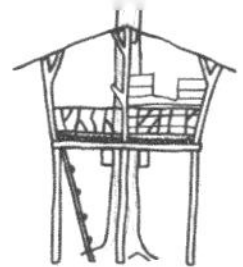

from a mild form of arachnophobia, something that reached its peak when I spent two months in Australia, where the spiders are *actually* dangerous.

The spider was not like any I could remember seeing before and, reluctant as the spider was, I eventually got it in a jam jar. My bookshelves in the tree house are bursting with identification books so I reached for the appropriate one and turned to the section on spiders.

What I read next was slightly disturbing: the little fellow I had just caught was capable of inflicting quite a nasty nip. It was a black or walnut orb weaver. Further research led me to a slightly more detailed description:

> *'Though bites occur rarely, the effects of a bite are likely to include an initial and possibly painful jab followed by some swelling close to the site of the bite and further pain lasting perhaps 24 hours; altogether it is unlikely to be worse than that of a wasp sting.'*

In actual fact, a dozen or more spiders that are resident in the UK are capable of inflicting rather painful and unpleasant bites – will we never be safe again? About a year ago I could have sworn I was bitten by a mouse spider while gardening: I felt a slight jab on my hand, and when I saw the spider and went to shake it off, it looked as if it was clinging on with its fangs. I had an itchy bump for a couple of days but thought nothing of it. This is England – the only dangerous wild things are meant to be bees and wasps!

I took the jam jar to the far side of the wood and tipped out the spider. From this day onwards, I will be a little bit more wary of spiders in this country. I used to be happy to handle them, knowing that they were about as lethal as a comfy chair and a good book, but now I know otherwise.

Clare came over for the night: it was our five-year anniversary and after recent events there was plenty to celebrate. On hearing of our engagement, people have sent us not only cards but also bottles of champagne, so we sat on the balcony of the tree house sipping bubbles and talking about the last five years. I wanted her to stay the night so I didn't tell her about my arachnid discovery …

FRIDAY 2ND OCTOBER

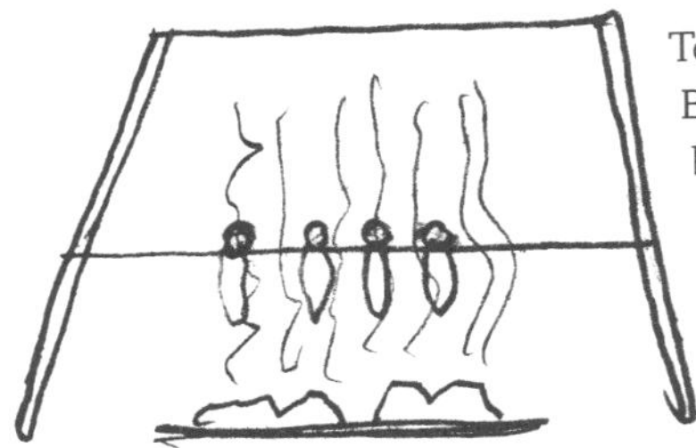

Today I have been smoking like a chimney. Because of my trip to Cornwall, all the pigeon breasts from decoying have been in the freezer at my parents' house. I lit Bertha and placed the solid block of 24 pigeon breasts on a chair in front to defrost, while I went downstairs to put together a basic 'A'-frame to hang the meat on during smoking. Once I'd finished, I went back upstairs to check on the pigeon breasts, which had defrosted completely, leaving a blood-soaked chair – nice.

I had picked up a few good tips from the smokery in Scotland so I put them into practice. Technically I was going to be air-drying this meat, with the aid of the smoke and heat from the fire underneath. It wasn't exactly the same method used in Scotland, but it relied on similar principles.

It took a long time, but that was fine with me: Clare had bought me some books for my birthday, so I sat in the hammock, read, and drank tea. By the time I was ready to move inside at 7pm the

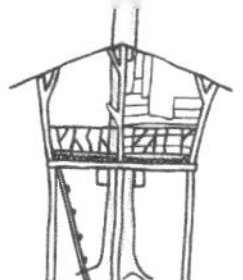

slices were still a little moist, so I took the four skewers on which I'd put the meat upstairs, and hung them with bungees over Bertha to finish them off.

It is not often I go outside to stand in the woods just to look around, but tonight there was a full moon. In the light of the head torch I could see my breath. When I turned off the torch to lose sight of the chill, the moonlight bounced off the waxy holly leaves, while all around me a light breeze kept the wood alive with the noise of falling leaves – the sound of the changing seasons.

SATURDAY 3RD OCTOBER

I feel full. I have just eaten two portions of the mushroom risotto I meant to cook for Clare on our anniversary. The field mushrooms are running out and there don't seem to be many other mushrooms coming through yet – probably because it's been so dry. I don't remember ever wishing for rain in the past …

I have started reading *The Wild Life* by John Lewis-Stempel. I am quite familiar with his diet – he spent a year eating only wild food from his 40 acre (16 hectare) farm. It must have been hard work – I find it difficult down here, and I have a few basic staples and a vegetable patch! I keep thinking that, compared to him, I'm not making as much effort as I could. But then again, he was living in a nice, warm, cosy house with central heating, electricity, running water and his family for company. I live in a hand-built tree house with *none* of the above (apart from Bertha). Still, cracking effort and a damn fine read.

SUNDAY 4TH OCTOBER

Today Clare and I went to the Autumn Game Fair at the South of England Showground. It was rubbish. There was about as much game there as there is at Borough Market – not a lot! There were only two highlights: one was the vegetable tent, where there were some very amusingly shaped vegetables and some enormous leeks, big enough to knock someone out with; the other was the poultry barn.

When I was nine my school sent our class to Normandy in France for a whole term. The idea was to get a feel for French culture and ultimately to learn the language. I loved the French markets, where you could find everything from fake Zippo lighters and flick knives to chickens, pigs and

HOW TO SMOKE PIGEON

1

2

1 I covered an 'A'-frame with two ponchos clipped together, and made a fire underneath. Once the fire was going, I laid two long oak limbs on top, which began smouldering. I looked inside to see the artificial chamber gradually filling up with smoke.

2 I cut each pigeon breast into four slices: I thought the process would be quicker if the pieces of meat were thin and there was plenty of surface area. I ended up with 96 slices and had to squeeze each one in a towel to remove as much moisture as possible before smoking. I seasoned half the meat with salt and pepper, and the other half with spicy piri-piri and a little salt, before threading the slices onto hazel skewers and placing them in the smoking chamber resting on the 'A'-frame.

2

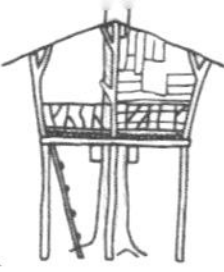

3 The smoking took a long time: I began at midday and by 6pm the meat was still slightly soft. I had to spend the whole afternoon sitting by the fire to maintain the steady stream of smoke.

As when smoking the mushrooms and the rabbit pelts, every time the fire got excited and flames began to jump, I doused the fire with a light drizzle of water.

vegetables – a far cry from the British farmers' market! I remember how cheap all the poultry was – the chicks were just one franc each! A friend and I very nearly bought some – but were apprehended by one of our teachers as we were telling the vendor what we wanted in our best stumbling French with appalling accents.

Ever since then, poultry for sale has always excited me – weird, I know. Clare and I walked about looking at all the birds for sale. I so wanted some, but I knew I wasn't in a position to care for them properly, and Clare just gave me that look that said 'Don't even think about it'. Back in May, I considered getting some chickens to keep down in the woods, but Frank and his pals would certainly have taken them off my hands – unless I had eaten them first.

I bought some more cartridges for the shotgun – the decoying had cleaned me out. I also got a couple of fishing lures for pike: it is getting to the time of year when they start to get a bit more active.

Back at the tree house I took Clare into the fields to show her how to use the shotgun. The noise and kick as she fired made her squeal with delight (and swear at the same time). With a little practice she could make a fine shot, probably better than me; in my experience girls generally are when it comes to shooting …

Clare's sister popped down with her husband to have a look at the tree house; she wanted her unborn baby at least to have visited weird Uncle Nick's tree house. They gave me a box of chocolates and I gave my future brother-in-law a taste of my beer. He loved it – until I told him about the unfortunate side effects.

I've got less than a month left at the tree house now and I'm not sure I want to leave. There is so much I still want to try. Time seems to have passed so quickly. I never stop learning down here, and there is always something new …

I spent some time in the field tonight taking some delay shots of the moonlit fields with my new camera. It's a great investment: no matter how little money you have for doing things, you can always go out and amuse yourself by taking pictures.

It seems to me, when you are inside you could be anywhere. But as soon as you step outside your whereabouts become apparent. Be it concrete or woodland, the same question always arises: am I happy? Am I content with my surroundings? At last, I believe I can finally say yes.

HOW TO MAKE CAT TAIL CANDLES

Although I had my lanterns, I was also interested in trying to create light by using natural materials. The cat tail, or reed mace, as well as being a good carbohydrate resource (the root), develops distinct cigar-shaped heads in July. I decided to see if it would be possible to turn these into candles – after all, they were the perfect shape, and the soft, fluffy flower heads should burn. I picked half a dozen from the carp lake to experiment with.

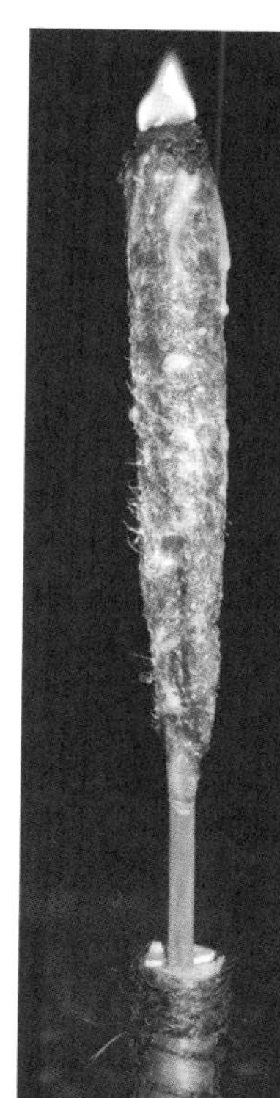

To help make the cat tail heads burn I melted some fat in a billycan over the fire (I had to buy in the fat, as not many of the animals I shot were that fatty), and then ladled it over the flower heads so they would soak up as much fat as possible and, hopefully, burn long and slow. Once coated and left to set, I fitted the cat tail candle into a length of hazel that was split at one end, and bound it together tight with twine.

It wasn't so easy to light, but when it eventually got going, the experiment was a success! With hindsight, perhaps a brief soak in paraffin would really get them fired up!

Mind you, I used to say that about London – perhaps old age is setting in. The younger, foolish version of me once enjoyed bars, clubs and vodka-Red Bulls; now I like cosy country pubs and a pint of fine ale. A kebab is the food of Satan, whereas a rabbit stew or pan-fried pigeon is the wholesome grub of comfort. People worry about turning 30, but at 28 I'm not that bothered. The only thing I really wanted to do before I turned 30 was move back to the country …

MONDAY 5th OCTOBER

Rain at last! Mushrooms to follow – hopefully. Due to the lack of rain, I have been collecting super-dry branches only as and when they were needed, and I have failed to gather a bounty of wood for my tree house wood store. There is plenty of kindling: all I have to do is split up all the small bits of timber left over from patching the walls. But big logs, essential for warmth, are few and far between – my 'cross that bridge' approach has fallen flat on its arse. I should be careful what I wish for …

Wood will always burn, however; it just needs splitting to expose the dry insides, and what better way to spend a miserable, rain-soaked afternoon than wielding an axe? I didn't go shooting today, it was far too wet, but I did spend some time looking out of the back window of the tree house with the air rifle. No luck there, so dinner was a vegetarian special, this time with burdock root instead of potato. The burdock was a pain to dig up considering I could have had potatoes, but I fancied a change of root.

10pm – still bloody raining!

TUESDAY 6th OCTOBER

I actually considered eating toad today; I know that they are used in Cantonese cuisine and are considered a speciality. The rain has turned the wood into a hopping frenzy of happy toads; it is difficult not to step on one of the warty beasts. I have always been a big fan of frog's legs and I never leave mainland Europe without a frozen packet of them. I decided to add toad to my wish list, after mole, for the next time I have a serious bout of culinary bravado …

This is the first time there has been two consecutive days of rain in the last five months – not such a bad summer after all! The relentless drizzle has made one thing perfectly clear: there was very little I could get done

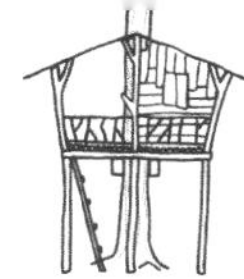

today. I must have read for hours: a mixture of *The Wild Life* and Nigel Slater's *Toast*.

I made a few more shotgun key rings for the forthcoming foraging fair, and cut and chopped more wood to keep the stove alive – Bertha loves oak more than anything. The prospect of another meatless meal forced me to look to my recently smoked pigeon for my dinner. The smoke-dried strips really were better than the very best biltong. I tore up a handful of strips and stuck them in a billycan along with some rice, beef stock, spinach and onions, and then thickened it with a little flour: good, warming, comfort food.

After supper I dusted off my emergency bottle of peaty Laphroaig, poured a dram and sat in front of the stove. I can't help but think that tree house living isn't quite as much fun when the weather is pants.

WEDNESDAY 7th OCTOBER

The rain is getting boring now. Clare and I went to meet the foraging day organisers at the Parham Estate – the fair is on Sunday. There were lots of pheasant and deer knocking about – I should have brought the gun!

> **'The best thing one can do when it's raining, is to let it rain ...'**
>
> HENRY WADSWORTH LONGFELLOW

Then we went to see Scott, a friend who owns a pub nearby. We had a quick drink and I dropped Clare home on the way back to the tree house. By this point the drizzle had been replaced by unforgiving, heavy rain. The deluge certainly highlighted the roof's weaknesses, and the sheep's wool was doing very little to keep the rain from entering the building. Strangely enough, the weak point is the enormous tree running through the middle of the house ...

I ran around the tree house like a deranged Charlie Chaplin, laying out newspaper and putting out pots to catch the drips. I always knew the oak tree would be the weak link: 60ft (18.3m) up, at the top of the tree, the branches catch all the precipitation and channel it down the limbs to the main body of the tree. That water then runs down between the grooves of the bark until it hits the edge of the roof, where it meets with a little interference, causing half of the water to trickle down the rafters, and the rest to run onto the floor. Fortunately this only seems to happen in torrential rain.

At first, when it was just the odd drip here and there, I found it hilarious. But gradually it got heavier, and when the water started to hit the bed, I stopped laughing. Eventually there I was, with the rain hammering on the roof and dripping into bowls that needed emptying every ten minutes. But Bertha was ablaze, a bottle of Château Tree House Meadowsweet 2009 was on the go, and a big stew with patch leftovers, dried ceps, dried seaweed and smoked pigeon was on the menu …

THURSDAY 8th OCTOBER

After drifting off to the drumming of the rain and avoiding the soggy side of the bed, I actually slept quite well. Too well! It was almost 11am when I got up, but then I had been on rain duty until 2am.

I stepped out of the tree house into another world. In the cold light of day, the sodden woodland felt different; *I* felt different. It wasn't easy to put my finger on. I don't think the rain had anything to do with it – it hasn't really bothered me apart from being a minor 'challenge'. As I scrabbled together what little dry wood I had left to start a fire, and got the kettle on, I tried to work out what was so out of place.

In the quiet wood the sun's rays filtered through the falling leaves. I felt an overwhelming sense of contentment. I have achieved everything I have set out to do and more, and although I felt there was still more to be done, I couldn't think of anything. I have been worried about leaving my life in the woods and waving goodbye to the comfortable existence I have created.

It is obvious the changing seasons are having a big impact on my lifestyle as well as my thoughts. The summer has been glorious – a snippet of rural bliss that felt like it could have come straight out of an H. E. Bates novel. My landlords are like a 21st-Century version of the Larkin family – they even have a boat on their pond called *Perfick*.

With winter drawing in, life in the woods doesn't seem to hold much enjoyment. Amongst all the positive feedback I received following the tree house's short burst of attention in the media, there was also the inevitable criticism, much of it regarding the fact that I am not going to be spending the winter in the woods, and that I am in the south of England and not a remote corner of the country.

I rather enjoyed the online attacks from faceless ranters who had probably never camped in a tent for more than two nights in a row, let alone built a

tree house and lived in it for six months. Some reeked of jealousy and hate – perhaps from a frustrated estate agent sitting in a dreary office somewhere in London.

With the wild larder providing me with 60% of my food, and the patch feeding me only until November, staying here for the winter would not provide the nourishment I need. I have always believed that if you are going to do something, you should enjoy it: I couldn't see winter in the tree house as being a barrel of laughs. I would spend most of my time collecting and cutting wood, sitting inside huddled next to the stove, and not really enjoying life. I feel ready to move closer to society; my time living as a tree-dwelling hunter-gatherer has almost run its course. I have gained so much from the experience, but it is becoming increasingly difficult to squeeze out any more.

I am also craving company: at first I relished the time alone, but as the weeks have gone on the solitary lifestyle has been harder to cope with than I anticipated. My trip to Scotland was certainly a contributing factor to my understanding that true happiness is best when shared; a conclusion also reached by Christopher McCandless in *Into the Wild*, shortly before he met with his fate. I have no intention of going the same way – although Alaska is slightly more inhospitable than Sussex.

Living here was never intended to be about cutting myself off from the outside world. If anything, it has been about self-sufficiency, trying to create a comfortable existence, and living well for next to nothing. I fear this happy lifestyle will not last into winter, but for six months I feel I have proved, to myself at least, that it has been entirely possible.

With the world around me changing, I had some toast and jam, put on a pair of wellies, and went on a nice long walk. The only mushrooms out were fly agaric and death caps – good eating if I wanted to remove myself from the gene pool!

Friday 9th October

The hustle and bustle of early-morning commuter trains is horrible: no seats, too many folk. Despite this, a few people seemed happy because it was Friday. Office hours had begun, and phones and laptops were already whirring into action. Is it live to work or work to live – I'm not sure?

Today I was in London for another series of fruitless 'brainstorming' sessions with television production companies before receiving the inevitable 'but …'

In the evening Clare and I had our engagement party in a pub we used to live next door to in Battersea. There's nothing like having an engagement to bring all your friends together. During my last year in London, it was virtually impossible to get everyone together. I suppose people thought they wouldn't be invited to the wedding if they didn't come to the engagement party – they'd probably be right.

Saturday 10th October

I feel absolutely shocking. Good party, great to see all our friends; not used to so much over-indulgence! Quite looking forward to getting on the train to head back to the country. Think I might steer well clear of anything fermented for quite a while – that goes for bread too.

Monday 12th October

The first thing I saw when I woke up this morning was my breath! It was bloody chilly, both inside and out.

I concentrated on nuts today. There seem to be plenty of squirrels doing the same, making the most of the glut before winter kicks in. I could also hear the constant 'tap tap' of nuthatches, as they wedged hazelnuts into the bark of large oaks, and pecked at them until they got to the tasty nut inside.

I went for a walk and gathered a basketful of acorns, sweet chestnuts and hazelnuts. The hazels are pretty bare, but acorns are plentiful – only the pigeons seem to be interested. When we were decoying, Tom told me that if you shoot a pigeon that has been feeding on acorns, it will drop out of the sky like a ton of bricks, and make a small crater where it lands.

I have read how unpleasant acorn coffee is so many times that I have never bothered to make it. The reason why it can be so unpalatable is that acorns contain high levels of tannins, which make them exceedingly bitter. As there is such a glut of acorns I decided to give it a try.

HOW TO MAKE ACORN COFFEE

The standard method of removing bitterness from anything is to boil it for some time in several changes of water. Boiling acorns not only helps to extract the bitterness, it also makes the skins easy to remove. I boiled the acorns for 20 minutes, removed them from the water, and let them cool down before peeling them.

After this, in an ideal world, you would dry the acorns for 48 hours, and then roast them. I decided to roast them whole for an hour in the clay oven, pound them using a pestle and mortar, and then roast the grounds for a further 30 minutes.

It worked perfectly and after the final roasting I was left with a light brown coffee substitute. I put the roast grounds in a jam jar and had a sniff – they smelt just like digestive biscuits!

I poured some of the grounds into my espresso machine, filled it with boiling water, and put it over a pan on the fire. It tasted really quite pleasant! There was a hint of bitterness, but no more than in normal coffee. I could get used to drinking it, but it wouldn't give me the caffeine kick I need first thing in the morning.

SLOE GIN

INGREDIENTS

1½lb (700g) sloes

8oz (225g) white granulated sugar

2 bottles cheap gin

1 First prepare your sloes. Some people are very meticulous and prick each individual sloe twice with a fork. I found it easier to lay them on a tray, take a fork in each hand, and go mad – it takes a minute, tops.

2 If you can get your hands on a demi-john (see photo) or large bell jar, these are best, but you can use ordinary bottles. Fill your chosen bottle halfway with the sloes, add the sugar, and fill the bottle to the top with gin. Seal and leave in a dark place for 2–3 months, turning occasionally. Decant through a sieve to remove the berries, and rebottle the gin.

3 Afterwards it is worth adding the gin-soaked berries to a bottle of sherry or vodka for an interesting liqueur, or using the sloes as an alternative to juniper berries in game stews and casseroles; after all, juniper berries are one of the prime ingredients of gin.

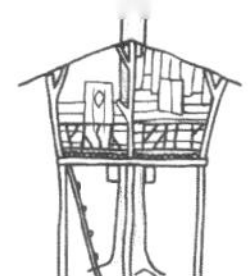

I shot a squirrel near the top of the wood and had it for early supper. I used my small quantity of hazelnuts to stuff the chest cavity of the squirrel – the pairing was genius. I seasoned the skin and roasted the squirrel whole in the clay oven, basting it from time to time with a mixture of olive oil, honey, seasoning and crushed herbs. After 40 minutes I took it upstairs and tucked in. The honey gave the skin a sublime, sticky glaze; I just wish there had been more of it. After supper I listened to the radio and read bits of books, while giving Bertha the occasional poke.

Tuesday 13th October

While I was out shooting some days ago, I came across a frost hollow where the hedge was packed with blackthorn, best known for its fruit: sloes. Sloes are only ripe after the first frost, which softens the skins and makes them more permeable, something that is necessary before you can make sloe gin – and that is why I wanted them.

Because of their position in the hollow the berries were already ripe, way ahead of their brothers and sisters in the other hedgerows. I arrived with that most versatile of foraging receptacles – the plastic bag – and began to fill it. The problem with harvesting sloes is the abundance of spikes on the branches next to the fruit – it is a bit like trying to pluck an olive out of a bag of toothpicks.

I didn't need to worry about using up my luxury item on the gin: the sloe gin, once put together, wouldn't be ready until Christmas.

Having just got engaged, Clare is about to leave me for a six-month contract in the south of France. It was her perfect job – designing girls' surf wear for a reputable brand. She *had* to go – after all, I have just spent the last six months living in a tree! I had also heard good things about the surf in Biarritz, so there are some perks …

She came to spend her last night in the tree house before she went. We roasted a big pheasant in the clay oven and ate it with potatoes, spinach and gravy. The pheasant took only about half an hour to cook and had a slight smokiness about it – for a change!

My air mattress has begun to deflate quite a bit and needed blowing up. It was the first time I'd had to do it since being down here. I undid the valves and gave it a pump. However, in the morning one side had completely deflated – I should have left it as it was!

Wednesday 14th October

I dropped off the kayaks at my old school and saw Chuck, who gave me a quick tour. It has changed quite a bit since I was there. We went down to the 'jungle' – the name we gave to the woods where I used to spend much of my time grubbing about building camps. The old outdoor swimming pool, in which we were forced to freeze off our extremities, had been filled in and had huge trees growing out of it. In fact, the whole place seemed a lot smaller than I remembered.

I have arranged to do a talk on 4 November: I plan to spend 45 minutes telling the children that you can get so much more out of life if you don't sell your soul to the business world. I'm not sure their parents would agree, but why not give the kids a balanced view?

In the afternoon I went on a long walk past the reservoir to some beech woods where I have picked loads of edible mushrooms in the past. I expected to see some hedgehog fungi but there were none. There were quite a lot of slippery jacks – from the same *Boletus* family as the cep – but when I got them home my identification guides said they weren't versatile enough for drying, which was why I had picked them in the first place. Oh, well.

On the way back I stopped at the pub I used to work in when I was 18, to have a quick ale and say hello to my old boss. I managed to barter some of my mushrooms in return for beer – good deal! I noticed the smell of the wood smoke straight away – funny, I don't notice it now when I'm at the tree house unless the smoke is blowing in my face.

The walk, the mushrooms and the beer (supped in front of a cosy inglenook fireplace) restored my appreciation of autumn a little. When I got back I fired up the clay oven to cook supper: slippery jack, wild garlic and onion pizzas with nettle pesto – yum! As I was cooking outside I had to dress up warm; my padded lumberjack shirt really came into its own, but I can't help feeling a bit like the Michelin man when I'm wearing it.

Clare left to go to France today. Don't really want to talk about it.

Made more shotgun key rings as a distraction and spent hours in deep thought while playing with a yo-yo I had found in a drawer at my mother's house. I finally mastered how to 'walk the dog'.

FRIDAY 16th OCTOBER

I spent today getting things together for the Parham Foraging and Countryside Day. They have printed up a big picture of the tree house and me – I definitely won't feel like a spoon standing next to that!

They want me to 'enlighten' the people of Sussex about the joys of tree-house dwelling and the simple life. I seem to have packed up half the tree house to take over as props. It has made me realise how much fun moving out is going to be at the end of the month – a proper sack of giggles!

CAULIFLOWER FUNGUS (SPARASSIS CRISPA)

DESCRIPTION **Associated with pine, and resembling a cauliflower – hence the common name – this species is yellow-cream in colour and can grow to the size of a football. The branches of the fungus are divided and flat. August–November.**

USES **Because of all the nooks and crannies, cleaning up a cauliflower fungus for cooking is a real pain – by far the easiest way to deal with it is to cut it into slices. These can then be fried in butter for five minutes, covered with grated cheddar, and grilled in the oven until the cheese has melted. Put it on a piece of toast, give it a dash of Worcester sauce and a sprinkle of parsley, and dig in!**

About this time last year, I found some enormous cauliflower fungi in a secret spot not too far from the wood. The fungi version is so much better than the vegetable – for starters, they don't smell of canned farts. They often appear at the base of large Scot's pines and can grow quite big, providing plenty of meals for the lucky finder.

I went up to the spot and was rewarded with three big ones – one was slightly bigger than my head! They do tend to go a bit harder as they get older, but if you catch them in their prime, they are easily one of the best fungi. And there are no other fungi you could possibly confuse them with – they are the ultimate safe bet.

As it was a Friday night, I put on my cleanest attire (of which there is very little) and met Chris and George for a few beers. My eyes are now well tuned to nature's tasty morsels: in the corner of the beer garden there were over 30 field mushrooms growing in pretty little rings. Against my better judgement I began picking them. I did wonder whether the chef at the pub was keeping them for his dishes but, judging by the poor, uninspiring menu, I doubt it.

SATURDAY 17th OCTOBER

Why is it that the animals around the tree house always know when I want them for my table? Today I spent ages looking for rabbits and squirrels for supper, and for a demonstration of a normal meal *à la* tree house at Parham tomorrow. The squirrels, usually out in force stealing all my chestnuts, were nowhere to be seen. There was no shortage of game, but ideally I wanted a couple of squirrels for the general public to taste. I think it is a meat we should be eating more of, not least because it would give the native red squirrels the breathing space they deserve.

However, I was not going to look a gift horse in the mouth, and when I came across a group of hen pheasants, I crept up and waited for them to follow the call of the nearest cock pheasant to roost. Once they began to take off, I shot the one nearest to me and it crashed down through the trees and into the nettles. This commotion prompted the cock pheasant to fly out from the tree so I shot him as well. Looks like it will be pheasant instead of squirrel for Sunday lunch, and pheasant with nettles for supper tonight.

For supper I roasted the pheasant whole in the clay oven, steamed the nettles, and pan-fried slices of the cauliflower fungus with wild garlic. I made a simple gravy with some stock and a bit of flour to thicken it, just

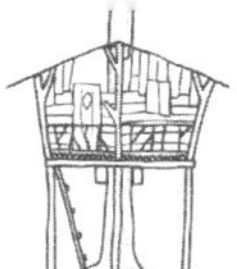

to add a touch of moisture to the meal. It was certainly at the high end of tree-house cuisine. I was so hungry I sucked every bone of the pheasant clean.

Despite Bertha's best efforts, it seemed unnaturally cold tonight, and to keep the tree house warm I was going through wood at an obscene rate. I don't think Bertha's firebox has ever been so full.

SUNDAY 18th OCTOBER ☼ FROST!

Parham. I woke at 6am. I had planned an early outing with the gun in a last-ditch attempt to bag some squirrel, but it was still pitch-black outside. I turned on the torch and not only could I see my breath but also my nose was frozen along with the rest of my head. I pulled a woolly hat down over my head, snuggled as far down into my sleeping bag as I could, doubled over the duvet, and went back to sleep for an hour.

It was just beginning to get light at 7am. I got up and made a fire in the dark, then set about the time-honoured tradition of the morning brew as the frozen dawn crept on.

After a much-needed caffeine injection the dawn chorus was well under way and the sun was peeking over the horizon. I went out in search of small mammals for lunch. The fields were coated in a thick layer of frost, which crunched underfoot, and the mist hung thick in the air.

It was so cold I struggled to grip the barrel of the gun. I saw a couple of squirrels, which disappeared before I could get within range. I shot a rabbit, but yet again it turned out to have myxomatosis – no good.

I got to Parham at 8.45am to set up my stall. It was turning into a beautiful crisp autumn day. The tree house banner was huge, and I did feel a bit of a plonker standing next to it, but it turned out to be really useful when I was describing the build to people.

Coffee Ritual

Coffee making was an important well-practised ritual at the tree house, ritual being the operative word. After my experience in the Cook Islands where I was without the black stuff for three months, I realised that, along with water, coffee is a basic human right: instant if you're desperate, but the real stuff if time allows. Sod it, you must make time! The ritual is just as important as the satisfying hit of caffeine on drinking. This is how my morning *Tinto* ritual was executed:

1. Boil kettle, fill billycan with 4–5 spoonfuls of coffee granules – Columbian or Costa Rican recommended! (Don't use the fine-grain stuff, it's a bugger to filter.)

2. Add water, give the coffee a good stir, and allow it to steep for 4 minutes – no more, no less.

3. Place the billycan back over the fire to reboil until bubbling – this is essential to bring out the maximum flavour. I was taught this by Tom, the Hungry Cyclist, who learnt it from an Israeli chap while on his travels. Trust me, it makes all the difference!

4. Remove the billycan from the fire and rest for 1–2 minutes with the lid on. Get a mug of cold water, dip your hand into it, remove the lid and flick drops of water over the surface of the coffee to make the granules sink to the bottom.

5. You are now ready to pour out the perfect mug of tree house coffee.

Most of the visitors were eager to learn more about my lifestyle. There were some great questions and I even met a few people who had been following my blog; one of them brought me a pack of lamb steaks – how kind! My stall was opposite the falconers, so I had a great view of the displays during the few moments I wasn't talking to people.

I had planned to do a few demonstrations, like making nettle beer and a fully foraged meal, but I barely had time to pan-fry a pheasant breast on the small fire I had been allowed to light. I had brought the coracle for a day out, my rabbitskin rug, the shower, and a selection of my processed wild foods and brews. I also brought 30 shotgun key rings to sell – I sold about seven. Glad I hadn't bothered to make any more!

Only one person rubbed me the wrong way: a spotty teenager who thought he was quite the comedian. He actually had the cheek to pick up an unopened bottle of elderflower champagne and open it. I'm pleased to say it exploded in his face and everyone laughed – serves the little bugger right!

The day wound up at around 5pm. I was absolutely shattered. I packed up the car and headed back to the woods. It was a good day, and hopefully I might have inspired a few people. When I got back I was starving, so I knocked together some flatbreads, and made good use of the lamb steaks I had been given. By 9pm I was out for the count.

MONDAY 19th OCTOBER

I spent some time this morning doing a scatty unpacking of all the stuff I took to Parham, and then I had a visit from Greg, a photographer friend of Al's. We had struck a deal: I needed some sequence shots done of me skinning and gutting a rabbit (a self-timer and blood-soaked hands aren't a great combo for any camera) and he fancied a night in the tree house.

I went to meet him at the top of the wood at about midday. He was much younger than I thought he would be and had a rather sinister beard – we hit it off immediately. He had obviously spoken to Al, and brought me a variety of bits and pieces: dry-roasted peanuts (for me, them birds ain't getting none), a packet of biltong, a box of Pop Tarts, four carrots, a pack of venison sausages, a half bottle of port, Stilton and crackers. It was a real spoiling! I haven't had Stilton for nearly six months – what sin!

We sat by the fire and got to know each other over tea and peanuts. I showed him around the tree house and talked him through the construction process. He was not camera shy in the least – his itchy trigger finger was shooting away throughout the tour.

Then we went on a walk with the gun to find some sustenance. Greg said he was eager to try squirrel for the first time, so we set our sights on bagging one. I wasn't confident – they have remained elusive for the last few days.

The rumours that I was out with the gun had obviously not started to circulate and we saw plenty of squirrels, rabbits and pigeons. But my eye was off and something didn't feel right. I was using the new cartridges I had bought at the game show so I switched to the two remaining cartridges I had left from my old batch.

As we walked into a cut maize field near the decoying spot, a cock pheasant was greedily pecking away at the leftovers. He stood up straight when he saw us climb over the hedge, and seemed to hesitate as if he was reluctant to leave the free food. As we got closer, he changed his mind and began his approach for take-off. Once he was in the air he was fair game and the shotgun brought him spinning down to earth with a thud. Never shoot pheasants on the ground or on Sundays – or (ahem) out of season.

On the walk back to the wood a squirrel presented itself over the pathway directly above us – Greg would get his taste of squirrel after all. We picked a few handfuls of sorrel – all that was left after the farmer's over-zealous trimming of the field. Back at the tree house I got the fire going and we tucked into the 'dangerous' meadowsweet beer sparingly: I was running low on toilet paper …

I peeled the squirrel and pan-fried it as a sort of tree house bar snack. Greg was a big fan, which came as no surprise; I've yet to meet someone who didn't like squirrel after having the balls to taste it.

After that we moved upstairs to cook supper on top of Bertha. I was planning to use only the breasts from the pheasant and I wanted to try a trick a young lad had taught me at Parham. Apparently, if you lay a pheasant on its back, put your feet over the wings, and pull the bird's feet firmly but slowly, the breast meat becomes exposed and there is no need to pluck it at all. It worked, but I didn't expect the bird to end up in two pieces! I was left with a big pool of blood on the floor of the tree house – right where Greg had planned to sleep.

For supper we had pan-fried pheasant breast with a few vegetables, cauliflower fungus and sorrel *verde*.

INGREDIENTS

A handful finely chopped sorrel
A handful finely chopped parsley
Juice of ½ lemon
1 tsp Dijon mustard
2 tsp red wine vinegar
Olive oil (enough to make it like a dressing)
Salt and pepper (to taste)
4 bulbs finely chopped wild garlic

SORREL VERDE

Mix all ingredients in a bowl and leave to rest for at least half an hour to let the flavours marry and mingle. Use with meat, fish or mushrooms.

We drizzled the sauce over the pheasant and cauliflower fungi; it was another exceptional tree house meal – tree-top cuisine perhaps?

I cracked open a bottle of birch sap wine that I had made back in March. By all accounts, it should be left for six months to a year before opening, but I wanted to know how it had turned out. It was bloody strong and slightly on the yeasty side (could have done with a bit longer), but overall it wasn't a bad effort.

We moved on to port, Stilton and crackers, and gorged until it was all gone. With our appetites fully sated, we talked for a while to let the digestive system do its thing before we turned in for the night.

Tuesday 20th October

Had Pop Tarts for breakfast: a blast from the past. As a child, every time we went to the supermarket I pestered my mother to buy some, and every time she flatly refused. She had a good point – it was like eating sugar-coated cardboard stuffed with molten goo.

We went up the river for a fish and took the gun with us just in case. I caught a good-sized pike in a narrow section of the river. Greg clicked away with his camera and asked if we were going to have it for lunch. As tasty as pike are – they happen to be one of my favourite fish – they are just the most evil-looking predators, cunningly fashioned for the kill and nothing else. I have always felt a strong affiliation with the pike, especially over the last six months where I have been at the top of the food chain (apart from the mosquitoes). There aren't many in the river, so I slipped him back into the water to let him follow his predatory instincts.

On the walk back, we turned a corner into a field and I spotted a rabbit just within range. I needed to shoot one to get my sequence photos. It was a long shot, and there was no cover to get closer, so I took careful aim and fired. The rabbit flopped over instantly.

For lunch we had venison sausages, rice, leeks and red onions, and then we did the rabbit photographic session before Greg had to head back up to town. A successful two days of hunter-gathering. I was pleased that my guest had been able to see so much in such a short time.

WEDNESDAY 21st OCTOBER

Heavy rain is expected this week but so far it is being elusive – good! I braved the shower this morning. Lately I have been having one every 2–3 days. It is not as bad as I thought it would be, just not quite as pleasant as a couple of months ago.

I had a good tidy this morning ready for another visitor, Kevin. I picked him up from the station at midday. We went up to my mushroom spot to check for hedgehog fungi. Still nothing – where could they be? Kevin had brought me some wild venison salami and some goat's cheese – great snack food. I took Kevin on roughly the same jaunt as I did Greg, even down to the squirrel, but sadly no pheasants presented themselves for the pot.

Oh, pants – my diary has run out of pages!

THURSDAY 22ND OCTOBER

I woke up to the sound of Kevin purging a dodgy prawn sandwich he ate on the train yesterday. A clear illustration of why it is good to know where your food comes from! We took a walk up to the dairy farm to get some milk for cheese making. The farmer told us to help ourselves, and as we walked away I overheard him explaining to his wife that I hadn't always lived in a tree!

Kevin was still not feeling great, so I told him to relax in the hammock and have a snooze, while I made some piri-piri cheese. By the time I dropped Kevin back at the station he was feeling marginally better. Back at the tree house I looked at my calendar – I've got Reuters News coming to film tomorrow so I'd better be on best behaviour.

I spoke to Clare this evening. She seems to be getting on well in France. I do miss her. I won't be heading out there until December – it seems ages away!

FRIDAY 23RD OCTOBER

'What's this structure here?', asked the Reuters News journalist. It was not quite the question I expected. It was quite clearly a bench – she could have made an educated guess …

I took the team up to the dairy farm so I could exchange my cheese for some more milk, shot a squirrel for lunch, and took them to see the patch. After a full week of showing people around, it was beginning to wear a bit thin. I want to enjoy my last week down here without having to play tour guide the whole time.

THE HOT TODDY

Many years ago, the good virtues of this wonderful golden liquid were instilled in me. Knowing it would be something I would enjoy as I got older, I never binged on it as a teenager! I decided that it would be an important addition to my 'medicine' cabinet. Germs don't like whisky – fact. The hot toddy is a superb restorative: honey has been used in medicine for thousands of years, the lemon contains vitamin C, and the whisky makes you feel better!

INGREDIENTS

1½fl. oz (40ml) whisky (just over a shot)

Juice of ½ lemon

Boiling water

2 tsp honey

1 The idea for a good hot toddy is to get the right balance between the sharpness of the lemon, the sweetness of the honey, and the strength of the whisky – let personal preference be your ultimate guide. If the lemon is a bit hard, give it a good roll on a hard surface to soften it before slicing it in half.

2 Put the whisky and lemon juice into the mug and fill with boiling water. Then add the honey – this way it simply melts off the spoon. Sit in front of an open fire in a big comfy armchair (if you have one) and enjoy!

After they left I had a quiet, reflective evening, sustained by a few hot toddies. Today I was asked about what I want to do next. I think I would like to build a house for Clare and me. It would have to be a low-impact and sustainable dwelling (solar energy, wind turbines, wood burning stove, etc.), so we would have next to no bills. Life for me from now on will always involve living close to the land: perhaps a few animals and a large vegetable plot. I would like a house built the old English way: timber-framed, wattle and daub, with a nice thatch to top it off. One day maybe …

SATURDAY 24th OCTOBER

While I had been living in a tree, Justin and Emma had spent the last six months organising a charity boxing event to raise money to build a school in Cameroon. Sixteen guys, who had never boxed before, had trained for six months, and then were matched up to fight in front of a roomful of paying punters who were dressed up to the nines. I went back to my mother's house and dug out my dinner jacket – a slight difference from my usual attire.

It was a fantastic night, and they raised enough money to build two schools! Justin was fighting, and then at the end he took to the stage in full Cameroonian tribal attire to thank everyone for their support. I stood next to the ring, snapping away with my camera so I could send some pictures to Clare. All of a sudden Justin got down on one knee in the boxing ring and asked Emma to marry him! I managed to get a photographic 'flicker book' of the whole thing! With the engagement announced and the crowd cheering, it was obvious that I was in for a long, heavy night. This engagement thing is catching …

MONDAY 26th OCTOBER

Six months sounds a long time, 24 weeks does not. So here we are, the 24th week, the grand finale of tree-house living. Mother Nature seems ready to be rid of me – she put the clocks back yesterday: it now gets dark at 5.30pm! Harsh.

Knowing that the freedom I have been lucky enough to experience over the last six months is shortly to come to an end fills me with sadness. I have enjoyed having my time dictated to me through the medium of light and dark rather than the hands of a clock. What is the right time to go to bed? When is lunchtime? I have got used to sleeping when I'm tired and eating when I'm hungry …

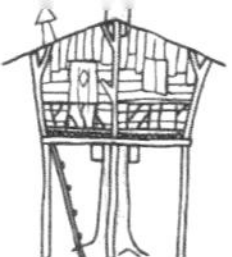

The concept of time is often dictated by food: time to go shooting, time to go fishing, time to check nightlines. I have been at the mercy of the changing seasons: both the vegetable patch and the wild larder provide me with food when they are good and ready and not a moment before. We live in an age where you can eat anything at any time of year, so learning to be patient was tough to begin with. But it all makes sense; adhering to this type of 'slow food' concept meant I was making the most of what was available and eating in tune with the seasons.

In 1986 Carlo Petrini, an Italian food and wine journalist, developed the 'slow food' movement, whose aim was to encourage people to protect their food traditions and preserve the pleasure associated with consumption of good, local produce. By nurturing the bond between producers and consumers, more people would look to local sources of food, rather than the supermarkets and the ever-expanding fast-food culture.

For many people, growing vegetables for the table and raising their own livestock for meat, makes them both producer and consumer, and removes the slightest sniff of a middleman. For a small amount of extra work the return is substantial, and they have the pleasure of knowing exactly where their food has come from and how it has been produced – they are at the very pinnacle of the 'food chain'.

But this is nothing new, and neither is living in the woods and trundling through life as a thoughtful hunter-gatherer. So what is the 21st-Century fascination with returning to the old ways? Have our lives become so ludicrously simple that we now wish to spice things up by getting back to basics? What was considered *de rigueur* as little as 90 years ago has now become all the rage – perhaps that was why the tree house received so much attention from the media.

It is a strange country we live in: trends and fads are as fickle as the weather, but I think the current ideal to move back to basics runs a little deeper than that. We don't want to lose touch with our past, our heritage, and what got us to where we are today. Of course, climate change has an awful lot to do with it, but let's not open that can of worms – yet.

It all boils down to the fact that food is our fuel: it keeps us alive and well. In an essay written by Ludwig Andreas Feuerbach in 1863, he said, as a literal translation, 'man is what he eats'. In another, earlier quote, much romanticised by the termites of the foodie class, Brillat Savarin said, 'Tell me what you eat and I will tell you what you are'. Neither man meant for us to take their words as gospel, they were just pointing out the obvious: whatever you put in your mouth has a direct affect on your wellbeing.

Fortunately I've had the luxury of identification guides to help me discern an edible wild plant from a poisonous one; the first hunter-gatherers would have played a Stone Age version of 'Russian roulette' with their foraging trips. As it turns out though, during my time here, my most alarming moments have occurred when man has tampered (deliberately or otherwise) with the wild larder: my poisoned nettle beer is a perfect example. Seeing first hand what the 'helpful' weedkillers did to my wild larder was disgusting, but when the crop reaches the consumer, is every trace of the contaminants gone? I doubt it …

I did think hunting, gathering and cooking would be the most enjoyable part of my experience, but in fact, building the tree house was by far the best bit. It is a permanent, tangible example of what I can achieve if I put my mind (and my back, arms and legs) to it.

TUESDAY 27th OCTOBER

I woke to a strangely warm day! Unlike during the heavy frosts a week ago, I didn't have an icicle for a nose when I opened my eyes. This morning I baked my final loaf of bread. I am looking forward to eating a slice of bread that doesn't contain dirt, twigs or leaves – I know roughage is a good thing, but sometimes tree house extras can be a step too far; my stomach must be rock solid by now!

Having seen some smart bent-hazel chairs at various country fairs, today I set about building an enormous chair as a thank-you to my landlords for allowing me the use of their land. Dotted around the wood were some small stacks of seasoned ash and hazel from the original tree house build. I opted for a true rustic chair and it slowly came together over the course of the afternoon – between tea breaks and smoky pieces of toast with tree house jam.

Darkness really crept up on me tonight. Having not yet adjusted to the clocks going back I very nearly missed out on supper. In the twilight, I positioned myself down by the river, underneath a tree frequently used by the pigeons for roosting. I had to squint to make them out among the disappearing leaves, but lucky for me, pigeons don't get comfortable straightaway and I was able to pick one out that was struggling to find the right sleeping position.

It was a good thing I wore my wellies – the pigeon fell straight into the river! I plucked the bird in front of Bertha, split the carcass down the middle, and cooked it in a pan with a few herbs from the hanging baskets.

I am going to miss having a limited larder – everything I cook tastes as it should and isn't drowned with too many flavourings. It is just simple, succulent food.

I sat in the flickering light of the hurricane lamps with my feet up in front of Bertha, drinking tea and reading *Wild Cooking* by Richard Mabey. How am I going to cope without the luxury of a real fire?

WEDNESDAY 28th OCTOBER

Today, like every day, began with a fire. Fire is something we all take for granted – it has become an element many of us don't even use anymore. Yet there is something about it that has transcended the ages; it is a symbol of warmth and comfort so powerful that we still have fireplaces in our homes today in order to enjoy its presence.

You only have to sit around a campfire at night with a bunch of people to see just how fascinated we humans still are with fire. Everyone has that primeval instinct that draws the gaze to the dancing flames and the glowing embers. Be it for cooking food, keeping warm or purifying water, fire will always remain mankind's most useful discovery.

When I first moved here I was a real purist when it came to making fire. I used only a flint and steel, and birch bark tinder or a dry cramp ball fungus. On a few occasions I even resorted to fire by friction, just to prove to myself I could still do it. After the first month though, the novelty began to wear thin, and I started using recycled newspaper and matches or a lighter to get the fire going. Fire is an integral part of my life down here and I needed it to be as instant as possible. Sometimes I felt slightly ashamed of myself for taking the easy option, but then again, it is still primitive – it is not as if I have a gas range or an electric oven.

In fact, anything that made my life easier down here, but still remained detached from the modern world, has been welcome. It is not as if I can cook at the flick of a switch – how to manage a fire for different uses is an important thing to learn: flames for boiling, embers for roasting, and different types of wood for different tasks. All of this used to be basic human knowledge; modern man doesn't know his arse from his elbow, and most things to do with fire-starting inevitably provoke the word 'petrol' or 'lighter fluid'. Other than bushcraft nerds and the woodsman fraternity, our true understanding of fire is slowly disappearing: ask a City banker to make fire from scratch and you will see my point (unless he happens to be a bushcraft nerd).

I spent most of the day working on the introduction to this book. I'm starting to get a little nervous about having only the next month to complete the manuscript. It's got to be good, as it's my first attempt at a book; if it isn't, I won't get a second chance … but then again, if you have got this far, it can't be that bad!

THURSDAY 29th OCTOBER

With my social secretary in France, it was down to me to try to put together a Halloween shindig to thank all the people who have helped me along the way. It was to be a small gathering, a sleepover with beer, fireworks and pumpkins.

Chris has given up the most time for the tree house build – he has helped with the foundations, the roof and the walls, and I am truly grateful for his assistance. Once again, he has offered to take tomorrow off work to help get things ready for the party and to help carve up the pumpkins.

I wanted things to go out with a bang, and as bonfire night is just around the corner, I blew £22 on a box of fireworks – rockets, to be exact. As it is going to be my last evening I am also going to treat myself to many of the culinary delights that I have been craving for the last six months: steaks, celery and cheese are at the top of the list. The list is actually pretty long and there is no way I will be able to get through it all in one night!

Tonight is my last night alone at the tree house. I took the gun out to bag my last wild supper. Rabbit was one of my first meals down here and I thought it only fitting that it should also be my last. As I wandered the fields I thought about how much everything has changed: I saw spring burst into life while I was digging the patch, summer took over as I moved into the tree house, followed by the gradual shift into autumn as I walked the fields and woods in search of mushrooms.

I really feel I have been part of the seasons rather than just a witness – my life has been so completely intertwined with them. My time here has been full of ups and downs. Simple tasks such as collecting water, chopping wood, watering the patch, and making a fire each morning became routine jobs that I didn't always enjoy. But, unlike a regular nine to five job, they really matter – they are the governing factors that allow life down here to continue.

Aside from the necessary routine jobs, life in the limbs has been unpredictable. I never knew what each day would bring, in terms of food, weather or activities. I liked not knowing; the best-laid plans don't allow for sporadic actions to take place on a whim. In the woods I had no one to answer to and only myself to depend upon. I had never felt so free from the confines of modern-day life, and the best thing about it was that for me … this *was* work.

I have never got tired of hunting or fishing – these are pastimes I will always enjoy – but they have become more than just recreational activities. The feelings of frustration over fading light and an empty bag have been some of the lowest points of tree-house living, which I could happily forget, but probably never will: they certainly helped me to appreciate the times I did have meat for the pot.

Supper came quickly this evening. Once again, I found it at the most productive of my meat stores: the copse. I squeezed the trigger of the air

rifle knowing full well that it would be a while before I shot for my supper again. I picked a few nettles, and took some leeks and the last of the red onions from the patch, to make a simple stew on top of my beloved Bertha.

I sat in the tree house in front of the roaring stove with rabbit stew bubbling away on top. This was what I was going to miss: cosy evenings sitting in a tree. I cracked the top off one of the last bottles of meadowsweet beer and filled my three-handled ceramic cider mug.

Producing my own grog has been an integral part of life in the woods, perhaps because it signifies the very pinnacle of self-sufficiency: the ability to create a luxury item from the hedgerows that is not essential to survival (although I'm not quite sure I totally agree with that last bit). My home brewing has come on in leaps and bounds. Despite the occasional mishap, I have enjoyed a varied cellar of wild brews throughout, and most of it has been shared with friends.

Before I went to bed I had to pump up the mattress again – thankfully it was for the last bloody time!

FRIDAY 30th OCTOBER

It all felt a bit strange today. It was going to be a day full of 'last times', but I tried not to dwell on it too much. I went through my usual coffee-making ritual and sat on the bench mulling over what had to be done for the evening.

Chris turned up at 11am with four large pumpkins. His carving efforts were much better than mine, so instead I concentrated on making the mix for some mulled wine with a few select ingredients.

We collected a big pile of wood and leftover bits of timber that were no longer of any use. We built a 4ft (1.2m) high bonfire and stuffed the inside with kindling and newspaper. Then I cleaned and tidied the tree house in readiness for my guests.

In a previous entry I said that the tree house wouldn't be finished until the very end. Funnily enough, I finished almost as I started – by hammering in some nails, this time to hang some lanterns. I sat down at the fold-out table to survey my finished house. It really did look like a proper house, and everything was where it should be.

Once darkness approached, I made the mulled wine and then lit the bonfire – for the first and last time with a petrol-induced 'whoosh'. As the flames leap high, fanning the few remaining hazel leaves, I can hear distant voices and clinking bottles, and see the twinkling of torches moving through the trees. Tonight is going to be a night to remember, and the last six months have been something I will never forget.

AFTERWORD

LOOKING back over my time in the woods I have asked myself lots of questions. What have I learned? What have I achieved? Has there really been a point to this whole exercise?

Truth be told, I have learned a lot, but I have only really scratched the surface; there is still so much more to learn. Practically every day I discovered something new: a plant I could eat, a plant I should avoid, the subtleties of animal behaviour, or even an easier way of doing something. If I were to write it all down, this book would be ten times the size! You may think I am a resourceful individual, but I'm no more so than you are. There is absolutely no reason that you couldn't go out and do as I have done, if you feel you are in need of a change. If reading this book means just one person decides that there is more to life than sitting in an office, or at least tries to build a clay oven in their back yard, then this whole experiment will have been worthwhile.

What became abundantly clear throughout my six months in the woods was the culinary versatility of Britain's native flora and fauna. I grew accustomed to treating rabbits, pigeons, nettles and hop shoots as if they were standard everyday ingredients. The flavours were new, different and unique to the palate, and gave me the chance to experiment with the more familiar vegetables from the patch. My diet was at the very forefront of what the 'slow food' movement is all about: fresh, local and seasonal.

With the exception of potatoes, flour, beans, salt and a few other extras, I was existing on the same diet as our Palaeolithic ancestors. This is the diet we ate as we evolved and it is correctly coded for our physiology; hence it is the healthiest possible diet we, as a species, can follow. I doubt I will ever follow such a pure diet again for a sustained period, although having had a taste, I will certainly strive to do so.

I found that I managed to keep my hunter-gathering activities to about 30–40 acres (12–16 hectares), despite having 250 acres (101 hectares) available. Britain has a total landmass of 59,672,730 acres (24,149,553 hectares) and a population (circa 2009) of 61,113,205. That works out as roughly 0.97 acres (0.4 hectares) per person. Putting aside factors associated with climate and landscape, would it be possible for us to survive off just under an acre of land each, or, like me, would we need a landmass 30–40 times that size to survive?

Of course, by today's standards the answer would be no. It is entirely possible for more than one person to survive off a smallholding of 1 acre (0.4 hectares) if managed intensively. The patch, a 14ft x 20ft (4.3m x 6m) plot for vegetables, was the only intensively 'farmed' part of my experiment. I could have put more energy into planting a larger variety of vegetables and grains, and reared livestock for meat. Then, rather than having to exploit a larger area of land, I would have had everything in one place,

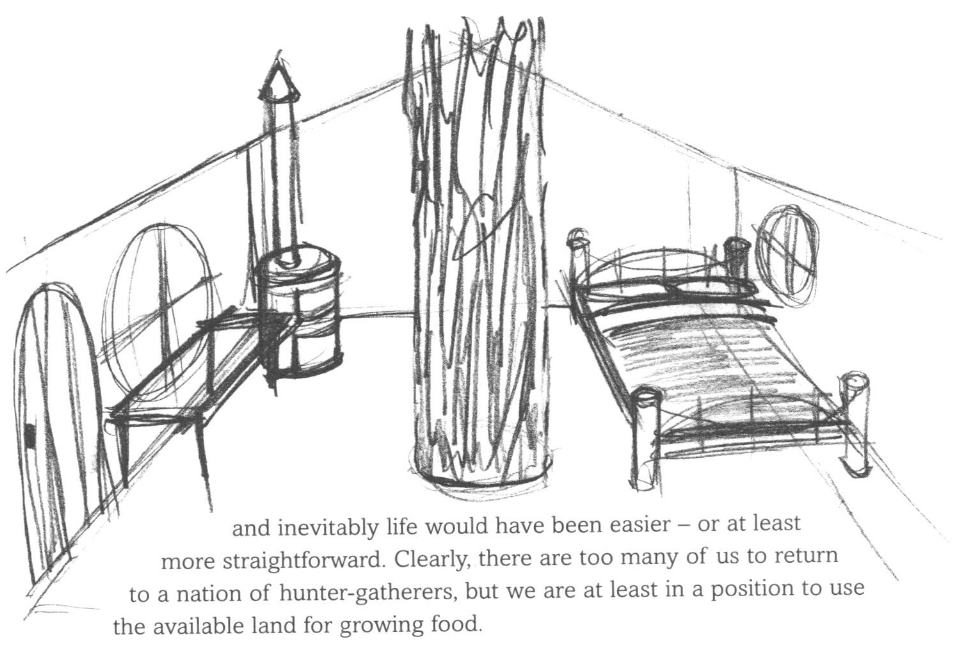

and inevitably life would have been easier – or at least more straightforward. Clearly, there are too many of us to return to a nation of hunter-gatherers, but we are at least in a position to use the available land for growing food.

Britain imports about 40% of all its food, and the convenience culture of today means we are more likely to use the supermarket than to grow our own or buy from local producers. If we are to avoid the food shortages that will eventually come because of climate change, and when oil production starts to decline, we need to become more self-sufficient in our approach to the way in which we live.

My bond with the countryside has become stronger than ever. I left the urban sprawl of London in the hope of rediscovering a life that was inexpensive, simple and straightforward, a life that was commonplace in the not so distant past. Now I have had a taste of rural living, I know there is little chance of me ever living anywhere larger than a village.

The hardest part was having the balls to step up and make a go of it in the first place. But the prospect of another wasted summer in the city, trying to scrub together the cash to pay the rent, was hardly an attractive thought. And so what began as an afternoon daydream on a sofa in Battersea gradually became a reality.

People debate over whether or not we have it good these days. The answer is yes, of course we do, but the best part is – we have options. It is down to the individual to decide how they wish to live out their days. Those who have a job they enjoy are the lucky ones, but for those less fortunate, is it wise to spend the best days of your youth slaving away in a mundane job you despise, chasing pennies to save for a better future that

may not exist? Is it possible that I could be part of the 'lost generation', one of the quarter-life crisis kids? Perhaps. But at least I know that while I could go out and explore the world around me, I did.

So what was the point of the tree house? I could have built a log cabin and kept my feet on the ground. I suppose the tree house was a way of rekindling the spirit of the child within, recapturing the days when there was nothing to worry about, and the feeling that anything was possible. This was my way out, my attempt at the good life, the chance to experience a new beginning I believed was better than the rut I was stuck in. I couldn't have been any closer to the truth: building the tree house has been the best thing I have ever done with my life, and signing the yellow piece of paper for that first delivery of the wood was how it all began.

To carve out an existence with your bare hands is a liberating feeling indeed; the lifestyle of the hunter-gatherer may be a thing of the past, but sometimes it is important to look back in order to see where you are going. I look to the future with open eyes and the excitement of the unknown, but now there is something that wasn't there before: a feeling of absolute content. No matter how bad things get or how desperate times become, I can always go back – back to the woods, the fields, and the places where the wild things roam free.

Acknowledgements

It would not have been possible to get this project off the ground (no pun intended) without the kindness and assistance of the following people. When living as a tree-dwelling hunter-gatherer, striving to live by a barter economy, you can give little in return other than your time and perhaps something made of wood!

I would like to begin by thanking the fellows who helped me during various stages of the build: Nick Sandham for his design geekery and skill with a chisel; Tim Macmillan for providing the van and giving up his weekend to put together a frame in a tree; Paul Burley for his banister-making efforts; Chuck Stanton for his skill with the gun and coracle binding; and, above all, Chris Whatley for his unfaltering efforts to help out wherever help was needed – thanks, Chief.

To my recycled wood providers, without whom I would have had no floor, walls or windows, I would like to thank Sue Slatter at Valley Builders and Pauline Comber for giving me free reign over their skips and scrap wood piles. I would also like to thank the team at Invisible Blue for not being able to give me any work so I could do this, and for the Perspex and plywood. Communications would not have been possible without the generosity of Lucy at Solio who donated a solar charger; and the good people at Hunter helped me avoid trench foot with their fantastic wellies. Also, thank you to all those who followed the blog and continue to do so; I will keep writing if you keep reading!

I would also like to thank Dan from Safari Britain for providing me with gainful employment over the summer, and the campers for their interest in all things 'wild'; Alan and Lynda Buckle for their encouragement and extras for the veg patch; Danny Goodwin for the milk and for enduring a camera crew; the folks at the cottages, Phil and Debbie and of course Sam for their banter and occasional lending; Tom for taking me decoying and topping up the meat store; Sarah Sands for commissioning my first column, without which the phone would have been barred; Daisy Dumas for kick-starting the media frenzy; and all the ensuing journalists and reporters who brought me a few treats and kept the location a secret.

Special mention must go to those who contributed to the photographs in the book, and who brought 'added value' down to the wood: Tom Kevill-Davies for his roof building, poultry, offal, and company on the Sussex waterways; Al Humphreys for his stories of faraway places and constant wood chopping; and last, but by no means least, Greg Funnell for photographically capturing the dismemberment of a rabbit so well, and for bringing out the port and Stilton.

It's not often that animals get a mention for their contributions, but they helped in their own way: Bangers the 'porcine rotivator'; Kochin and his harem of hens for the eggs; Frank the fox for his efficient waste disposal; and Jeff the pheasant, for his company and skill in avoiding the pot – rest in peace, buddy.

This book would not have been possible without the fine folk at Anova, so thank you to Caroline King, Gemma Wilson, the person whose pens I stole, but, most of all, Katie Cowan for spotting a bargain and keeping the faith in a person living in a tree. Also, thanks to Martin Hendry for his excellent design work and to my editor Katie Hewett for her sterling work in keeping me on track, pointing out the dos and don'ts, and making my bumbling prose legible for publication. I would also like to thank my agent Annabel Merullo and her assistant Tom Williams for supporting my crackpot schemes and making things happen.

It is rare indeed to find two people with the warmth and generosity of Ray and Summer Driftwood, who not only allowed me to hunt, gather and grow on their land, but also provided me with a beautiful slice of the Sussex countryside in which to live. It must be said that without them, this whole adventure and experience would never have happened. Thank you so very much – you made my dream come true.

Finally I would like to thank those closest to me: my mother for always being there, teaching me to cook, and housing me during the writing stage; my brother, ever the voice of reason and source of inspiration, and for helping make sense of things; but, above all, to Clare for all her support, giving the tree house a woman's touch, and for saying 'Yes'.

References

FURTHER READING

Food

James A. Bateman, *Trapping: A Practical Guide* (David & Charles, 1979)
Isabella Beeton, *Mrs Beeton's Book of Household Management* (Oxford University Press, abridged Edition, 2000)
Anna Del Conte and Thomas Laessoe, *The Edible Mushroom Book* (Dorling Kindersley, 2008)
Clarissa Dickson-Wright and Johnny Scott, *The Game Cookbook* (Kyle Cathie, 2009)
Keith Erlandson, *Home Smoking and Curing* (Ebury Press, 2003)
Hugh Fearnley-Whittingstall, *A Cook on the Wild Side* (Pan Macmillan, 1997)
Patrick Harding, Tony Lyon and Gill Tomblin, *How to Identify Edible Mushrooms* (HarperCollins, 1996)
Larousse Gastronomique (Hamlyn, 1998)
Leon W. Kania, *The Alaskan Bootlegger's Bible* (Happy Mountain Productions, 2000)
Mark Hix, *British Regional Food* (Quadrille Publishing, 2008)
Miles Irving, *The Forager Handbook* (Ebury Press, 2009)
Richard Mabey, *Food for Free* (Collins, 1983)
Richard Mabey, *Wild Cooking* (Vintage, 2009)
Ray Mears, *Outdoor Survival Handbook* (Ebury Press, 2001)
Ray Mears and Gordon Hillmann, *Wild Food* (Hodder & Stoughton, 2007)
Ian Niall, *The New Poacher's Handbook* (Heinemann, 1960)
Roger Phillips, *Wild Food* (Pan Books, 1983)
Karen Solomon, *Jam it, Pickle it, Cure it* (Ten Speed Press, 2009)
Eric Treuille and Ursula Ferrigno, *Bread* (Dorling Kindersley, 2007)
John 'Lofty' Wiseman, *SAS Survival Handbook* (HarperCollins, 1996)
John Wright, *The River Cottage Mushroom Handbook* (Bloomsbury, 2007)

The patch

Dr D. G. Hessayon, *The Vegetable & Herb Expert* (Expert Books, 1997)
Sarah Raven, *The Great Vegetable Plot* (BBC Books, 2005)

The tree house

Jack Hill, *The Complete Practical Book of Country Crafts* (David & Charles, 1979)
Ben Law, *The Woodland House* (Permanent Publications, 2005)
Peter Nelson and David Larkin, *The Treehouse Book* (Universe, 2000)
David and Jeanie Stiles, Cabins: *A Guide to Building Your Own Nature Retreat* (Firefly Books, 2001)

Reading matter

Joseph Conrad, *Heart of Darkness* (Penguin Classics, 2007)
Daniel Defoe, *Robinson Crusoe* (Longman, revisied Edition, 2004)
Guy Grieve, *Call of the Wild* (Hodder & Stoughton, 2007)
Alistair Humphreys, *Moods of Future Joys* (Eye Books, second revised edition, 2007)
John Humphreys, *Poacher's Tales* (David & Charles, 1991)
Richard Jeffries, *The Gamekeeper at Home – The Amateur Poacher* (Oxford University Press, 1948)
Tom Kevill-Davies, *The Hungry Cyclist* (Collins, 2009)
John Lewis-Stempel, *The Wild Life* (Doubleday, 2009)
G. W. Maunsell, *The Fisherman's Vade Mecum* (A & C Black, 1959)
Bruce Parry, *Tribe: Adventures in a Changing World* (Michael Joseph Ltd, 2007)
Charles Rangeley-Wilson, *Somewhere Else* (Yellow Jersey Press, 2005)
Nigel Slater, *Toast* (HarperPerennial, first printing edition, 2004)
Robert Louis Stevenson, *Treasure Island* (Pavilion, 2009)
Paul Theroux, *The Great Railway Bazaar: By Train Through Asia* (Penguin, 2008)
Paul Theroux, *The Happy Isles of Oceania: Paddling the Pacific* (Penguin, 1992)
Edward Thomas, *The South Country* (Little Toller Books, 2009)
Henry David Thoreau, *Walden; or Life in the Woods* (Forgotten Books, 2008)

INTERNET RESOURCES

www.thetreehouseguide.com Practical tips on building tree houses, as well as links to other people's projects. Thoroughly useful.

http://www.countrysidemag.com/issues/88/88-6/W_Wayne_Robertson.html Instructions on how to build a wood burning stove – Bertha's birthplace!

http://www.communicationagents.com/chris/2004/04/14/cool_fridge_without_using_electricity.htm How to build a pot-in-pot fridge without electricity.

INDEX

S

T

V

W

Y

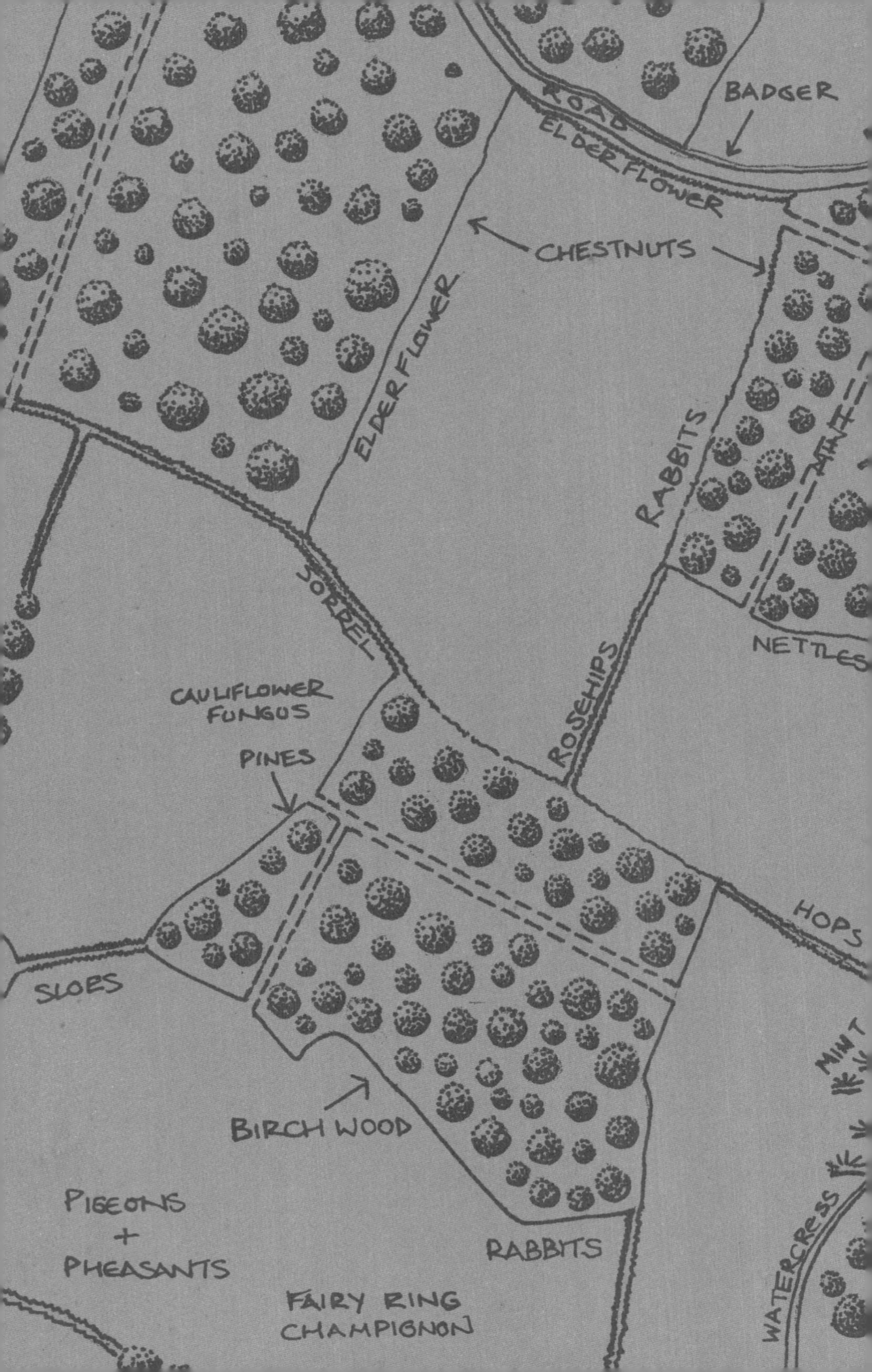
BADGER
ROAD
ELDER FLOWER
CHESTNUTS
ELDER FLOWER
RABBITS
MINT
SORREL
NETTLES
CAULIFLOWER FUNGUS
ROSEHIPS
PINES
HOPS
SLOES
MINT
BIRCH WOOD
PIGEONS + PHEASANTS
RABBITS
WATERCRESS
FAIRY RING CHAMPIGNON